FROM I
TO BUDDHISM ...

Answers to Questions

FROM BEETROOT TO BUDDHISM...

Answers to Questions

RUDOLF STEINER

Sixteen discussions with workers at the Goetheanum in Dornach between 1 March and 25 June 1924

English by A.R. Meuss, FIL, MTA

RUDOLF STEINER PRESS
LONDON

Rudolf Steiner Press
51 Queen Caroline Street
London W6 9QL

First published by Rudolf Steiner Press 1999

Originally published in German (with an additional lecture dated 8 May
1924) under the title *Die Geschichte der Menschheit und die
Weltanschauungen der Kulturvölker* (volume 353 in the *Rudolf Steiner
Gesamtausgabe* or Collected Works) by Rudolf Steiner Verlag, Dornach.
This authorized translation is based on the 2nd, revised German edition
edited by Paul Gerhard Bellmann, and is published by kind permission
of the Rudolf Steiner Nachlassverwaltung, Dornach. The line drawings
by Hedwig Frey are based on Rudolf Steiner's blackboard drawings

A catalogue record for this book is available from the British Library

ISBN 1 85584 062 6

Cover by Andrew Morgan
Typeset by DP Photosetting, Aylesbury, Bucks.
Printed and bound in Great Britain by Cromwell Press Limited,
Trowbridge, Wiltshire

Contents

Main Contents of the Discussions

die. Jesus and the Christ. Ritual and teaching bound up with one another in the ancient mysteries. 'Fathers' and 'children', sons of gods and sons of man. What the Christ has brought into the world. Hidden similarities between languages.

root on intestinal parasites. Root diet. Powers of moon influencing reproduction and growth. Inner animal forces depending on sun. Thinking and the whole of our inner life depending on Saturn. Moon has relationship to plant aspect in humans, sun to animal aspect and Saturn to the part of us that is wholly human. Star wisdom of ancient Babylonians and Assyrians. All minerals have once been plants. Metals and planets. Ancient knowledge eradicated between the fifth and the eleventh and twelfth centuries. Commodus an 'initiate'. Parchments of Constantinople and what has become of them. Copernicus the father of modern astronomy. Copernicus' three theses. Svedberg and alchemy. How can we understand Paracelsus? Misery of science of today. Star wisdom needs to be combined with human wisdom.

11   *Discussion of 10 May 1924*
The Sephiroth Tree
What the ancient Jews meant by the Sephiroth Tree. Powers of the world influence human beings from all sides. Ten powers (*sephiroth*) act from outside. Three shape the human head: *kether* (the crown), *chokmah* (wisdom) and *binah* (intelligence); three others act more on the middle human being: *chesed* (freedom), *geburah* (strength) and *tiphereth* (beauty); three more act on the lower human being: *netsah* (overcoming), *hod* (empathy) and *jesod* (the fundament on which the human being stands), and the tenth is the outside world of the earth influencing the human being: *malkuth* (the field). The Jews represented the world of the spirit through the ten *sephiroth*, which are a spiritual alphabet. Raymond Lully and supersensible perception. Spiritualist seances. About the alphabet.

12   *Discussion of 14 May 1924*
Kant, Schopenhauer and Eduard von Hartmann
Study of Kant in his youth. How Kant saw the world. Kant's *Critique of Pure Reason*. Kant's 'thing in itself'. Kant maintained, on the basis of thought, that the thing as such cannot be known, and our whole world is made up of the impressions we gain of things. Schopenhauer following Kant. Consequences of Kant's teaching. Kant's transcendental deduction of space and time and his proof that human beings have transcendental apperception. Kant's strange statement: 'I had to let knowledge go to make room for

faith.' Kant's *Critique of Practical Reason* and his teaching concerning belief in God, freedom and immortality. Kant bringing sickness to knowledge.

Publisher's Foreword

The truly remarkable lectures—or, more accurately, question and answer sessions—contained in this book, form part of a series (published in eight volumes in the original German)* dating from August 1922 to September 1924. This series features talks given to people involved in various kinds of building work on Rudolf Steiner's architectural masterpieces, the first and second Goetheanums. (The destruction by fire of the first Goetheanum necessitated the building of a replacement.) A vivid description of the different types of workers present, as well as the context and atmosphere of these talks, is given by a witness in the Appendix to the first volume of this English series, *From Elephants to Einstein* (1998).

The sessions arose out of explanatory tours of the Goetheanum which one of Steiner's pupils, Dr Roman Boos, had offered. When this came to an end, and the workers still wished to know more about the 'temple' they were involved with and the philosophy behind it, Dr Steiner agreed to take part in question and answer sessions himself. These took place during the working day, after the mid-morning break. Apart from the workmen, only a few other people were present: those working in the building office, and some of Steiner's closest co-workers. The subject-matter of the talks was chosen by the workers at the encouragement of Rudolf Steiner, who took their questions and usually gave immediate answers.

---

* 347–354 in the collected works of Rudolf Steiner in the original German, published by Rudolf Steiner Verlag, Dornach, Switzerland. For information on English translations, see the list at the end of this Forword.

After Rudolf Steiner's death, some of the lectures — on the subject of bees — were published. However, as Marie Steiner writes in her original Preface to the German edition: 'Gradually more and more people felt a wish to study these lectures.' It was therefore decided to publish them in full. However, Marie Steiner's words about the nature of the lectures remain relevant to the present publication:

> They had, however, been intended for a particular group of people and Rudolf Steiner spoke off the cuff, in accord with the given situation and the mood of the workmen at the time. There was no intention to publish at the time. But the very way in which he spoke had a freshness and directness that one would not wish to destroy, taking away the special atmosphere that arose in the souls of those who asked the questions and him who gave the answers. It would be a pity to take away the special colour of it by pedantically rearranging the sentences. We are therefore taking the risk of leaving them as far as possible untouched. Perhaps it will not always be in the accustomed literary style, but on the other hand it has directness and vitality.

In this spirit, the translator has been asked also to preserve as much of the original style, or flavour, as possible. This might necessitate that readers study a passage again, trying to bring to mind the live situation in which the talks were given, before the whole can be fully appreciated.

S G

Rudolf Steiner's lectures to workers at the Goetheanum

GA (*Gesamtausgabe*) number

347 *The Human Being in Body, Soul and Spirit* (New York/ London: Anthroposophic Press/Rudolf Steiner Press 1989)

348 *Health and Illness*, vol. 1 (New York: Anthroposophic Press 1981) and *Health and Illness*, vol. 2 (New York: Anthroposophic Press 1983). Revised translation forthcoming, Rudolf Steiner Press

349 Publication of English translation forthcoming, Rudolf Steiner Press

350 Four of the sixteen lectures in the German edition are published in *Learning to See Into the Spiritual World* (New York: Anthroposophic Press 1990). Full edition forthcoming, Rudolf Steiner Press

351 Nine of the fifteen lectures in the German edition are published in *Bees, Nine lectures on the Nature of Bees* (New York: Anthroposophic Press 1998)

352 *From Elephants to Einstein, Answers to Questions* (London: Rudolf Steiner Press 1998)

353 *From Beetroot to Buddhism, Answers to Questions* (London: Rudolf Steiner Press 1999)

354 *The Evolution of the Earth and Man and the Influence of the Stars* (New York/London: Anthroposophic Press/ Rudolf Steiner Press 1987)

Translator's note

I have added a list of German names and terms that appear in the text, with indications as to how they may be pronounced. Reading the lectures aloud, in a group, for instance, people often feel they would like to pronounce the words properly, and I hope this may be a help.

Pronunciation of German names and terms

Alp	alp ['a' sound as in father]
Basel	baa sl
der Bruder, die Brüder	da brooder, dee breeder [French u if you can manage for the ee, otherwise just the English ee sound]
Burgenland	boorken lunt
Burle	boor le
Dollinger	dollin ga [hard 'g']
Donar dröhnt im Donner	doner drunt im donna [first 'o' as in 'hole', 'u' as in 'burn'; second 'o' as in 'lot']
Eisenstadt	icen stut
Erbsmehl	airps male
Gau	gow
Guericke, Magdeburg	goo eric e, mug de boork
das Holz, die Hölzer	dass [as in 'ass'] holts [short 'o'], dee heltsa
die Holzer	dee holtsa [short 'o']
Jachin	ia<ch>in [<ch> is like the rough h in 'human']

Karfreitag	car fry tug
Neudörfl	noi derfl
rentenmark	ren ten mark
Tageding	taage dink ['aa' as in 'father'; 'dink' as in 'Dinky']
umlaut	oom lout [keep oo short]
vertagedingt	fer tage dinkt ['a' as in 'father']
verteidigt	fer tidikt [first 'i' as in 'tide']
der Wagen, die Wägen, Wäge	da vagen ['a' as in father], dee vaygen, vayge [all with hard 'g']
Walther von Habenichts	vul ta fon hub nichts ['vul' as in 'vulture'; ch as the rough h in 'human']
Wotan weht im Winde	votan veight im vinde ['o' as in 'hole'; 'veight' like 'weight' but starting with a 'v'; 'i' in 'vinde' as in 'in']
Ziu zwingt Zwist	tsi-oo tsvinkt tsvist [German 'z' is a 'ts' in English; all three 'i' sounds as in 'in']

Effect of cemetery atmosphere on people. How the ancient Indians, Egyptians, Babylonians and Jews saw life

Good morning, gentlemen! Has something come to mind for today?

Mr Dollinger: I would like to ask why people living near a cemetery are often less lively and look so pale. (He gave an example that seemed to bear this out.) I'd like to know how the rhythm is in the bodies, and if it cannot also do something good.

Rudolf Steiner: Well, I reckon I can answer this question quite well, because I lived right next to a cemetery from the age of 7 until I was 17. So I must have looked terribly pale in those days. It was a little bit true. Considering what you have said, this should have been the case, particularly for me.

The cemetery was that of a small place[1] with a population of about 600, and so the cemetery was moderate in size. But it was right next to the house and the railway station where we lived. And people lived right next to it all around, as was usual in such places. You had the church, with the cemetery around it, and then the houses [drawing on the board]. It was always possible to see the state of health of the people who lived around the cemetery. Well, it is fair to say that there were considerable differences between the people, and that the priest, for instance, who lived not far from the cemetery, was neither pale nor frail; he was quite corpulent and also looked pretty good. So that is what I saw at the time.

But one comes to see that, providing healthy conditions are created in other ways, and this was often done in places where you had cemeteries around the churches, you cannot assume that this is so terribly harmful. Many walnut trees would grow in those villages. The scent of walnut trees spreads, and it is extraordinarily good in strengthening health. You have to assume that people had pretty good instincts in villages where this was the general custom, and so they would plant chestnut or walnut trees, and above all also lime trees in places where the cemetery was right in the village. Limes and walnut trees counteract the harmful effects of a cemetery, balancing them out.

Something else to be considered is this. You see, if you go into more detail with the things Mr Dollinger wants to know, that is, the effect on the higher bodies, we have to be clear that only the physical body and the ether body have a vitalizing effect, whilst the astral body and the I* do not have a vitalizing but essentially a paralysing effect; they are active in soul and spirit. And you will know from many other things I have said that the physical body and the ether body are like a plant; they grow, and organs develop. If we had only these two, we would be in a continual faint. We would have a sleep life, like the plants, if destructive processes were not continually at work in us; it is only because of these that we do not have the sleep life of plants. The astral body and the I destroy, they atomize. There is continuous production and destruction in the human being. And the astral body is the most destructive in our human nature. All the products we eliminate—I have spoken of these—have really been broken down by the astral body and I. The ether body is only involved a little in this, as I have told you.

Now you see, gentlemen, the atmosphere that rises in a cemetery is related to the principle that is destructive in the human astral body, and it encourages the destructive processes. People are more subject to destruction if they live

---

* These terms are used in a technical sense. See further in Rudolf Steiner, *Theosophy*, New York: Anthroposophic Press 1994.

near a cemetery than if they live out in the woods some-where. If they live in the woods, the productive forces are stronger; if they live near a cemetery the destructive forces are. But, as I said,[2] if we did not have those powers of destruction we would be stupid all our life. We need those powers of destruction.

Then there is something else. I have told you that I can speak on the subject because I know it from personal experience, having known it especially in my young days, a time when so many things develop. I have always had a tendency to think clearly. And I am convinced that I owe this to the fact that destiny made me live close to a cemetery. So that is the good thing about it, gentlemen, and it has to be taken into account as well.

You'll agree that it is the dead bodies which are harmful in a cemetery. Those dead bodies merely continue in the process of destruction. When we die, the productive process stops. And because of this the astral body is really encouraged to think clearly when close to a cemetery. This, too, cannot be denied.

In the area where I grew up, called the Burgenland today, villages everywhere had their cemeteries at the centre. The Burgenland is an area that was much fought over. There are a few larger towns, Eisenstadt and others, but these lie far apart, and villages are to be found every-where, always with the cemetery in the middle. And it is true to say that people there had a certain rustic cunning. Nor can we deny that this cunning really developed under the influence of the cemetery atmosphere. They kept the harmful influences away by planting walnut trees and limes everywhere.

It was also a wine growing area. The atmosphere created by the vine also helps to balance out bad effects. As you know, lime blossom is quite powerful, and walnut trees also have a powerful scent; this has more of a vitalizing effect on the astral body. And the atmosphere created by the vine has more of a vitalizing effect on the I. So there you get a powerful effect also on the higher bodies.

Of course, we cannot deny that things change as civilization progresses. The moment the villages grow bigger, with many houses built, which reduces the effect of the trees, a cemetery begins to be harmful, and then you do, of course, see those pale faces around a cemetery. It can no longer be balanced out and the result is that people suffer from the cemetery influence. This has in turn led to a natural instinct, which is to put the cemetery outside when villages have grown into towns.

Something else also has to be considered. It is something that happens when the effect goes further, affecting the ether body. You see, everything that rises as a subtle vapour in the atmosphere influences the astral body and the I. Both the subtle smell of bodily decay that is always present in and around a cemetery and the scent of walnut, lime and chestnut, which is particularly vitalizing, can really only influence the higher bodies; they do not reach the ether body to any marked degree.

But the situation is that the water in a region acts particularly on the ether body. And the water in the area surrounding a cemetery contains slight seepage from the dead bodies. This water is drunk by people, it is used in cooking. And if the water in a village where the cemetery lies close to the dwellings is contaminated, trees do not help! Nature helps very little in that case. And the consequence is that people will easily get tuberculosis and suffer very severely from that disease.

You see, this is something I was well able to establish. There was a village some hours away from the one where I lived — a small village. Almost everybody lived around the cemetery. These people were naturally slow to act. They had weak muscles, weak nerves, everything was flaccid;

they were pale. And then I did wonder why. And, you see, this is most interesting.

In our village of Neudörfl the people living close to the cemetery were relatively healthy. So that is a big question for someone who looks at the country and considers the conditions under which people live. You had a village where people lived around the cemetery, and all they did was to plant walnut trees; they did plant them, that was a very healthy instinct — but apart from this they would very often take the water they used in cooking from the village stream! Here would be the row of houses [blackboard drawing], between them the village stream; here the cemetery, here the church; this was where we lived, here the priest, this was the school house; then there was a row of houses here, with a stream in between, and walnut trees everywhere. People would simply take their water from the stream; that stream did of course contain residues and bacteria, bacilli, from the seepage coming from the cemetery. People, and especially the people who lived there, were not outstanding when it came to cleanliness; there were houses with thatched roofs and everywhere the dunghill right at the front door, with the pigsty also right there — you got a wonderful combination of pigsty and dung heap — again draining into the village stream, so that when you stepped into it you were wading in a brownish sauce. So you see, it was not exactly hygienic, as we would say today. And in spite of this the people were healthy. One has to say they were healthy.

In the first place, if the people are healthy, the dead bodies, too, are not so bad, to begin with, compared to a place where people are sick. But this still left a big question. Why were these people healthy when those others were feeble and not fit to live? The explanation is as follows. Near this village was another place — very small but a health resort with a mineral water spring.[3] The whole village went and got its drinking water from that place. And the drinking water from there, being carbonated, also helped to counteract the contaminated water from the cemetery. The people in the other place, which was far away from the spring, did not have this water. So it was possible to see directly that carbonated water – as I once told you, it acts strongly on the I and on thinking – influences the I and the ether body, and in the ether body balances out the destructive effects of the cemetery seepage.

Of course, if there is still a cemetery once the village has become a town, there is basically nothing there to help transform the cemetery atmosphere, at least not unless spring water is brought in from a long distance away. If a town is situated in such a way that the cemetery is still at the centre, and if water is still drawn from wells, you do, of course, have the worst possible conditions for health, for in that case the ether body is under attack; and the ether body is a principle that cannot be coerced any further by anything coming from the astral body and the I.

You see, sanitary conditions are most interesting, especially from this point of view. Of course, we also have to take into account that the people who live around a cemetery, if they are still believers and have not yet become unbelievers, continually see the funeral ceremonies. These again provide a counterbalance. They influence the I. They have a strengthening effect. This, too, must be considered from the health point of view. It does balance things out.

I suppose this is more or less what you wanted to know? Perhaps someone else has thought of something?

Well, gentlemen, in that case I'll go on with this question, taking it from quite a different angle. You see, we have considered many things so far. Today let us take the insights we have gained and consider the following.

If you look at a map, your interest may go in a direction where you say: Here one nation lives, and here another. We take an interest in the different nations living next to one another. But you may also say: Today I'll look at the map to see how humanity has evolved. And then the map really gets very interesting.

Let us look at a bit of a map. I'll just make a rough drawing of it [blackboard drawing]. Going over to Asia, for instance, we have India here, Peninsular India – I have drawn this before when we were studying the races[4] – and here Arabia; this is Asia Minor. There Asia merges into Europe, and we are practically in Europe, the islands that look across to Europe. There we have Greece. Then we come to Africa here. And there we have a river; that is the Nile; here is Egypt – completely under British control today, as you know – it was a free country once. Now you see, different nations live in all these areas. In India the Indians, who are now struggling to their feet. They were ruled by the British for a long time, still are today, but they are getting on to their feet, and people with some insight in Britain are terribly afraid that the Indians may one day become independent. There is a major Indian movement today. Mahatma Gandhi[5] has stirred up such a movement in India. He was locked up, but has been released again now, for health reasons. Here in the Arab countries live people who have also been more or less under British rule; that is still a fairly impassable terrain in the Arab countries. As you know, one of the things that caused the Great War was that a railway was to be built through Turkey, going this way, and a route established to India in one direction and Arabia on the other. This German plan aroused the envy and jealousy of many other countries, the intention being to build the Berlin–Baghdad Railway through Turkey and down into Asia. And this is where Syria used to be.[6]

You see, there are all kinds of aspects where it is interesting to ask ourselves: People have been living everywhere from time immemorial; they lived very different lives. We need only mention a few things to realize how different their lives were. In India for example there was strict segregation in castes, compared to which anything by way of classes in Europe is a mere shadow image. In India you would be born into a caste. The highest caste were the Brahmins, priests and scholars. The children of the Brahmins all went to school in those early times. They were the ones who were able to write, the uppermost caste. Priests came from this caste, but not rulers. They came from the second caste, the military and the rulers. But it would never be possible for someone to rise from the second to the first caste; it was all strictly segregated. The third caste were peasants, country people, and the fourth caste were the people who did menial work. These castes were kept strictly apart. If it would ever have happened that someone moved from one caste to another in ancient India, it would have been as if a lion were to turn into a lamb. The castes were considered to be separate just as individual animal species are separate. And people had nothing against this. It would have seemed as crazy to them to see someone move from the third caste to the first, as if a lion had turned into an ox. The situation was entirely natural to them in ancient India.

Let us move on to Egypt; they had castes, too. What I am telling you now, gentlemen, you can consider to have been at a time that was about 3000 or 3500 years, perhaps even 4000 years before the coming of Christianity. We thus have to go back five or six millennia to look at the time of which I am speaking. In Egypt, they also had castes, but not so strictly adhered to; there it was possible for someone to move from one caste to another. But the situation in Egypt was that the whole organization of the state came from the priesthood. The priesthood arranged everything. It was the same in India, but there the division into castes determined everything, while it was less strict in Egypt. But they made sure that everything by way of law came from the priests.

The other peoples in Syria, in Asia Minor, correspondingly had their own particular ways; they differed.

To show you the role things we have been learning play in human history, let me tell you something else about these particular nations. Let us take four of them — the Indians, then the Egyptians, and then the peoples who were in this area. Here Euphrates and Tigris enter the Persian Gulf, and the people who lived there were later called the Babylonians. They will be the third group we look at.

And then, as you know, a nation emerged here that was later to play a great role in history — the Semites, the Hebrews, the Jews. They went across to Egypt, later moved back again to live here in Palestine, a relatively small nation but one that played a great role in history. We may thus consider the Indians, the Egyptians, the Babylonians and the Jews.

You see, a special characteristic of the Indians was that they really looked at the people who lived there as distinct groups, like animal species, and divided them into four castes. Then there was the particular religion the Indians had in earlier times. They saw no difference between the world of spirit and the world of physical bodies; at the time when this Indian population first evolved in India, no difference was made between spirit and body. A tree would not be differentiated the way many other peoples did — this is the physical tree, and a spirit lives in it. No such distinction was made. The tree was at the same time a spirit, only a somewhat coarser spirit than a human being or animal. An animal was also not divided into body and soul; it was soul to the ancient Indians, as was the human being.

And when an Indian of earliest times asked after the soul — and he knew that we inhale, inhale air — then to him the air that is inhaled was the spirit. And he would know:

The air is out there; that is the spirit that is all around the earth. And when this spirit, which is around the whole earth, began to flow, to waft, he would call the spirit that moved everywhere on earth Varuna. But the spirit in him was also Varuna. When there were gales outside, it was Varuna; and inside — also Varuna.

People often say today that those Indians had nature worship, venerating wind and weather, and so on. But it would be equally right to say they worshipped the spirit, for they saw the spirit in everything. The Indians had no notion of a physical body, and this being the case, every part of the human being was also a spirit: the liver was spirit, the kidney was spirit, everything was spirit. They did not distinguish between body and spirit. The secret of ancient Indian wisdom is that no distinction was made between body and spirit. Liver was liver spirit, stomach was stomach spirit.

You see, if we consider the stomach today we find that there has to be something in the stomach if it is to digest things properly. We call this substance pepsin. If it is lacking, digestion does not take its proper course; we have to put in some hydrochloric acid in that case. The ancient Indian would say to himself — he did not yet have a name for it, but he knew that there was a spirit there — the stomach is like this: that is the stomach spirit. Today we still know the term 'stomachic spirits or elixir' for some medicines. They are of course called by their inventors' names now, Hoffmann's tincture (spirits of ether) or the like; but you will still find words used that refer to the spirit.

The Indians thus saw the spirit everywhere. They therefore also took no offence at the caste spirit, seeing it as a spiritual principle, just as the different orders of animals were seen as a spiritual principle.

If one goes more deeply into those Indian views, it is interesting to see that the Indians had accurate knowledge of all human organs. It was merely that they saw them as spirit. The human being was made up of many different spirits: lung spirit, stomach spirit, kidney spirit, and so on; they would only consider the physical body. With regard to the ancient Indians, therefore, we may say their whole thinking was in terms of the physical body. They saw it as something spiritual.

1   Indians   physical body   spiritual

This is very interesting, for we have now discovered a people who in the first place had accurate knowledge of the physical body.

Let us move on to the Egyptians. Here it is a strange story. The Egyptians had the Nile which we may say is really the father who feeds the country. Every July the river rises above its banks, returning to them in October. All an ancient Egyptian would know, therefore, was that the Nile held water; the waters would recede during the cold part of the year and then rise to flood the land again for the benefit of humanity. When the waters receded in October, fertile mud was left behind—the Egyptians do not need to use fertilizer. They would sow their cereal grains and so on in the mud; these would germinate and grow and be harvested before the Nile flooded again. And so the Nile really prepared their fields for them year after year. And the Egyptians were deeply conscious of the beneficial nature of water. They gave much thought to water in the world of nature. You see, today we admire the skill of engineers who are able to channel the waters. Well, the Egyptians were very good at this thousands of years ago! When the Nile rose above its banks and flooded everything, it would of course sometimes also go to places where it should not go. They therefore created a lake, one of the earliest man-made lakes, to control the flooding. Any excess water would collect in the lake. The

Egyptians thus controlled nature. With all this, their attention focused on water to an extraordinary degree.

Now I already told you when answering Mr Dollinger's question that water has a tremendous influence on the human ether body. The Egyptians still had the instinct that enabled them to say: The human being has not only a physical but also an ether body. This is interesting. You see, over yonder in India were some of the oldest nations; many of them had later migrated via Arabia to Egypt. A kind of old civilization existed in Egypt that had come from India. When the Indians came to Egypt they appreciated the beneficial qualities of water. And they said to themselves: This does not act on the physical body, which we got to know in India, but on a higher body in the human being. And so the Egyptians—and with them the Indians—really discovered the ether body through their experience of water.

Having discovered the ether body the Egyptians developed the whole of their religion as a religion of the ether body. The most important aspect of ancient Egyptian religion is presented in the following legend. The Egyptians would tell this story everywhere, just as the Gospel stories were told all over Europe at a particular time. *There is a sublime god*—they called him Osiris. *This sublime god is the benefactor of humanity. He is the source and origin of everything that comes to humanity through the element of water. But he has an enemy. He works for the good of humanity, but he has an enemy. This enemy lives in the hot wind coming from the desert.* The desert was there [pointing to the blackboard]. The Egyptians thus had two gods: Osiris and Typhon, his enemy. To them, everything they saw in the natural world could also be seen in human life. But unlike the Indians they ascribed it not to the physical body but to the ether body.

The legend continues. *One day Typhon killed Osiris and carried him away. Then Isis, wife of Osiris, brought the body back again, burying different parts of it in different places. Monuments were built over them. From then on Osiris was the ruler of the dead. Before, he had been ruler of the living, now he was the ruler of the dead.* The Egyptians did already consider death.

As you know, for I have told you, the human ether body departs a few days after death; after this the human being gradually gains consciousness again. In the legend we hear that Osiris went away and was brought back again by Isis. The human being regains consciousness after death.

We may say, therefore, that the Egyptians discovered that the human being has an ether body. This is most interesting. The Indians still took the physical body to be a spiritual principle. The Egyptians discovered the ether body and saw it as spirit:

2 Egyptians   ether body   spiritual   Osiris Typhon
                                                      Isis

Everything the Egyptians believed, everything they worked for, was really for the ether body. This determined their view of things.

Something Egyptian you have certainly seen already are the mummies. I spoke of them recently, when I said that when medieval physicians spoke of mummies this was something spiritual; I explained this to you.[7] Today people only think of Egyptian mummies when they use the word. The bodies were skilfully embalmed and preserved. Why was this done? The Egyptians knew only of the ether body and would preserve the physical body so that the individual would find it again when he returned to life. If they had already known about the astral body and the I they would not have thought it necessary to preserve the physical body. They knew only the ether body, and this in a highly spiritual way. If they had known of the I and the astral body they would have said: They create their own physical body. But they only knew the subtle ether body and therefore believed they had to preserve the physical body so that the individual would find it again on his return. The Egyptians thus discovered the ether body.

We now come to the third group, the Babylonians. They developed the ability to think to such a high level that much of their thinking still exists today; and above all they developed astronomy. They built great towers from which to observe the stars. And they realized that human beings depend not only on the things that exist on earth but also on the things to be found in the stars. They made special efforts to perceive the influence of the stars on human beings, and noted how the year is divided. The year in turn has great influence on humans through the stars. The Babylonians were thus the first to go beyond the earth in looking at life, creating astronomy and astrology, knowledge of how the stars influence human beings. This also made them aware of having to divide everything by 60 and 12 and so on.

They divided their money into units of 60 and 12, for instance. The decimal system only came later. You still have this Babylonian system of 12 in the English shilling. This system was brought down from the heavens by the Babylonians. The question is, which part of the human being is specially influenced by the stars? It is the astral body, gentlemen. This is wholly and completely under the influence of the stars. But modern astronomers do not want to know about the astral body and therefore do not set out to observe the way the stars influence human beings. The things they calculate really have no particular influence on human beings. But the Babylonians had a fine science of the stars. And this led them to discover the human astral body. This is truly marvellous. We are able to say that the Babylonians discovered the astral body, spiritually.

3 Babylonians   astral body   spiritual

The astral body actually owes its name to this. It was first discovered by the Babylonians. And it was called 'astral body' because they discovered it from the science of the stars—astrology, astronomy. So you see that successive nations made their discoveries out of the spirit—the Indians discovering the physical body, the Egyptians the ether body and the Babylonians the astral body.

If we look to see what lies behind all Babylonian legends we find it is the stars. Don't let modern scholars and their books confuse you. There is one expert who says all religions had their origins in star worship, which must therefore be regarded as the original religion. Another will say: No indeed, religions evolved from the veneration of nature. Wind and weather were venerated. A third will say that all religions developed from the elements, from water and its effects. Well, gentlemen, why is it that people say such things? The one who says religion comes from star worship has only studied the Babylonian age and thinks it was the same everywhere as it was in Babylon. The one who says religion is based on the elements has only studied the Egyptians. He therefore 'Egyptianizes' everything. And he'll say: all religions derive from veneration of wind and weather. So the reason is that people are rather limited, studying only individual aspects. Religions have a wide range of sources.

Now there is also, as I have told you, a small nation over there in Palestine—the Hebrews, the Jews. You see, they lived among those other nations and were not satisfied with anything they found there. You can read it in the Bible, in the Old Testament, how the Jews were never satisfied and came to a spirit who is completely invisible. The physical body is, of course, completely visible. The ether body came to expression in the floods, in the watery activities of the Nile; these were tangible. The astral body of the Babylonians would not be visible on earth, but could be found by studying the stars. The Jews wanted none of that, they wanted an invisible god. This invisible god influences the human I. Therefore,

4 Jews	I	spiritual (Yahveh)

The Jews found the I as a spiritual principle and called it Yahveh.

So we now have history. You can read as much as you like in history books. You will not understand how the peoples of antiquity developed. You'll read about all kinds of things, wars and kings, and have chaos and confusion in your minds; for you'll have no idea what it is all about. Religions may also be mentioned, but no one knows where they come from. If you know, however, that the human body consists of physical body, ether body, astral body and I, and that these were discovered one after the other, depending on the way people looked at life, you find that the Indians discovered the physical body, the Egyptians the ether body, the Babylonians the astral body and the Jews the I. It gradually emerged that the human being has these different bodies. This did not come suddenly, out of the blue, but was discovered in relation to the way people lived.

1 Indians	physical body	spiritual	
2 Egyptians	ether body	spiritual	Osiris Typhon Isis
3 Babylonians	astral body	spiritual	
4 Jews	I	spiritual	(Yahveh)

The Indians—and many people migrated through there, so that they differ in race—discovered the physical body. The Egyptians, who had to concern themselves a great deal with water, discovered the ether, and therefore the ether human being. Among the Babylonians, who took everything they needed for the astral body from other peoples, the priests got the idea of building high towers; they gained knowledge of the stars. And the Jews, who were always on the move — read the stories of Abraham, Moses and so on — were not inclined to venerate anything visible, be it above or below; they found Yahveh, the invisible god who created the human I and influenced it.

Now the whole has meaning! You can see how humanity gradually found itself. The story continues, and we'll look at the rest of it. Well, gentlemen, today is Saturday, so we'll meet again next Wednesday.

Aspects of human life that are not physical. Greek culture and Christianity

Well, gentlemen, has someone thought of something for today?

Someone asked about the purpose of the Shrovetide carnival, if Rudolf Steiner could tell them something about it. What were the origins and the significance.

Rudolf Steiner: You mean, what is the purpose of the Shrovetide carnival? Well, you see, the Shrovetide festival cannot really be understood if one asks about its purpose, for I think you'll admit that as the years go by people could manage without it, at least the way it is celebrated now. It would be fair to say that from the present-day point of view the Shrovetide carnival is essentially pointless. This is because it has lost its original meaning. The same thing has happened to it as to the orders, habits, etc. of old. They had meaning and purpose once but this has gradually been lost. The other festivals of the year are also gradually vanishing; little by little they lose significance unless they are given new meaning. So far nothing much has been done to give it meaning again. If it regained its original meaning, which it had in ancient Rome, for instance, it would have a profound influence on the whole of our social life.

Let us go back to ancient Rome. People had different roles then, just as they have today. One would be a civil servant, another a soldier, the third a workman, and so on, and the divisions were much sharper then, at least socially, than they are today. A human being who was a slave could actually be bought! So we may say the differences between people were still very marked in ancient Rome. But there were to be at least a few days every year when people could forget that they had a particular social position. Today we speak of democracy and think that all people are equal, at least in theory. The ancient Romans believed no such thing; for them, someone had to be born into one of the upper classes before he would even be considered to be a proper human being. To this day some people still believe the old saying that to be human you must at least be a baron, meaning that anyone less than a baron is not a human being.

This was a powerful thing in ancient Rome. They did not yet have a nobility in the sense that was to develop later on—for this is a medieval principle arising from the feudal system. But there were marked class differences in ancient Rome. For a few days in the year, however, people were to be equal and democracy should reign. It would not do, of course, for people to show their ordinary faces, for then they would have been recognized; so they had to wear masks. They would then be what their masks indicated them to be. One individual would be the carnival king and he could do anything he wanted during those days. He could issue commands where normally he would only be given them. And the whole of Rome went mad, topsy-turvy, for a few days. People could even behave differently to their superiors and did not need to be polite to them— just for a few days, to make people equal. This meant, of course, that people did not exactly weep or mourn on those days; for they were delighted to live like that for a few days. This developed into the carnival pleasures we know today. People would only do mad things for the few days when they were free. That was the origin of our carnival.

People liked it so much that it survived to this day. But things survive without people knowing the original meaning. And so the carnival is now a time when people let things go topsy-turvy. Then the Church thought it necessary to let Ash Wednesday come immediately afterwards, when people are conscious of their sins, not allowed to do anything they want, and so on, and since Christians had developed the custom, at least in earlier times, that people should go without things, the fasting period of Lent was established. And it was sensible to let Lent follow on from the carnival time, when people had to restrain themselves as little as possible, doing anything that pleased them, in so far as it was possible. And afterwards it is much harder not to eat things one has been eating before. And so the two events came together.

In Rome the carnival came much earlier, at about the time of our Christmas, for everything was afterwards moved to a later season. And so today's carnival has survived. I think the date is based on the date for Easter in most areas, but in Basel it is celebrated about a week later, as far as I know. I also hear that all this means is that people celebrate twice!

So that would be what I can say in reply to this question. It can be said of many things in human life that they originally had meaning but that this was then lost as time went on. And one asks oneself why all this should be.

Does anyone else have a question today?

Someone wanted to ask if Rudolf Steiner would continue with the look at history from the last time.

Someone else: *I wanted to ask Dr Steiner if such a thing would be possible that people insult another person or cause him pain, that is, have an influence on them. Mrs A. had a 3-year-old child who would always see spirits come in through the door and the windows. The child often had disturbed nights, especially when the woman had washed their body linen – the woman would take things from the house – and then the child would always grow disturbed. In the end there was no more of this; the woman died later. I would like to ask Dr Steiner if such a thing might be possible.*

Rudolf Steiner:. These are, of course, things that affect all kinds of areas, and because people are superstitious, superstition would also play a role—superstition and also the facts. You simply have to understand that there are situations in the world that are not open to direct physical observation. Let me begin with some quite simple situations.

Think of a grape harvest. You gather the grapes and press them, putting the wine in barrels in the cellar. You will find that it grows restless at the time when the next year's wine is fermenting. A connection is there, although there is no physical link. This is a simple fact and it shows that there are connections in the natural world that cannot be observed using one's eyes and so on.

Today we have a method by which ordinary visibility can be bypassed. Even in lifeless nature we have situations today where visibility with the naked eye—not visibility of a more subtle kind—is done away with. Just think of wireless telegraphy. This is based on an apparatus that generates electricity that is not connected by wires but stands there by itself. Somewhere else, and in no way physically connected with it, is an apparatus with parallel plates that may be set in motion. It is called a coherer. To begin with, there seems to be no visible physical connection, but if you produce an electric current here, the signs move there; and if you link this up with an apparatus, you can receive telegrams, just as you can pick up electricity with wires. We know this is due to electricity spreading, but this is something we cannot see; it spreads without there being any tangible physical link. Here you have a connection in lifeless nature where we may certainly say: The visible sphere has been overcome, at least to some extent.

We can take this further. Think of a pair of twins. There is no physical contact between them when they have grown older. One may be in one place, the other in another. Yet it is possible to see especially in the case of twins that one may fall ill, for instance, and the other, who lives further away, likewise. Or one may feel sad about something, and the other one too. Such things show that there are effects in this world where we cannot say they are due to a direct physical influence.

When we come to the animal world, we soon find that animals have perceptions, for instance, that humans do not have. Let us assume an earthquake or a volcanic eruption is about to happen that will do great harm to those who live in the area. The people will stay where they are, feeling no disquiet; but the animals can often be seen to leave the area, sometimes days beforehand. This shows that animals may sense something that cannot be perceived by the physical senses. If it could be perceived in that way, the people, too, would know what was coming.

You can see from all this that it is possible for connections to exist in the world that are not physical. If we go into these more subtle connections we find that people, too, will sometimes sense something that they have certainly not been able to perceive with the physical senses. Let us take an example. Someone gives a sudden start and sees some kind of image before him—this is only a dream, of course. He shouts: 'My friend!' But the friend may be far away. The person may have the experience in Europe when the friend is perhaps in America. 'My friend! Something has happened to him!' As it turns out, the friend has died. Such things do certainly occur. It is possible to establish that they happen, though there is no physical link.

It has to be said, however, that it is a good thing for humanity that these things are none too common. Just think what it would be like if your head enabled you to perceive all the bad things someone else is thinking or saying about you—that would be a bad business! You know that when one has a telegraph, this has to be set up first, the wire has to be switched on, and then you get a transmission. With wireless telegraphy, too, this part must be functioning properly [pointing to the blackboard] or you get no transmission. Normal, healthy people are not connected to all the currents there are; they are switched off. In special cases it may however happen that someone is connected and able to receive something.

Let us assume, therefore—I cannot go into your particular case and there is good reason for this, for you probably do not know how well it is proven to be true. I'll consider a similar situation, and this should also explain yours. I always want to speak only of things that are properly authenticated, otherwise it may well be just talk. You probably did not know the people involved personally but read or heard about it?

Let us assume a woman, Mrs A, had a dispute with a Mrs B whilst she was pregnant. It happens, does it not, that people have disputes. Perhaps Mrs B, who lives in the neighbourhood, really cursed Mrs A, and Mrs A got a terrible fright when Mrs B was making such a hullabaloo. The result may be that the child, when it is born, shows a certain dependence on Mrs B, and Mrs B also on the child, and it may well happen that this makes the child sensitive to what is given to it as body linen or the like, with Mrs B washing it. Feeling some regret at what she has done to Mrs A, Mrs B needs something from her house, to soothe her. If the object is taken from her she will try to get it back by all possible means. People sometimes take all kinds of things though they are not thieves by nature. They only steal those things; they do not steal otherwise, but seek to get hold of those things by all means. And it may indeed happen that if it is taken away from them they sicken and die from a kind of inner consumption, a consumptive fever, for human health is also influenced by elements of soul and spirit. Or they may die of a heart attack or a paralysis. This may certainly be the case.

We may say, therefore, that these things happen, and they can be explained because under certain conditions one person certainly has an influence on another even if there is no physical contact. But one must always be able to consider the cause. In the case you mention the cause may have been completely different. But if there had been a row during Mrs A's pregnancy that might have been the reason for the later connection between Mrs B and the child.

Well, gentlemen I have been asked to continue with the subject I spoke of last week. I showed you that people's lives were completely different in ancient India, perhaps four or five millennia ago. Due to the special nature of those peoples, and the way the nations came together, the ancient Indians developed their view of the human physical body.

The Egyptians, whose lands were completely under the influence of the Nile, and who owed everything they were to the Nile, as it were — a situation that makes people aware of the ether — developed a view of the human ether body.

The people of Assyria and the Babylonians lived at some altitude where the air was particularly clear and the stars could be easily observed. They developed a view of the astral body.

The Jews, who had to move from place to place in earlier times, and initially had no lasting abode, thought and felt more out of inner human nature. They developed a view of the human I.

We thus see the gradual development of human awareness of the physical body, the ether body, the astral body and the I. You see, Yahveh actually means 'I am the I am'. That is the meaning of the word. And if Yahveh is worshipped as the greatest god, such recognition of the greatest god clearly points also to the human I.

If we follow the evolution of history in this way, we find that all those peoples essentially gave expression in thoughts and feelings to the way they experienced life.

Indians knew a rich, fruitful world of nature, a continual flowering and abundant growth. They really perceived the riches of the physical world and out of this developed their view of the physical body. The Egyptians saw that help came to them only from the Nile, which one can see; they therefore developed the concept of the ether, and so on. All those peoples really developed their views from their life experience.

This was different with another nation. We may say [blackboard drawing]: Here ancient India, here Arabia; here then Egypt, this is where the Nile flows. Then over here we have a land that extends towards Africa and connects with Europe. This is where Assyria would be, as I showed the last time, here Egypt, here India; here we would have Palestine, where the Jews lived; and here we have Greece. People coming from many different parts of Asia and Europe settled and intermingled here in Greece. There were original inhabitants, but as time went on the Greek nation evolved on this European peninsula. The Greeks, we might say, were the first to open their eyes and see something of the world that was not purely inner experience. Indians knew the natural world from inside; the Egyptians had living experience of ether activity; the Assyrians gained experience of the astral body from the stars; the Jews had living experience of their I. The Greeks were really the first to look at the world outside. The others did not actually look at the world. We are thus able to say that the Indians, Egyptians, Babylonians and Jews did not have a real view of the natural world; they did not know much about it because they did not open their eyes to look at it. A view of the natural world developed among the Greeks because they actually looked. And humanity did not really perceive the outside world until the Greeks did so.

You see, the Indian view was like this: 'This physical world here is part of the whole world, and I came from the

realm of the spirit at birth and shall return to it when I die.'
The Egyptians did believe it was necessary to preserve
mummies so that individuals might be able to return to
them; but they also had their particular view of the spirit.
The Babylonians saw the will of the spirits in the starry
heavens, the astral sphere, which they observed. And you
know that the Jews held the belief that Jehovah, Yahveh,
would take them back to the time of the Fathers. Essentially
they were therefore also concerned with something that
connects human beings with the world of the spirit.

This changed in ancient Greece. The Greeks were really
the first to grow fond of the outside world. They thought a
great deal of it; there is a Greek saying that it is better to be a
beggar in the upper world—meaning Greece, here on
earth—than a king in the realm of shadows, meaning the
dead.[8] The Greeks, then, came to love the world above all
things, and thus were also the first to develop a view of the
natural world.

The other peoples developed a view of the human being.
The Indians in particular, had a certain view of the human
being in very early times. But they did not gain this by
dissecting dead bodies! If that had been necessary the
Indians would never have gained a view of the human
being. They sensed how the liver, the lung, functions in a
particular part of the human body; this was still possible at
the time. The Indians gained great wisdom because they
knew from an inner sense and feeling how the liver functions, and so on. Today we only know how a bite of meat
tastes in the mouth. The Indians knew from inner experience how a bite of meat behaved in the intestines, what the
liver did, what the bile did, just as today we have experience of the bite of meat in the mouth.

The Egyptians developed geometry because they needed
it. They had to establish the position of their fields over and
over again, for the Nile would flood everything year after

year. This, too, is something we produce out of the head. The Babylonians developed astrology, knowledge of the stars, again something beyond earthly concerns; they had no great interest in earthly things. The fact that the Jews had no great interest in earthly things is evident from the way their real interest lay anywhere except with the world we perceive through the senses. They were well able to think but had no real interest in the sense-perceptible world.

The people who had the greatest interest for the world perceived through the senses were the Greeks. If one goes into this, it is interesting to find that they saw the whole world differently from the way we see it today. This is most interesting. We see a blue sky today. The Greeks did not see blue the way we do; their sky was much darker, almost blackish, with a slight tinge of green. They were particularly conscious of the colour red. Our perception of red is so weak, we can hardly imagine the impression that colour made on the Greeks. Humanity only gradually developed a feeling for blue, and with this humanity has come away again from that sensory impression. The Greeks therefore developed a particular liking for things that existed outside themselves. And because of this they specially developed something we call a mythology today. The Greeks venerated a whole world of gods — Zeus, Apollo, Pallas Athene, Ares, Aphrodite; they saw gods everywhere. They venerated those gods because the natural world around them, which they loved, seemed to them to be filled with life and with spirit. Not as dead as it is for us, but filled with life and spirit. They thus venerated the gods everywhere in the natural world that had become dear to them.

Because of this, people who depended on Greek civilization, culture and spirit in those ancient days forgot the things the Indians, Egyptians and Babylonians had known in mind and spirit.

You no doubt know the powerful effect Greece has had

on the whole of human development. It continues to this day. Anyone able to send his son to grammar school today makes him learn Greek. This was much more widespread earlier on. You were an ass in those days if you did not know Greek or were unable at least to read the work of the Greek writers and poets. Greece has had a tremendous influence on the world because this was the first nation to take an interest in this outside world.

Whilst the Greeks developed this interest in the outside world, the significant development happening in Asia was that the Mystery of Golgotha spread from there. This was when Greece had been conquered and everything was essentially under Roman rule. What was the significance of this Roman rule? It was full of the Greek spirit. Educated Romans would all know Greek, and the educated people in Rome knew Greek as a matter of course. The Greek spirit had the greatest influence everywhere. Whilst Greek culture was thus spreading, something else happened in Asia, in a little-known Roman province—that was Palestine at that time, with the Jews conquered. A man had appeared, Jesus of Nazareth, who said something very different from what people had ever said so far. And as you can imagine, because it was something different, people did not immediately understand him. At the beginning very few people understood what he said.

What did this Jesus say, when he appeared in Palestine? He said, in the way he was able to put it in those days: 'People everywhere believe today'—this was the today of that time—'that the human being is a creature of the earth. He is not, however. He comes from the world of the spirit and will return to it on his death.' Christianity has had an influence for almost 2000 years now, and so it may seem strange to hear of such a thing being said in those days. But the situation was very different. Asian and African ideas of the spirit were little known then; they had not spread far.

People were more interested in the world. And what Jesus of Nazareth was teaching at that time was tremendously important, especially compared to the worldly Greek culture of the Romans.

With this, however, Jesus of Nazareth would have done no more than bringing back to life what earlier peoples — the Indians, the Egyptians and so on — had already said in the past. It would merely have been a return of the things I have told you, things that were already known. But Jesus of Nazareth did not merely rehash something that was already known, for he also said the following. He said: 'If I had only listened to what people are able to tell me today, I would never have found the teachings of the spirit, for the truth is that people really no longer know anything about the spirit. This is something that has come to me from beyond this earth.' He had thus become aware that he was not only Jesus, but that a spirit had arisen in his soul who was the Christ. Jesus was to him the individual born of a woman here on earth. The Christ was the spirit who had entered into his soul at a later time. Then the truth arose in his soul that human beings are spiritual by nature.

At this point we must ask ourselves how the ancient teachings of India, Egypt, Babylon and the Jews were kept alive. If you consider the life of mind and spirit today, you find the Church on one hand and schools on the other. At most those who rule the Church are in dispute with those who govern the schools as to how much influence the one should have on the other. They are, however, separate establishments. This was not the case among the ancient Indians, Egyptians, Babylonians or Jews. Anything connected with religion in those times was also connected with the schools; church service and school service were one. Much of this has continued on to the present time, but it is no longer the case, as it was then, that the priest would also be the teacher. Priests were teachers in India, Egypt,

Babylon and so on. And they taught in the places where religious rites were also held. The religious rites were completely bound up with the teaching work. Those were the mystery centres. People did not have churches and schools but places that were both, places we now call mystery centres.

The general view was, however, that one had to be cautious in what might be learned. You see, the ancient view was that people had to have the necessary maturity before certain knowledge was given to them. This is something that has been lost today. And the people who held the highest rank in the mystery centres were known as the Fathers. A remnant of this is that in the Catholic Church, for instance, certain priests are still called Father. In those early times, the Fathers were those initiated into knowledge in India, Egypt, Babylon and so on. And those they taught — people who had been admitted because the Fathers believed they could make them ripe for knowledge — would be called the sons. All other people, who were not admitted to the mysteries, were called the children of the Fathers, or also sons and daughters.

You will understand that this created a certain attitude, which was that people — much more capable of belief at that time than people are today — truly felt those who served the mysteries to be their Fathers; they were glad to have them as their Fathers in the spirit. And above all people believed that these spiritual Fathers were communing more closely with the gods than those outside the mysteries who had to receive the message from the Fathers. People gradually became very dependent on those Fathers. A situation which, I believe, the Roman Catholic Church would dearly like to create today was taken as a matter of course at the time. This was so in all countries. And no one would object to it. People would say: 'To be truly human you either have to be a Father, and commune directly with the gods, or you have to learn about the gods from the Fathers.' You would be human therefore in so far as those who served in the schools, in the mysteries, told you something.

A difference developed between children of God and children of man, sons of God and sons of man. Those who were part of the mysteries would be called sons of God, because they looked up to the gods as they did to the Fathers. Those who lived outside the mysteries, who were merely told what came through the mysteries, were called children or sons of man. Thus the distinction arose between sons of God and sons or children of men. This may seem almost ridiculous today, but at the time is was perfectly natural. Today a difference is made — perhaps not in Switzerland, though for all I know a bit of it exists here as well, but in neighbouring countries — between excellencies and ordinary people, the barons and the ordinary people. It is a bit less now, but not long ago it was taken as a matter of course. In earlier times it was a matter of course that a difference existed between sons of God, children of God, and sons of men.

The individual who then called himself Christ Jesus, and who was called this, said: 'You do not become a son of God, a child of the spirit, through another person. Everyone becomes this through God himself. It is only a matter of being aware of this.' People of old would say that the Father from the mysteries must make them aware of it. Christ Jesus said: 'You have the seed of the divine in you, and you merely have to make the effort and you can find it in yourself.'

He thus showed what makes people all over the world the same in their souls. And the biggest difference to be overcome by Christ Jesus was the one between sons of the gods and sons of men.

This was later widely misunderstood — in the old days because people did not want a time to come when no distinction was made between sons of gods and children of men, and later because people no longer knew what was meant by it. Just as people later no longer knew what the carnival meant, so they no longer knew what was meant by 'sons of gods' and 'sons of men'. This is why we find all the time in the Bible that on one occasion Jesus Christ is called Son of God and on another Son of Man. All the passages where reference is made to the Son of God and the Son of Man really mean that the two terms may be used to say the same thing, which is why they are given in alternation. If one does not know this one cannot really understand the Gospels. And they really are very poorly understood today, especially by those who declare their belief in them.

This, then, shows the principle that really came into the world through Christ Jesus at the level of feelings. Considering things in a more superficial way today, I have to say: You see, there were also other great differences between people everywhere. Just think of ancient India where a distinction similar to those between classes of animals was made between Brahmins, priests, peasants and workers. The Egyptians had a whole army of slaves. Their castes were not so strictly separate, but they did exist. Even in ancient Greece and Rome a difference was made between freeborn people and slaves. These outer differences have only been wiped away in more recent history because the difference between children of the gods and children of men had been removed. What happened in Palestine through Christ Jesus thus had a tremendous influence on the whole social life of humanity.

Now we may indeed ask in the light of all this: Is it true that one can find out where the spiritual principle comes from that exists in the human being, having come from beyond this earth? You see, it is extremely difficult to speak of this today, because everything is considered in material terms. Think of language. You know people in different countries speak different languages. In spite of this all languages secretly have something in common. This may not be as clearly apparent as it is in Germany and in England, in Germany and in Holland. But it is indeed true that languages, however different, show a certain similarity. You may find, for instance, that if you enter into the language that is spoken in India, you may not immediately understand, but the shapes of individual words show similarity, for instance, with the German language.

How do people try to explain this? They'll say: 'Well, such and such a language evolved in one place on earth — for everything is said to come from the earth — and then people migrated, taking their language to some other place, where it changed a little. But it all comes from one language.'

That is the most misguided belief scientists have produced in recent times. For you see, gentlemen, the misguided beliefs of scientists are exactly as follows. Imagine someone living in India getting hot in the sun. The view then arises that a person may grow hot. Later on people in Europe discover that they, too, can grow hot in summer. And now they do not use their brains but their senses and say: 'The fact that we get hot is something we cannot explain in terms of the present situation; but people got hot in ancient India and they emigrated to Europe, transplanting the ability to grow hot to Europe.'

Well, gentlemen, anyone saying that is, of course, mad. But that is what the language experts say! They do not say that there has been the same influence coming from outside the earth in India and in Europe; they say the language migrated. When people get hot in two parts of the world we don't say they have brought the ability to get hot with them when they migrated. Instead we look at the sun which shines in both places and makes people hot in both India and Europe. If you find two languages that are far apart geographically but show similarities, this is not due to migration but to a common influence, just as the sun's influence exists for the whole earth. Coming from beyond the earth it affects peoples in very different parts of the earth. People simply do not want to admit that there is such an influence on mind and spirit, and they therefore think up all kinds of things where one simply does not notice that they are crazy because they are so scholarly. If people were not afraid of being taken for mad they would also deny that the sun makes us hot; instead they would say: 'In very early times the capacity for getting hot developed, and this has been transplanted to all parts of the globe.' They would deny the sun's influence, except that this would be crazy. This is something to consider when we seek to understand how Christianity arose.

It is too late today to take this further. We'll continue next Saturday.

Christianity coming into the world of antiquity and the mysteries

Good morning, gentlemen. I'll continue today with the things we have been considering before. You need to be really clear. Asia is over there in the east [drawing on the board]. From Asia people came to Europe in antiquity, to Greece, along a whole chain of islands. This was as far as Asia went; here came Africa; and there was the Nile—I have told you a lot about it. Here is Greece, the Adriatic Sea, here Italy and Sicily, the island. Many islands would be here— Samos, Rhodes, Cyprus and so on, and people came to Greece from Asia via these islands. This would be Greece, this the Roman Empire, the Italy of today.

Now you need to call to mind the following, gentlemen. You see, from about the year 1000, 1200 before Christ, everything I have told you developed in Greece. With people learning to look at the world. Very soon, however, from the fourth and third centuries before Christ, Greece gradually lost its dominance, and this went to Rome, the capital. What happened was that Greeks who were more or less dissatisfied with conditions in Greece emigrated in growing numbers in very early times, settling down here in Sicily and southern Italy. For half a millennium, four or five hundred years, they brought Greek culture to these regions, so much so that Sicily and southern Italy were known as Greater Greece in those days. They would refer to their old homeland simply as Greece, calling the rest Greater Greece. Not only discontented people went there but also people like the great philosopher Plato who wanted to establish an ideal republic there.[9] The people who were most important in developing that civilization really all lived in southern Italy and we have to say that life in that region was refined, with people highly educated. The brutal dominance of Roman civilization, as it came to be called, spread from the region above this.

You know that the original population of Rome has a most peculiar origin. Chieftains, one of the best known of them being Romulus, called together all the rogues and scoundrels in the area, and effectively created the first robber state. This robber mentality continued under the first Roman kings. Soon, however, under the fourth and fifth kings, a northern tribe, the Etruscans, came and settled in Rome. They brought a human element to Rome, inter-marrying with the descendants of the early robbers. But the whole dominion over the world later established by Rome, all the lust for power that continues even into our own time, really originated — we should be under no illusion here — from the original colony of rogues on the seven hills of Rome. All kinds of other things were added on top; the whole business has been much refined, but we cannot really understand how things were done in later times unless we know that originally a band of robbers had been gathered from the woods. All the lust for power and so on that spread over the whole of Europe and still plays such a great role today came from this. Something else that developed in Rome was the thinking through which the Church became increasingly tied up with worldly government. Medieval times evolved from this, and so on.

Now you see, at the beginning of our era there was the Mystery of Golgotha. The Roman rule I have spoken of was established in the eighth century before Christ. At the time of Golgotha, Roman rule, established seven centuries earlier, spread far and wide, including the area where the Mystery of Golgotha took place. The Jews living in Pales-tine, among whom Jesus of Nazareth appeared, were also under Roman rule. It will be good, having said so much about the Mystery of Golgotha, to take some account also of what really had been happening on the Italian peninsula from very early times.

It is absolutely true to say that Europeans really only understand the things that go back to Roman times. 'Educated' people have of course learned Greek, but there has really been very little understanding of Greek culture in Europe. You see, it is most interesting that a hundred years after the Mystery of Golgotha Tacitus, one of the most important Roman writers,[10] wrote only a single sentence about Christ Jesus in his vast historical work. A hundred years after Golgotha, Tacitus wrote about the ancient Germans, for instance, in a way that simply was no longer possible afterwards. His works include a single sentence about Christ Jesus, which says: 'The Christ, as he was called, founded a sect among the Jews, and was later sentenced to death and executed.'[11] So this is what Tacitus, an educated Roman, had to say a hundred years after the founding of Christianity in Palestine. So you can imagine, ships went to and fro all the time, all kinds of trade and cultural links developed, and a hundred years after the event no more notice was taken of Christianity in Rome than to make a note that a sect was founded and its founder condemned to death and executed!

There was, of course, the aspect that the idea of the state developed from Roman culture. We cannot really call the Roman Empire a state in the proper sense, for the idea of a state as we know it only developed in sixteenth-century Europe. Thus we may say that Tacitus was already thinking so much in terms of state that the most important thing to him was that Christ Jesus was properly condemned and executed. That is one thing.

You also have to consider that in its early days Christianity was not what it became later. Originally it had a real air of freedom. It would be fair to say that people had all kinds of different views, and only came together in that they saw Christ Jesus to be something special; apart from that they had very different views.

Well, gentlemen, you'll only be able understand what came into the world with Christ Jesus — and why it was after all necessary for me to show you that the surroundings of our earth have an influence on it, even in language — if I now attempt to show you how Christianity developed as teaching, as a view, a view of the world and of life, and how Christ Jesus came into this evolution of Christianity. It is really something very special to see that Christianity was founded there in Jerusalem, and a hundred years later the most erudite Roman author knew no more about it than I have told you. People were, however, always migrating from Asia via Africa to Italy. And this Christian sect was spreading beneath the surface, I would say, of human affairs as they were seen in Rome. When Tacitus wrote those words, the Christians, Christianians as they were called, had long since spread among the populace, which would not interest a noble Roman.

But what did they do with the Christians? Well, you see, the descendants of Romulus the robber, too, had gradually reached a point where they were 'really educated'. Their education consisted among other things in building vast arenas where fights with wild animals took place. They took great pleasure in throwing those whom they did not consider to be part of humanity in the Roman sense to the wild animals and delighted in watching them being eaten, having first been forced to fight. That would be a 'noble' pleasure. The despised sect called the Christians were particularly suitable for throwing to the wild animals at the time when people thought like this in Rome; they were also particularly suitable for being painted with pitch and set fire to, so that one could see them as torches in the circus.

But the Christians still found ways of surviving. They did so by holding their ceremonies and so on in secret. They would spread what they felt it was important to spread below ground, in the catacombs. Catacombs are large underground spaces. There the Christians buried those of their dead whom they loved. So there would be the graves, and the divine services were held over the graves.

It was generally the custom in those days to hold divine services over the graves. You can still see this today if you look at the altar in a Roman Catholic church. It is in fact a burial place [sketching], with relics such as the bones of saints kept inside. In earliest times the altar was an actual gravestone, with divine services performed on it. Below ground, in the catacombs, the Christians of those early centuries were able to hide the things which they had to do.

A few centuries later the picture had changed a great deal. What happened then was this. You see, the Romans were up above in the early centuries after the founding of Christianity, amusing themselves in the way I have told you, and below, in the catacombs, were the Christians. A few centuries later the Romans had gone and the Christians began to rule the world. The question as to whether they did better or worse is something we can discuss on another occasion; but they took over world rule. It proved extremely harmful to Christianity to be thus connected with world rule, for as world history progresses the religious life is less and less compatible with the state system and world rule.

The matter is as follows. We can only understand the evolution of Christianity, the involvement of Christ Jesus in the evolution of Christianity, if we understand the nature of religious life in earlier times, when it was part of everything. I have told you of the ancient mysteries. To use a modern term, the mysteries were institutions where everything a person could learn was learned. And at the same time they were the religious institutions and the art institutions. All cultural life came from the mysteries. And people did not learn the way they do today. How do people learn today? People have things drummed into them in grammar schools and secondary schools; they then go through some years at university and this leaves them the same as before. But in the mysteries you became a different human being. You had to gain a new relationship to the whole world. In the mysteries you had to grow wise. The institutions we have in the modern world do not make anyone wise; at most you can become learned. But two things may be compatible or not compatible; wisdom does not go with stupidity, but learnedness can easily go hand in hand with great stupidity. So that is the situation. In the ancient mysteries people were made into wise human beings and truly cultured. They became human beings who could take the spiritual realm seriously. They had to go through seven stages, with only very few reaching the highest stage. Those seven stages had names which we must learn to understand so that we shall know what the individuals who had reached them had to do.

If we translate what a person had to do when first admitted to the mysteries, we arrive at the term 'Raven'. The first stage thus were the Ravens. Admitted to the mysteries you became a Raven. What did Ravens have to do? Well they primarily had to maintain communications between the outside world and the mysteries. They did not have newspapers then. The first newspapers only came thousands of years later when printing was invented. The people who taught in the mysteries had to gain information by sending out trusted individuals who would observe the world. The Ravens may be said to have been the confidential agents of the people who served the mysteries. And this was something you had to learn first, to be someone who could be trusted. Today political parties and so on employ many confidential agents, but one has to ask oneself if they can always be trusted! Those employed as Ravens in the mysteries were only accepted as confidential agents after being tried and tested. Above all they had to learn to take the things that they saw seriously and report them truthfully. But in the first place it was also necessary to learn what truth signifies in human beings. I am sure people were no less deceitful in antiquity than they are today. But today lying and deceit come into everything; whereas in those days you first had to learn to be a true human being. This was what you had to make your own in the years of being a Raven, a confidential agent of the mysteries.

The second stage was something people find most unacceptable today. It was the level of the Occultists. Occult means hidden, secret. They would not be sent out but had to learn something modern people do not like to learn—to be silent. One level of learning in the ancient mysteries was to learn to be silent. You'll think it grotesque, a real joke, that people had to keep silence for a year at least, or even longer. But it is true. You learn a great deal from keeping silence. It is something that can no longer be done today. Imagine schools were required to make young people between the ages of 17 and 19 be silent for a year instead of having to go into the army. It would indeed be very useful for the gaining of wisdom, for keeping silence would make them terribly wise. But it can no longer be done today.

Something else can be done, however. I know you cannot stop people talking, they don't want to be silent but want to chat, and everyone knows everything, and if you meet someone today he has above all what we call a 'point of view'. Everyone has a point of view, of course, but the world looks different from another point of view, and this is nothing new for anyone who knows the world; it is understood. If you stand here, the mountain looks different compared to the way it would look if you stood over there. The same holds true in cultural life. Everybody has his point of view, and every person is able to see something else. And if you have a dozen people they will, of course, have thirteen opinions! That need not be so. But it need not surprise us that they have twelve points of view; only they should not take it so seriously. Everybody considers his own point of view to be most important, terribly important! In earlier times people simply had to keep silence about the things they were to learn; they were merely listeners. One could not call them anything but 'Listeners' in the occult world, for they had to listen. Today the students at German universities are called 'hearers' and no longer pupils.[12] But they often do not hear, for they chatter. Some actually consider it more important to chat to their fellow students than to listen in the lecture theatres. And sometimes listening is no longer something that makes people particularly serious.

This, then, was the second stage. People learned to keep silence. And when there is silence it happens — this is like a cause and effect relationship — that the inner nature of the human being begins to speak to him. This is the way. Imagine you have a basin of water; if you use a hose to siphon off the water, the water will run away — if you have a basin, not a spring — and then there is none left. And this is what happens when people chatter all the time. Everything runs away with those words, and nothing is left. The ancients knew this, and because of this their Listeners were first of all made to keep silence. They thus learned to appreciate the truth and then to keep silence. The silence came afterwards.

The third stage was one we might translate as the 'Defenders'. Now these people were allowed to talk. They were now permitted to defend the truth they had learned by keeping silence in the mysteries. Above all they were asked to defend the spirit. 'Defence' is the word we may reasonably use for this third stage. The people who were at this stage had to know enough to lend weight to anything they said about things of the spirit. It was therefore not permissible in the mysteries simply to talk about the spirit; you had to learn about it first and have become a proper Defender.

People would then advance to the fourth stage. We may translate this as 'Lion'. That is how it is usually translated. It would be even better to say 'Sphinx'. The word signifies more or less that one has become a spirit. You would still go about in a human body but you would behave among people the way gods behave. People did not make a great difference between humans and gods; you simply became a god as you progressed through the mysteries. The ancients had a much more open way of looking at things. People of later times saw the gods as always being above humanity. That was not the view held by the ancients. Today people say: All right, man is descended from the apes. Du Bois-Reymond, a famous scientist,[13] actually said there had been a giant leap from anthropoid apes to humans, a giant step also in the size of the brain. The brain was suddenly larger than it was in the anthropoid apes. That was a strange statement for a modern scientist to make. One would assume that someone who says such a thing would have dissected an anthropoid ape and know how big the brain was. But if you look it up you'll find that scientists have to admit that the anthropoid ape has not yet been discovered! Dr Du Bois-Reymond, the famous scientist, was therefore referring to something that has not yet been found, something nobody has seen so far—the anthropoid ape. That is the kind of 'conscientiousness' applied in science today. People would never think that Du Bois-Reymond might speak of something he has never seen. They think a famous scientist knows everything! People are more credulous today than they were in antiquity.

The ancients thus certainly believed that human beings

can develop and are able to gain the conscious awareness of gods.

Someone who had reached the fourth stage and was a Sphinx would no longer speak like a Defender of the third stage but use a language in which he expressed himself in such a way that it was really difficult to understand him; you had to reflect on how he should be understood. It is difficult for people today to get an idea of the language spoken by the Sphinxes because we no longer see things the way they saw them then. Even in the Middle Ages, in the seventeenth century, for instance, something of that language still survived. At that time, two hundred years ago, they had the Rosicrucian schools, for example. In them, certain initiates would speak in a language that was slightly veiled and had to be studied first; they would above all speak in images. Two hundred years ago you would still find an image—you may find this interesting—that was used everywhere to explain the human being to some extent. This image [blackboard drawing] was a human form with a lion's head, and next to it a human form with an ox head. Speaking to the people under instruction they would refer to the relationship between the two as 'the creature with the ox head', 'the creature with the lion's head', meaning man and woman. They would not use the words 'man' and 'woman', but 'the creature with the ox head—meaning the man—and 'the creature with the lion's head'—meaning the woman. The relationship between ox and lion was seen to be like the relationship between man and woman. This sounds funny to people today, but the tradition has survived. And the Sphinxes always used the names of animals to give clearer and more characteristic expression to anything that lives in a human being. This, you see, would have been the language of the Sphinxes, who were already speaking more out of the spirit.

There followed the fifth stage. These people were obliged

to speak only out of the spirit. Depending on which nation they belonged to they would be called 'Persian' or 'Indian' or 'Greek'. In Greece, it was they who were the real Greeks. People would say to themselves: 'Someone who belongs to a nation has private interests, wanting this or that; wanting something different from someone belonging to another nation. It is only when he has advanced to the fifth stage that he no longer wants something for himself but only what the nation as a whole wants; this is also what he wants. He has become like a spirit of the nation.'

Those spirits of the nations in the ancient mysteries, and still in ancient Greece, were exceedingly wise people. They would not say: 'When something comes up I'll stand there and have my own point of view, knowing everything.' No, although they had advanced to the fifth stage they would go through long periods of exercises that would allow them to judge situations. You see, if you have a modern statesman, a point may be raised in parliament and he has to answer. Just think what it would be like if things were done the way they were in those earlier days, when someone required to answer would say: I must first withdraw from the world for a week, go into myself, so that I may form an opinion. Well, I'd like to know what the parliamentary parties would say to Mr Stresemann[14] or to other bodies if someone asking a question were to be given the answer: 'To give a considered opinion on the issue I must first withdraw for a week.' That is how it was in those days. People believed in the world of the spirit and knew that it would not speak to them in the hustle and bustle of life but only when they were able to withdraw from this. One will then of course also develop the ability to withdraw in the midst of the hustle and bustle; but it has to be learnt first. Once it had been learnt, the individual would progress to the sixth stage.

At the sixth stage the individual no longer had an earthly point of view, not even that of his people. He would say to himself: I am a 'Greek', my brother initiate who has reached the fifth stage in Assyria is an 'Assyrian', the one who lives even further away a 'Persian'. But those are all one-sided points of view. The sun moves through Persia and then on to Greece; it shines on us all. Initiates of the sixth stage no longer wanted to learn from what a nation was saying; they wanted to learn from what the sun was saying. They became Sun People, no longer people of the earth but of the sun. You see, those Sun People would seek to consider everything from the sun point of view. People have no idea today of the things that were done in those days, for they know nothing of the secrets of the world.

To gain insight into such things we have to consider the following, for example. Some time ago a man came to me and said: 'A strange book has appeared in which it is shown that the Gospels were written in a numerical code.' If we were to take a particular word in the Gospels, let us say the word 'beginning' in John's Gospel: 'In the beginning was the Word. And the Word was with God, and the Word was a God', and divide the phrase up, and we were to find that one particular part was twice the length of another, and each word had a numerical value—there you have a word with a numerical value of 50, followed by 25, another word, 50, and another word, 25. And one would be able to calculate which word should be written in which place.

It is interesting to see if this works. Let us take a word— I'll use one that we also have in German—the word Eva. Let us assume the E has the value 1, the V a two, the A a three. Let us assume it is so. In the past every letter had a numerical value; it was not only a letter and people knew that if you had an L, for instance, this also meant a number. You can still see the numerical values in Roman letters:

I = one, V = five, X = ten
i v x

These are letters but they also have numerical value.

So with Eva as an example, it is not really 1, 2, 3, but we'll assume it is:

1 2 3

E v a   is the mother of all that lives. Now we turn it round:

3 2 1

a v e   and we have 'ave', which means the end of life. Going in opposite directions, read in reverse from the back:

1 2 3   3 2 1

E v a   a v e

Changing the numbers you'll always find that figures and letters agree.

And so there is a numerical code. We may say, let us look at the first line in John's Gospel. The numbers are these. Let us look at the second line. The numbers are in a different order, and that signifies something. Now you see, gentlemen, people are amazed at this. But, you know, a man called Louvier[15] launched himself at the 'Sphinx': 'The riddle is solved'. He applied these numerical relationships to Goethe's *Faust* and it worked. Goethe never thought of composing his *Faust* on the basis of some law of numbers. But it works nevertheless, because all composition involves numerical elements. But if you just try and say something I can also apply a numerical code to your statement; this is something that lives in speech itself. A spiritual principle is at work in your speaking.

And that, gentlemen, is the element from beyond this earth, the sun influence. These Sun People therefore studied the secrets of the sun. The pyramids were probably not just built to be royal tombs, for instance, but had specific openings where a sunbeam might enter at a particular time of the year. The sunbeam would write a figure on the earth.

The Sun People studied this figure and let it inspire them. In this way they studied secrets of sun life. Someone who had become a Sun Person was able to say he did not go by earthly things at all but by the sun.

And when he had been one of the Sun People for a time and had taught humanity about things beyond this earth, he was elevated to the rank of Father. This was the highest rank, and few attained it. These were the people who had full maturity, people who were obeyed and followed. Others would obey them firstly because they had grown old in years — for by the time you had gone through these seven stages you had grown old in years — and because they had wisdom of life and also wisdom of the world.

Mysteries

1 Raven
2 Occultist: listener
3 Defender — defence of the spirit
4 Sphinx
5 Greeks: spirit of a nation
6 Sun Person
7 Father

Now just imagine, gentlemen, that Christ Jesus, Jesus of Nazareth, lived at a time when people everywhere in Asia still knew something about those mysteries. It was still known, for example, that there were people who taught sun wisdom. Jesus of Nazareth wanted people to be enlightened and to understand not only within but also outside the mysteries that what the sun does for human beings is already there within them, it is there in every human being. That is the most important thing about Christ Jesus that he is sun truth, teaching the sun word, as it was called, to be held by all people in common.

You need to note the great difference between Christ Jesus and the other Sun People. If you do not understand this you'll never gain insight into the Mystery of Golgotha. For you see, it is like this: What did people have to do to become Sun People in those early days? They had to be Raven first, then Occultist, Defender, Sphinx, Soul of a Nation — before they could advance to being a Sun Person. There was no other way. You had to be admitted to the mysteries. What did Jesus of Nazareth do? He had himself baptized in the River Jordan, as was the custom among the Jews then. And on this occasion, that is without having been in the mysteries first, the wisdom came to him that was held by the Sun People. He was therefore able to say that his wisdom had come from the sun itself. He was the first to relate to heaven without the mysteries.

What did a Sun Person in the mysteries say when he looked up to someone who had reached the seventh stage? He would say: Behold, that is the Father. That individual would be standing at the altar in the white garment of a priest. That was the Father, the Father among those who had gone through the different stages in the mysteries. Christ Jesus did not go through the mysteries but received it from the sun itself. This is why he said: 'My Father is not on earth' — meaning not in the mysteries — 'but my Father is up above in the world of the spirit.' He was thus clearly speaking of the Father in the world of the spirit. Christ Jesus wanted to make people, who in the past had received all things of the spirit from the earth, aware of the spiritual sources that lie beyond the earth. And this has always been misunderstood. People would say, for example, that Christ Jesus taught that the earth would perish and a kingdom of the spirit would come very soon that would last a thousand years. The clever people of today, sometimes feeling benevolent towards the ancients in their cleverness, say: 'Well, this is something current at the time and Jesus quoted it; after all, he was a child of his time and would accept what people said.'

But that is nonsense, for the thousand-year kingdom did indeed come, only it did not look the way people thought it would. It was like this. In earlier times people gained ideas and also experience of the spiritual world by the means I have described. It was the custom in those days, when people were different. This had ceased at the time when Christ Jesus lived, and people had to find the spirit in a different way. The spirit had to be found by direct means. Christ Jesus did so. And if he had not done what he did, humanity would have gone into a complete decline. Life would have become meaningless. This is not to deny that much that is meaningless has later emerged particularly through Christian institutions; but originally there was none of this. So people would have become witless. The mysteries would have perished the way they did indeed perish; but people would not have known anything of what was taught in the mysteries.

Take the Sun Person of old. What was said of him? People knew that he had the knowledge to be gained from the viewpoint of the sun, that he had died where life on earth was concerned. Speaking of a Sun Person, they would say he had died where life on earth was concerned. This was the reason why a ceremony imitating death and burial was performed in the mysteries before someone became a Sun Person. Christ Jesus put death and burial openly before the whole world; what happened publicly at his death was something that had always been part of the ritual in the mysteries. It had been a secret of the mysteries, and then it was there for all the world to see on Golgotha. You see, it really was true that a Sun Person had died where the earth was concerned. Because of this he was in between, between death's world of decline and the world of resurrection, the world of the eternal.

Things sometimes remind us of old customs where we can no longer perceive the meaning. Think of canonization in Rome, for example. It is a major ceremony when someone who died hundreds of years earlier is canonized in Rome. The ceremony is as follows. First the Advocatus dei, the defender of the divine, appears. He presents all the good qualities of the person to be canonized. Then the Advocatus diaboli, the devil's advocate, speaks of all the bad qualities of the saint. The decision lies between the two; I am not saying it is always the right decision, but it lies between the two. The ceremony is still performed today. When someone is canonized, for instance Joan of Arc, the two advocates appear. The saint stands between the two advocates, in the spirit. You remember that in pictures of Golgotha one always has Christ Jesus on the cross that is in the middle, and beside him the two thieves, or robbers. But the strange thing is that the Christ said to one of them: 'Today you'll be with me in Paradise.' This one went up above, therefore, and the other one went below. Lucifer and Ahriman are those two advocates.

This also held true for the Sun Person of old. He made the acquaintance of Lucifer and Ahriman, meeting the principle that wants to draw us up into the world of the spirit, making us wholly spiritual — which is not the right thing for a human being — and the principle that wants to take us down into the earth's sphere, which also is not right for a human being, for the human being is at the in-between stage.

In the Mystery of Golgotha, the whole world could see something that had only happened in the mysteries before, where it was only a metaphor, for the initiates would not really die. They became Fathers. The Christ did really die. But he said: 'My spirit does not die; it goes to the Father, for the Father is now no longer working down here as the ancient Father; he is working in the world of the spirit.' This is something that came entirely from the mysteries. We must look in the old mysteries for the Father idea, and only then do we really understand how Christianity evolved.

Now you see, gentlemen, everything I have told you was very much the custom over there in Asia. It also had an influence on the founding of Christianity. But even the Greeks knew extremely little of this, for they were developing outer civilization. And the Romulus people, descendants of a robber colony, knew nothing at all of this; they knew only about ruling the world in outer terms. They knew so well how to rule the world that the Roman Caesars, or emperors, behaved as if they were initiates. One of the early Roman emperors was Caligula.[16] Now you see, in the 1890s a German historian wanted to describe the German emperor Wilhelm.[17] But this could not be done, for anyone writing such a description would have been put in prison. The historian therefore wrote a small book entitled *Caligula*.[18] He wrote about the Roman emperor Caligula but every trait applied to Wilhelm II! Everybody who knew about these things realized: that is our Wilhelm II. That was the only way of doing it. Caligula had also been an initiate, for by that time it had all become outer form. It was possible to understand the function of the Ravens by seeing what the princes did, at least at a superficial level. Caligula had become a Sun Person but only superficially, more or less the way a 5- or 6-year-old becomes a 'general' by putting on a uniform. Caligula was also supposed to initiate others. And during one of those ceremonies it happened that when one of the Sphinxes was given the symbolic stroke of the sword, Caligula actually killed him with the sword.[19] This, of course, would not have been a problem for a Caesar. Everything had become outer form with the Romans, and they did not understand the inner meaning of any of it. No wonder they were quite unable to understand Christianity.

In Rome, therefore, Christianity became connected with worldly, or temporal, rule. When Christianity came to Rome, they had a temporal ruler who, however, saw himself as a god — naturally, for you became a god if you were an initiate. Augustus[20] was considered to be a god, and so were his successors. They also had the pontifex maximus, the 'great bridge builder'. He was the spiritual ruler but gradually faded away to a mere shadow in Rome, having no real role to play; the temporal ruler had all the power. This was only to be expected in a nation descended from Romulus who gathered all the rogues together. And then, you see, Christianity became worldly exactly through its connection with Rome.

This is what I had to tell you today concerning the outer aspect of Christianity. I'll speak about the inner aspect, the true influence of the sun on Jesus, the next time, which will be next Wednesday.

Star wisdom, moon and sun religions

Today we'll continue with our study of the Mystery of Golgotha. I have told you that further evolution must be such that what happens on earth depends not only on the earth but on the whole world. The notion of such dependence of earth events on the whole world is difficult for modern minds to accept. Yet we cannot really understand even the simplest event in human life unless we know that influences are reaching the earth all the time from cosmic space. I have spoken of this to you with regard to quite a number of different things. Today I must speak of it in relation to the Mystery of Golgotha.

I have spoken of the Jews as the fourth nation in the process of evolution. They really discovered the fourth aspect of human nature, the human I. They saw it to be the divine element in man and called it Yahveh. And they also established a certain relationship between this Yahveh, the cosmos and the starry heavens.

You know that Christianity had its origin in Palestine. Jesus of Nazareth lived in Palestine, in a Jewish environment. The Jewish religion was dominant there; politically they were under Roman rule, but in countries as far away as Palestine the Romans were not able to abolish the local religion as well. The Jewish religion was thus part of the environment in which Jesus of Nazareth lived.

What was the nature of this religion? You'll find it easier to understand if I first tell you some more about the people I mentioned before I spoke of the Jews—the Babylonians, Assyrians, who lived in Mesopotamia, which lies further to the east, in Asia. These people, neighbours of the Jews, had a well-developed star religion. Today people will say that the people in Assyria venerated the stars. They actually did not venerate the stars but having the instinctive wisdom of their age they knew more about the stars than people do today.

People think they know everything about the stars today, but you may have read recently that this certain knowledge of the stars is in danger of being lost. The discovery has been made that the earth is not surrounded by empty space. At an altitude of 400 kilometres, the earth is surrounded by nitrogen crystals! We have to assume, therefore, that modern scientists will gradually come to see that the ancient Greeks had the right idea with their crystalline heaven. Things like this make truly intelligent modern people see how little we really know about the world of stars.

You only have to consider the following. Imagine an inhabitant of Mars — astronomers believe Mars to be inhabited. Looking down at the earth he would not see human beings. Unless our Mars dweller has highly sophisticated telescopes he will not see human beings; he will see the earth shining out into cosmic space, giving off a greenish light. Yet the earth is alive with human beings, who are connected with spiritual entities. The same holds true for the other stars. And just as the physical forces of the stars have an influence on the earth, so do their spiritual powers also have an influence on the earth, and above all on the human being. The Orientals with their ancient, instinctive wisdom knew very well that there are spiritual entities in the stars. In their own way they venerated those spirits, not the physical stars. The religion of the Near East was a star religion in this sense. People believed for instance that there were spiritual entities on Saturn and that these had a certain influence on human beings. Jupiter would have spiritual entities, and so on, and all these spirits would have a certain influence on human life on earth.

The Jews took little interest in the other stars but took the idea of the moon influence from those ancient religions. They saw their Yahveh in relation to the spiritual aspects of the moon. In the original Jewish religion Yahveh, who lives in the human I, was dependent on the moon.

This, gentlemen, is no mere legend, nor is it mere religious superstition, for it can be shown to be true, using scientific methods. During a period that is important for their existence on earth, during pregnancy, when they are still embryos in the womb, human beings are entirely dependent on the moon. This is something that has been known for a long time, and the period of pregnancy was therefore reckoned to be ten lunar months. It is quite a recent development to convert the lunar to solar months, making it nine months. This idea of the ten lunar months, which was entirely the right idea for the period of pregnancy, still reflects the fact that human beings are dependent on the moon during the embryonic period.

The question is, in what way are they dependent on the moon. It is something I have spoken of before. You see, the fertilized ovum initially contains earth matter that has been destroyed, pulverized, and nothing would ever come of it if it were subject only to earth forces. It only becomes something because the moon has an influence on the earth. And we may indeed say that human beings enter into life on earth through the powers of the moon. The Jews, who saw Yahveh as a moon god, really wanted to show that human beings depend on moon powers when they enter upon the earth.

The Babylonians, Assyrians further to the east assumed there were other influences as well as those of the moon. They would say, for instance, that Jupiter had some effect on whether a person grew clever as he developed or remained stupid, and so on. The Jews were not interested in such lesser effects. They venerated the one God, and that was a moon god. It is generally considered a great advance in religious life that the Jews progressed from many gods to one God.

Jesus of Nazareth also met this one God, Yahveh, venerated by the Jews, in the Jewish religion that was part of his environment. He was instructed in this, as it were.

As you can imagine, when people venerate only the moon god, on whom human beings depend during the period when they are in the womb, they will obviously think that we bring the whole of our human nature, the way we are, and so on, with us when we come to earth. And this is what we find in the old Jewish Yahveh religion. If you had asked one of the ancient Jews who had got ill, let us say, why he got ill, he would say: 'Yahveh has willed this.' If his house was set on fire, he would say it was the will of Yahveh, and so on. He recognized only the one God through whom human beings entered into life on earth and would ascribe everything to him. This gave the Jewish religion a certain rigidity. All their lives people would feel dependent on what they had brought with them on coming to earth.

Jesus of Nazareth also got to know other religions where it was said that human beings are influenced not only by the moon but also by the other stars. The Gospels give a hint that there was a connection between the star religions of the East, of Asia, and the lands where the Jews lived and where Jesus of Nazareth was born. We hear that the wise men from the East saw a star that guided them to the place where Jesus of Nazareth was born.

Now the way we read it in the Gospels today is the result of a misunderstanding. The situation was that the wise men from the East had their star wisdom and saw from the position of the stars that an important event was going to happen. The star wisdom of the East, of Asia, thus touched Jesus of Nazareth at his birth, and the connection continued to exist.

The main aim of Jesus of Nazareth was to give human beings also an inner nature as they walk about on the earth. The Jews would say that everything came from Yahveh. But Yahveh only has a major influence until we are born; once a human being is born and walks about on the earth he does not merely continue in the Yahveh impulse. The most important thing Christ Jesus brought into the world was that human beings are not just like a ball that keeps rolling, continuing the momentum given by Yahveh when they were in the womb, but that they have an inner will during life and with this are able to make their own inherent nature, their individual nature, better or worse. This was a tremendous idea at the time. For, you see, the star wisdom had really been kept very much a secret, and no one knew about it in Palestine, let alone in Rome. Star wisdom had been kept a secret. It was a significant deed when Jesus of Nazareth, pointing first of all to the sun, not the other stars, said: 'Human beings are influenced not only by the moon but also by the sun.'

This was a major deed at the time. But you have to remember that such things should not be considered as mere theories but in their reality. What influence does the moon have when a human being is in the womb? Well, gentlemen, it is a spiritual principle, soul and spirit, that comes in from the moon. In his soul, a human being comes down from the moon which is in the world of heaven. And what did it mean when the Jews said: 'Yahveh is influencing the human being during pregnancy'? They meant that everything of a soul and spiritual nature in the human being came from the moon; the creator of the human soul was in the moon. When people walked around on earth, therefore, the Jews would say: 'Well, the physical aspect of the human being, anything material, comes from the earth; everything by way of soul and spirit comes from the wide world through the moon.' The human spirit truly enters into the human being through the moon. And what they really meant was that when they met another person they had to think: 'Your soul has entered into you through the moon, and anything that lives in your soul has been given to you via the moon gods.'

Jesus of Nazareth taught: 'Yes, that is true, the human being has such a soul; but this soul can still change as life goes on. Human beings have an element of free will. The human soul can change as life goes on.'

What made him say this? That is the big question. To answer it, we consider the following.

As you know, we distinguish the Jews from the rest of the earth's population. The difference has arisen because the Jews have been brought up in the moon religion for centuries, refusing in their hearts to accept any other influence. Here we have to consider a particular trait of Judaism if we want to understand the situation. Look where you may, the Jews have a great gift for music and very little talent when it comes to sculpture, painting, and the like. The Jews have a great gift for materialism, but little for recognition of the spiritual world, because out of the whole world beyond this earth they venerated only the moon, really, and hardly knew that they did so any more. Jewish and Greek nature are complete opposites. The Greeks were mainly concentrating on sculpture and painting and architecture—at least as far as sculpture went. The Jews are the musical people, the priest nation where the inner life is essentially developed; and that is due to gifts originally developed in the womb.

This characteristic was very highly developed at the time when Jesus of Nazareth lived. You see, the Jews we meet in Europe today have lived among other nations and acquired things from them. But anyone who is able to judge this can still distinguish the special nature of the Jewish spirit from that of other people. It does not mean they are less good, but there is a difference. How was it with the Jews? It was like this: they concentrated with all their heart and soul on the moon. Because of this they developed everything connected with the moon but not with the sun. The sun was completely forgotten. And if Jesus of Nazareth had continued in the Jewish way, he could not have taught anything but the moon religion. But he developed another impulse as life went on, and a direct spiritual influence came to him from the sun.

You see, because of this he may be said to have been twice-born. All the early eastern religions had this aspect of being twice-born, which has since been forgotten, become merely an item of information. People no longer understand it. Jesus of Nazareth knew a particular moment when he felt: 'Now I am born again, as it were; just as in the womb I received my soul through the moon, so my soul has now been given new life from the sun.' Among initiates, the individual who was Jesus of Nazareth was known as Christ Jesus from that moment. And they would say: 'Like other Jews, Jesus of Nazareth has become a human being, a Jew, through the moon powers; but because he received the sun influence at a particular moment in his life he was born again as the Christ.'

Unless they are able to understand this in the spirit, modern people really cannot make anything of this. It does not mean anything to them that before birth, in the womb, human beings are united with their souls through the moon, so that their souls come from the outside world. It means even less to them that Jesus of Nazareth received a sun influence, and a second individual entered into him, as it were. Just as the first individual nature enters into the womb, so did Jesus of Nazareth draw sun nature into himself as a second individual nature.

The Roman Catholic religion has completely forgotten these things in the words it uses. But if you attend mass and it is a solemn mass, you will see the 'sanctum sanctorum', the monstrance, on the altar. The host inside, and here rays [Fig. 1]. What does it represent? It is the sun, and inside it the moon. The whole monstrance tells us in its form that Christianity arose from a view in which people acknowledged not only the moon, as the Jews did, but also the sun. As human beings are under the moon influence at birth, so was the Christ under the sun influence at his birth.

One might say that in that case every human being could be born twice, coming under the sun influence in the course of life. But it is not quite like that. The influence on Christ Jesus was directly on the human I. Where does the moon influence go when we are in the womb? Well, gentlemen, I told you that human beings consist of physical body, ether body, astral body and I. The moon influence is on the astral body, so that the astral body, which is at an unconscious

Fig. 1

level in the human being, is influenced by the moon. The sun influence in the Christ was on the I. The I, however, is independent.

What would happen if the sun influence were the same as the moon influence on human beings? Well, as individual human beings we do not have much say where our birth is concerned. We are simply sent into the world at birth. If the sun influence were exactly the same as the moon influence we might receive it, say, at the age of 30[21] and we would have no say in it at all. We would suddenly be another person at the age of 30, and would actually forget what we did before. Just imagine that you would be going about as young people until you were 29, and then you would reach the age of 30 and you would all be reborn. You then meet someone who has not yet reached the age of 30 and he would say: 'Good morning, Erbsmehl!' 'Huh? I don't know him! I've only been here from today. I don't know anything about it.' That is how it would be if the sun would influence everyone in their 30th year, say. You'll find this highly improbable, gentlemen, but it is nevertheless true. It has merely been forgotten because history is always being falsified, so that people do not hear of this.

Something very similar to this existed in earlier times, though it was not as drastic as that. But in very early times, about 7000 or 8000 years ago, it really was the case that in India, for example, people would no longer know about the earlier part of their life once they reached the age of 30; they would then be completely new people. And others would be kind to them and say: 'Go to the local authority' — I am using modern terms — and there they would be told who they were and what their name was. This transformation gradually grew less and less marked, but it did happen. Even in ancient Egypt the situation would be that people simply did not remember their childhood when they were 50 years old, their memories only went back to the age of 30;

they would hear about the rest from others, just as we hear from others in the family how we behaved as babies or at the age of 2. Historians do not tell us about humanity changing such a lot on earth, but it is nevertheless true.

Due to special circumstances Jesus of Nazareth was the last human being to receive the sun influence at a time when others could no longer do so. It says so in the Gospels, but people tend to misinterpret it. You see it says in the Gospels that Jesus asked John to baptize him in the River Jordan. A dove descended during the baptism. This was a sign of the sun influence. Sun nature thus entered into Jesus. And that was the last time. He was the last to receive this sun nature. Other people in his time could no longer do so because their bodies were no longer ripe for it. He was the last.

Let us go back to the people who lived in the ancient Orient. There everyone was able to say: 'In the course of life the sun has an influence on the human being; a new nature is gained with this.' At the time when Christ Jesus lived it was generally no longer possible to say so. The priests only knew it because they had heard about it from others, not from inner perception.

Something had to take the place of sun veneration. In earlier times, before the time of the Jews, people had venerated the sun because they knew that the sun had this tremendous influence during their lifetime. Now they were no longer able to venerate the sun because they no longer received its influence. Who took the place of the sun? Christ Jesus himself! Christianity was such that people had a sun religion as well as their star religion; it pointed directly to the sun. When Christ Jesus had received this sun influence as the last human being to do so, people could only point to him and say: 'The sun spirit dwells in him.'

This was a tremendous change. It was an unbelievable revolution to think that Christ Jesus had brought down to earth the element which until then had only been seen in the sun. In the old days, and in the early days of Christianity, the Christ was therefore always called the Sun. You still find the term 'the Sun, the Christ' everywhere in the Gospels, for people knew about this. Later it was forgotten. You can see it in the monstrance at every solemn mass. But when someone actually says that it is so, for you can see it, he is considered a heretic and persecuted as a misbeliever. For it was always considered dangerous in the Christian Church to tell the truth about the stars and also about the sun.

Well, gentlemen, why should that be so? Here we must go back to the ancient mysteries and compare them with Christianity. You see, not everyone would be admitted to the ancient mysteries. I have told you the stages of initiation — Raven, Occultist, Defender, Sphinx, and so on. They knew that the influence came from the stars. And the priests of the mysteries watched with care that not everyone would be enlightened and enlightenment was only found with them, in the mysteries. For knowledge certainly is power, though this is often suppressed. But when the priesthood still had power, then knowledge was power.

Star wisdom had been lost. And then came Christ Jesus. He brought it back, though in a new form, saying: 'You must bring the sun god down to earth.' He brought back the sun religion. And if it had happened that he had gained the day with his teaching, the whole of the ancient star religion would have been there again, as sun influence. This was very often the case in the early days of Christianity. The ancient mysteries had come into flower again. Christ Jesus brought a tremendous revolution, making the knowledge of the ancient mysteries known to all. And this would have been for all people on earth. Well, every effort to get people to accept these things I am telling you was in vain.

In the fourth century the Roman emperor Julian, called the Apostate,[22] wanted to bring back the old star religion.

He was murdered when on a campaign in Persia. What happened in Rome can be told as follows.

Star worship, which had really been brought back by Christ Jesus, was called superstition in Rome, and indeed worse than superstition, belief in the devil. The very thing to give true insight into the spiritual aspect of the world was given a bad name; it was cast aside, as it were. People were to believe only in the external, historical event concerning Christ Jesus in Palestine which was proclaimed by the Church. In the eyes of the faithful, this made the Church the highest authority in questions of belief. You see, Christianity did not reach Europe in its true form via Rome, only an amended Christianity did so that limited itself to the external event in Palestine and left aside the whole cosmic context. How did this come about?

Rome really began with a band of robbers who had gathered there. And something of this attitude remained an influence for a long time. Rome therefore always wanted to grab religious as well as worldly dominion. This was a definite trait. The Pope has taken the place of the pagan high priest of ancient times, the Pontifex Maximus, taking only his title. During the Middle Ages the Pope gradually took the position of the Roman emperors, gaining dominion of the world as well as dominion of people's minds. On one occasion only, at the beginning of the eleventh century, a German emperor tried to do something similar with regard to Julian who was called the Apostate, the dissenter. This was Henry II.[23] It is most interesting. Henry II was initially seen as a kind of saint, being an excellent representative of the Christian faith. He reigned from 1002 to 1024, and was called Henry the Saint. You will still find him listed among the saints in a Roman Catholic priest's breviary. But he, too, wanted to speak of the old truths. He wanted to preserve the view that the sun spirit lived in Christ Jesus. He wanted a non-Roman Holy Church, an *ecclesia catholica non romana*.

Remember this was at the beginning of the eleventh century. If he had succeeded in establishing a non-Roman Catholic Church, Christianity in Europe would have had its cosmic significance, and religious life at the time would have given people true knowledge of the spirit. But Rome, religious and Caesarean Rome, won the day, and the Roman Catholic Church continued to rule. Emperor Henry II wanted to have Church and State completely separate.

You'll have to admit this would have been a tremendous achievement, for there would have been none of the persecution of heretics that followed. All such persecution comes entirely from the desire to control people's thoughts. In reality it is not possible to control thoughts. Just think about it. Can anyone truly control your thoughts? They can only be controlled if there is State control, forcing people to go to particular schools where they are taught specific things, and forcing them to belong to a certain class. The class then gives them their opinions, and so on. Thoughts cannot be controlled. No Church could ever become harmful unless assisted by a government that controls people as physical beings. A Church can only teach, and it is up to people whether they accept its teaching. That was the situation Henry II wanted to create. But, as I said, the old Caesar, the Caesar in the Pope, won the day. As you know, temporal rule, the State, was very powerful at that time. We may think this a bad thing, but the fact is that in Henry II's day temporal rule was tremendously powerful. If it had proved possible to establish a non-Roman Catholic Church, the teaching of the Church would have been separate from temporal affairs.

The Crusades had essentially the same aim.[24] It is generally stated that they were at the behest of Rome, and they are usually described like this. When those horrible Turks had conquered Jerusalem, pilgrims to that city could no longer say their prayers in peace. Then Rome sent out Peter the Hermit[25] to preach that people should go on a Crusade; the aim was to get many people to join up and go to Asia, to Jerusalem. A large army of Crusaders was raised and led by Peter and by Walther von Habenichts.[26] You can imagine why he bore that name, he was indeed as much a have-not as we all are. We, too, could not manage to raise the funds for a Crusade to Asia. The whole army of Crusaders perished on the way, however; it did not achieve anything.

But then others set out under Godfrey of Bouillon. They did not serve Rome, and their aims were similar to those of Henry II. They wanted temporal rule to be set aside. So here we have Italy [drawing on the board], here Greece, the Black Sea, Asia, Palestine, Jerusalem. This was where the Crusade was to go, and Jerusalem was to be the centre of the Christian religion. Rome was to be deposed from the first real Crusade onwards. These Crusades were actually against Rome. And again the aim was to make *ecclesia*, the Church, independent of temporal rule.

None of this succeeded. Romance princes were involved in later Crusades. You can read about it in the history of the Crusades.

What happened was that this whole foundation of the Christian faith, with the magnificent idea that Christ Jesus brought the power of the sun down to earth, and that everyone who recognizes this can thus become free—'You shall know the truth, and the truth shall make you free'[27]— has essentially remained unknown throughout human evolution. Today we must rediscover true Christianity through the science of the spirit. It is not surprising that those who represent Christianity as it is today turn against a Christian faith that truly goes back to Christ Jesus and teaches what he taught. Their aversion does not, however, relate to Christianity. In the social sphere, Christianity has brought tremendous progress in that slavery has gradually disappeared. And indeed, gentlemen, if it were not for

Christianity, we also would not have the whole of modern science. Most of the major discoveries were made by monks. Only the air pump came from Guericke, good burgomaster of Magdeburg.[28] Copernicus,[29] who developed the Copernican system, was a canon. And all schools were really run by monks.

There was something else, however. You see, monasteries were not all that popular in the Church of old, because the monks had retained much of the old knowledge. Among the monks—who were not allowed to open their mouths, however—you could find knowledge of the old star wisdom. You just have to look for it. The things I have told you about—last time I did you a drawing to show how men and women were told apart even as late as the seventeenth century—were passed on through the monasteries in the past, not through the temporal powers. And it was really only in the seventeenth or eighteenth century that monastic tradition was finally put down. The Middle Ages were not as dark as is generally thought. Only the things one is generally aware of were dark. But secretly people had a great deal of wisdom; it is just that modern people fail to understand this, even when they read the old writings. You'll remember I told you that no one knows today what the term 'mummy' really means.[30] I explained this to you.

And it is indeed the case that the great idea of Christianity is the one that speaks of the sun's power coming down to earth.

You see, gentlemen, it is only because of this that history, as we know it, developed. In the Orient they had great star wisdom but thought nothing of history. The people who had the knowledge in the ancient East always said that creation was out there in the distant heavens. They did not concern themselves much with anything human beings did on earth. The Jews did have a kind of history, but it was a history that began with the star wisdom, for the 'seven days of creation' are star wisdom. And then there was chaos. Real history, with the whole of Earth evolution divided into the pre-Christian and Christian eras, only came with Christianity.

This is what I was able to tell you today. I'll add a little more next Saturday.

What did Europe look like at the time when Christianity spread?

Gentlemen, let us continue today by my showing you some other ways in which Christianity came alive in Europe.

In the early days after its founding, Christianity first of all spread through the south, across to Rome and then later, from the third, fourth and fifth centuries onward, to the north. Let us take a look at Europe as it was when Christianity spread, that is, the time when it was founded and a little after. The question I want to consider is, what did Europe look like at the time when Christianity came to it?

Let us think of Asia over there [drawing on the board]. Europe is like a small appendage, a small peninsula. As you know, it looks like this. Here we have Scandinavia, then the Baltic; here we come across to Russia, and here is Denmark as it is today. Here we come to the north coast of Germany, here into Dutch and then French territory. We move on to Spain, and across to Italy. We now come to regions we know already: the Adriatic, Greece and the Black Sea. We then come to Asia Minor, and down there we would have Africa. Here, on the other side, we would have England and Wales, and here Ireland, which I'll just indicate here.

I am going to try and show what Europe looked like at the time when Christianity gradually spread and then reached it. Here, Europe is closed off from Asia by the Urals. We then have the huge Volga river, and if at the time when Christianity came up from the south we had gone to the regions that are now southern Russia, the Ukraine, and so on, we would have found a people who later disappeared completely from there, moving further west and merging

with other peoples: the Ostrogoths [eastern Goths]. You'll
see in a minute how all these peoples started to migrate at a
particular time. But at the time when Christianity was
coming up from the south, these peoples lived in this part of
Europe.

Now if you take the Danube, you have here, further
along, the Romania of today, and this is where the western
Goths were. Over here, where western Hungary is today,
north of the Danube, were the Vandals. Those were the
names of the peoples in those days. And in the area where
we have Moravia, Bohemia and Bavaria today were the
Suevi, the Swabians of today. Higher up — this is where the
river Elbe rises which then flows into the North Sea — here it
was all Goths. But here — this is the Rhine, which you know
well, with today's Cologne about here — here in the region
around the Rhine lived the Ripuarian Franks and up near
the mouth of the Rhine the Salian Franks. Over here,
towards the Elbe, were the Saxons. They were given their
name by people to the south of them who had noted that
they lived preferably or almost exclusively on meat and
therefore called them 'meat-eaters'.

The Romans had spread to these regions here, including
modern France, Spain, and so on. Here, too, you would find
Graeco-Roman peoples everywhere. Christianity spread
first among them, before moving further north. We may say
that in these areas Christianity reached the northern parts
earlier than it did in areas further to the west. One of the
early bishops among the Goths was Ulfila, or Wulfila,
meaning 'little wolf'.[31] Ulfila translated the Bible into
Gothic at a very early stage, in the fourth century. His
translation is particularly interesting because it differs from
those that came later. It is found in a most valuable volume
at the Library in Uppsala in Sweden.[32] We can see from this
that Christianity spread earlier here in the east.

Looking at the blackboard we thus see that the Greeks

and Romans were there; but in very early times you still had here everywhere a much older European population and this is of great interest. This population—I have marked it in red—had already been pushed further west at the time when Christianity came. Originally they lived more to the east. You have to visualize them living on the border between Asia and Europe. The Slavs of today were even further into Asia in those days.

The question is this. If we were to go back to the times before the origin of Christianity, I would have to hatch this whole map of Europe in red, for an ancient Celtic people also lived everywhere in Europe. Everything I have drawn on the board for you only came across from Asia later, a few centuries before and after the founding of Christianity. So the question is, why were those peoples migrating? At a certain point in world history they started to move, pushing across into Europe. The reason was this. If you look at Siberia as it is today, it is really a vast, empty, sparsely populated space. Not that long ago—not long, a few centuries, before the coming of Christianity—Siberia was much more low-lying and relatively warm. It then rose. The land does not have to rise by much and it will be cold where it was warm before, the lakes dry up, and it grows desolate. Nature herself thus made people move from east to west.

The Celtic population of Europe were most interesting people. The peoples migrating from the east found them there, a relatively peaceful population. They still had the original gift of clairvoyance. If they took up a trade they would think the spirits were helping them in their work. And when someone felt he was good at making boots—they did not have boots then, but something to protect the feet—he would see his skill to be due to help from the spirits. And he would actually be able to perceive the element from the world of the spirit that gave him help. The way those ancient Celts saw life was that they were still on familiar terms with the world of the spirit, in a sense. And the Celtic peoples produced many beautiful things. They also went to Italy in very early times and brought beauty to it. This softened the rough edges of the original robber mentality at a time when the Romans had achieved a high life-style. The influence of the Celtic peoples softened the brutal nature of the Romans.

In earlier times, therefore, Celts were to be found everywhere in Europe. To the south you then had the Roman and Greek, Romance-Greek, Graeco-Latin peoples. And, as I said, when Siberia grew colder, these peoples moved west. As a result, the map of Europe looked like this at the time when Christianity moved northwards from the south [pointing to the board].

It is a strange thing, gentlemen — certain characteristics of peoples survive well, others less so. Among the peoples coming to Europe from Asia were the Huns, for instance, with Attila the most powerful of their kings.[33] Attila was, however, a Gothic name meaning 'little father'. Many of the peoples whose names I have written on the board also accepted Attila, the king of the Huns, as their king, and that is why he was given a Gothic name. The Huns were, however, very different from the other peoples. You see, the wilder peoples migrating to the west had originally been mountain tribes in Asia. The slightly less wild people, such as the Goths, were more plains people. And the wild doings of the Huns, and later also of the Magyars, were due to the fact that they had originally been mountain people in Asia.

As the Romans extended their rule more and more to the north — this was independent of Christianity — they encountered the peoples coming from Asia. Many wars were fought between the Romans and the peoples here in the north. I have mentioned Tacitus to you, the important Roman historian.[34] He wrote a great deal about Roman history and also a truly tremendous little book called *Ger-*

mania,[35] in which he described the tribes who lived there so well that they truly come to life. I have also told you that Tacitus, a highly educated Roman, had no more to say about Christianity than that it was a sect established by a certain Christ over there in Asia, and that the Christ had been put to death. Writing in Rome at a time when Christians were still suppressed and lived in their underground catacombs, he did not even get this right.

At that time Christianity had not yet reached these peoples in the north. They had their own religion, however, and this is very interesting. Please call to mind, gentlemen, how religious ideas arose among the peoples in the south and the east. We have spoken of the Indians who considered above all the physical body, that is, one aspect of the human being. The Egyptians considered the ether body — another aspect of the human being. The Babylonians and Assyrians considered the astral body — yet another aspect of the human being. The Jews considered the I in their worship of Yahveh — again an aspect of the human being. Only the Greeks — and the Romans took this over from them — looked less at the human being and more at the world of nature. The Greeks were truly magnificent observers of the natural world.

These peoples in the north, however, saw nothing of the human being as such, of the inner human being; they saw less even than the Greeks. This is interesting. Those people in the north completely forgot the inner human being; they did not even have memories of any thoughts people might have had before about the inner human being. The Greeks and Romans at least still had memories, being the neighbours of peoples all over the Near East — Egyptians, Babylonians and so on. They remembered what those ancient peoples had thought. The peoples of the north looked only at the world around them, outside the human being. And they did not see nature but the nature spirits. The ancient

Greeks saw the world of nature; the peoples here in the north saw the nature spirits. And the most wonderful stories, fables, legends and myths arose among them, because they always saw the spirits. The Greeks would see Mount Olympus rise high, and their gods dwelt on Olympus. The people in the north did not say: gods live on a mountain. They would see the god himself in the mountain top, which did not look like a rock to them. When the rosy dawn shone on the mountain top, making it golden all over, and the morning sun rose, these people did not see the mountain but the way the morning sun moved across the mountain, and this they felt to be divine. It seemed to have spirit nature to them. It was quite natural to them to see spirit nature spread over the mountains.

The Greeks built temples for the gods. Everywhere over there in Asia people built temples for the gods. The peoples of the north would say: 'We do not build temples. What would be the good of building temples? It is dark in there, but up on the mountains it is light and bright. And the gods must be venerated by going up the mountain.'

Their thoughts about it were like this. When the light shines in the mountains it comes from the sun; but the sun is most beneficial in midsummer, when St John's-tide — as we call it today — approaches. They would then go up into the mountains, light fires and celebrate their gods not in a temple but high up in the mountains. Or they would say: 'The light and warmth of the sun go down into the soil, and in the spring the powers the sun has sent into the earth rise from the soil. We therefore must venerate the sun also when it lets its powers rise from the soil.' They were particularly aware of the beneficial gifts of the sun coming from the earth in their forests, where many trees grew. They therefore venerated their gods in the forests. Not in temples, but on mountains and in forests.

These peoples saw everything spiritualized. The ancient

Celts who had been driven away by them had still seen the actual spirits. These peoples no longer saw the spirits but to them everything that was light and warmth in the natural world was divine. That was the old religion of the German tribes which was then driven out by Christianity.

Christianity reached those areas in two ways. On the one hand it penetrated southern Russia and the areas which are Romania and Hungary today. This is where Ulfila translated the Bible. The Christianity that came to the people there was much more genuine than the Christianity that spread from Rome, which was the second route. There it had more the character of dominion. It would be fair to say that if the Christianity that spread over here, moving up through Russia in the east, had spread there at a time when the population was not yet Slavic, it would have been very different, more inward, having more of an Asiatic character. The Christianity that spread from Rome was more superficial, finally becoming dead ritual because the significance was no longer understood. I have spoken to you about the monstrance with the host, which is really sun and moon, but that was suppressed; it was no longer given any significance. And so a ritual spread that had no reality to it. This was taken to Constantinople by a Caesar who also had no reality; Constantinople was founded. And later this altered Christianity also spread through other countries.

The Christianity that exists in Ulfila's Bible translation, for instance, has completely vanished from Europe. The more superficial, ritual Christianity spread more and more. And in the east, too, this ritual, with little inwardness, spread even more when the Slavs came.

The things I have told you about religious ideas of these peoples later went through a change. It is always the same. Initially people know what something is about; then a time comes when they no longer know what it is about and it becomes mere memory. Some outer aspect remains. And so the gods that had once been seen by people, the spirits found everywhere in nature, became three main gods.

One was Woden or Odin, who was really still thought to be like the light and air that floats above everything. He would be venerated, for example, when the weather was stormy. Then people would say: Woden blowing in the wind.

Those peoples tended to express anything they experienced in nature in their language. And so they venerated Woden blowing in the wind. Can you feel the three Ws when I say these words?[36] It made those people shiver when a storm came and they imitated the storminess in those words. These are the words as we say them today, but they were similar in the old language.

When summer came and people saw lightning flash and heard the rumble of thunder they saw a spiritual element in this, too. They would imitate this in words, calling the spirit who rumbled in the thunder Donar, Thor: Thor thunders in thunder.[37]

The fact that this came to expression in speech shows that these people related to the outside world. The Greeks were less strongly connected with the outside world. They looked for these things in rhythm rather than in the shaping of speech. With these northern peoples, it was in the speech itself.

And when these peoples went across into Europe and first met the Celts, there were constant wars and battles. Making war was something people did all the time during the centuries when Christianity spread. They saw spiritual elements in the blowing of the wind and the rumbling of thunder, and in the roar of battle. They had shields, and would rush forward in closed ranks carrying their shields. That was still their way when they met the Romans. And when the Romans opposed them as they rushed down from the north, the Romans would above all hear a terrible cry.

The people from the north would shout into their shields from a thousand throats as they rushed forward. And the Romans were more afraid of the terrible war cry than they would be of the enemy's swords. In present-day words the war cry was something like *Ziu zwingt Zwist.*[38] Ziu was the spirit of war and the ancient Germans believed him to be rushing before them. The Romans would hear the dull reverberations of the cry roaring above their heads. As I said, they were desperately afraid of this, more than of bows and arrows and the like. A spiritual element was alive in the courage and thirst for battle shown by those tribes.

If they were to come again today — and they do, of course, because there is reincarnation, but they'll have forgotten all about the past — and if they still were the way they were then, they would look at people today and immediately put a nightcap on everyone's head, saying: 'It's not right for people to be such sleepyheads. Let them put on a nightcap and go to bed!' They looked at life in a very different way; they were mobile.

There would of course also have been times when those tribes could not go to war. In that situation they would lie down on bear skins and drink — they were terrible drinkers. That was their second occupation. It was considered a virtue in those days; and their drink was not as harmful as drink is today; it was relatively harmless, being brewed from all kinds of herbs. Beer came to be produced later, and was of course very different. They would feel truly human when mead, a beerlike sweet drink, coursed through their bodies. You sometimes still see people who feel themselves a little bit to be descendants of those ancient Germans. I met a German poet once in Weimar who drank almost as much as the ancient Germans. We started to talk and I said to him: 'Surely no one can be as thirsty as that!' He answered: 'Ah thirst — I drink water when I'm thirsty. I actually drink beer when I'm not thirsty. When I drink beer it is not for the thirst, it is to get merry!' and that is how it was with the ancient Germans. They grew merry and active when the sweet meadlike drink coursed through their limbs as they lay on their bear skins.

Their third main occupation was hunting. The tilling of the soil was very much a secondary occupation performed by subjugated tribes. When such a tribe gained new territory they would subjugate others who then had to till the soil. They were unfree. In war they had to take up arms, and so on. The difference between free and unfree people was enormous at that time. The free people, who went to war, hunted and lay on their bear skins, would meet to organize affairs. They would discuss judicial or administrative matters and so on, whatever was necessary. Nothing was written down, for they were unable to write. Everything was by word of mouth. Nor did they have towns or cities. People lived in scattered villages. About a hundred villages would form a community and be called a 'hundred'. Several hundreds would make a *gau*. The hundreds had their meetings, as did the *gaus*. The whole was truly democratic among those who met, which would be the free people. Their name for it was not parliament, diet or the like, which would be a much later term, but a *Thing*, which was a meeting on a fixed day. You often hear English people say 'thing' when the name of something does not come to mind. The word has fallen into discredit today. I got into trouble once about this word. I had been asked to set up a resolution that had been discussed, and included the word 'thing'. The chairman, a famous astronomer, took this very much amiss because the word is so poorly regarded today; it should not be used, he said, when people meet to discuss serious matters. But in the old days it was called a *Thing*. People would not say they were going to parliament, or the diet, but to the *Thing*, the *Tageding*. When someone spoke about something, they would say he *vertagedingt* the matter, which has later become *verteidigt*, defended. That is how words evolved. Today one usually has a 'defender' in court, and here in Switzerland they don't say defender but advocate.

This, then, was how those tribes lived with one another and with their gods. And the peoples from the south brought Christianity to them.

Again there were two ways in which Christianity arose over there in the west. Part of it came directly from Rome; but there was another route — from Asia through all those more southern regions where the Graeco-Latin element had not gained much influence, through Spain and on to Ireland. Christianity spread in a very pure form in Ireland in the early centuries and also over here in Wales. Christian missionaries then went to Europe from there. They brought Christianity to some, whilst others had it from Rome.

You'll remember I said that in the monasteries and also in the early universities people still had much of the old wisdom, and Christianity was thus linked with the old wisdom. The old star wisdom that survived, only to disappear completely from Europe at a later time, really all came from Ireland. What had come from Rome had really only been ritual. Later, when central Europe turned to the Gospels, these were added on to the ritual. But much of what lived among the people had come from Ireland. You see, in Europe Christianity gradually became part of temporal rule. And the good elements that existed here in the upper areas, where Ulfila produced his Gothic translation of the Bible, and those that had come from Ireland had more or less disappeared later on. Quite a bit survived into the Middle Ages, but then it largely disappeared. You see, the people who came from Rome were very clever.

The tribes whose names I have given, originally forced by natural conditions to migrate from an Asia grown desolate to Europe, developed a certain wanderlust, a desire to be on the move. And it is strange to see what happened.

Here we have the River Elbe, for instance. The people who lived there soon after the coming of Christianity were the Lombards. They lived to the north-east of the Saxons, on the Elbe. Soon after, about 200 years later, we find them down there by the river Po in Italy! They had migrated. Before the coming of Christianity the Goths, the Ostrogoths, were to be found here by the Black Sea. A few centuries later they were here, where the Vandals and the western Goths had been before. The western Goths had moved further to the west and after some time could be found in Spain. The Vandals had been here, on the Danube. A few centuries later they were no longer to be found in Europe, but over there in Africa, opposite to Italy. The peoples were migrating. And as Christianity spread they moved further and further to the west. The Slavs only came much later.

What was happening in the west? The Romans already ruled the world when Christianity evolved. They were really very clever. At the time when these tribes moved westward and encountered Roman civilization, the Romans had grown feeble, quite worn out, and really could not do much more but stand with quivering legs when the roar of *Ziu zwingt Zwist* rolled into the shields from up there. They were quaking in their boots. But they were crafty, arrogant and proud in their heads.

The difference between them and the tribes was enormous. They had their lands, their fields, were settled, with something to fall back on. The tribes did not care much about places. They were on the move. The Romans would take in the tribes that came rushing south and give them land, of which they had more than enough. The tribes then changed from being hunters and warriors to being tillers of the soil. The Romans had their own way of giving land, however. They remained in control, running the administration, and in this way gradually became the rulers. Their rule was most powerful here to the west. In the area later populated by the Germans, people resisted for a long time. But tribes like the Goths went down to Italy, mingling with the people who lived there and becoming dependent.

The Roman, Latin people were clever, therefore. They said: 'It no longer works so well if we take up the sword.' They had grown feeble. So what did they do? They made the peoples who came from the north into warriors. The Romans waged their wars by sending the Germans — who were given land but had to fight in return. The ancient Germans who had remained in the north were thus fought by their own former warriors. And in the early days when Christianity spread, wars were really waged by the southern people, the Romans, with the help of those ancient Germans who had joined them. Only the generals of the Roman armies were normally Romans. The mass of soldiers really consisted of ancient Germans who had become Roman.

It was then a question of introducing the religious element in a way these people would accept. In those very early times people were much more attached to their religion than later. And so the following would happen, for instance. You see, those people always saw the light and air in the natural world as something spiritual. They felt it was hard when the snows came in October or November, covering the ground, so that everything spiritual really had to disappear. But they specially venerated the time when we celebrate Christmas today. They could feel that the sun was returning. This was the feast of the winter solstice, when the sun returned to humankind again. These tribes therefore were inclined to accept the spiritual element in nature.

The Romans, who had already made Christianity part of their system of rule, let the tribes keep their solstice. But they said it was not to celebrate the solstice but the birth of

Christ. The tribes were thus able to celebrate their feast as before, but it had been given a new meaning.

The ancient Germans always perceived a spirit in any tree that stood out more. The Romans made the spirit into a saint. Essentially they took everything of the old pagan religion and gave it a new name. People would not notice this so much, and that is really how Christianity spread among the ancient German tribes. Feasts like those of the returning sun and so on were celebrated, taking account of the fact that the tribes liked to celebrate their gods in the open air, in mountains and forests.

We may thus say that cleverness was the main principle in the founding of Christianity coming from Rome. Essentially Europe has been governed using such cleverness for centuries—Roman cleverness. This went so far that the Romans preserved the old Latin language in the schools, with the vernacular really only spoken among the people. When the Romans introduced scholarship with their Christianity, this would not be in the vernacular but in Latin. The vernacular only came into scholarship in the eighteenth century. Roman culture thus persisted in its original form for a long time.

To the west, going through Spain, France and finally Britain, Roman culture remained alive. A language has developed in which it lives on. Here, in central Europe, the Germanic element gained more of the upper hand. The German languages developed. Over here the Romance element prevailed and therefore Romance languages. But in their origins all those people were really German, those who went to Spain and also those who went to Italy. I mentioned the Ripuarian Franks, the Salian Franks. They went over there later, German tribes settling in France. And the Romance language spread over them like a cloud. French has evolved from it, and so has Spanish. There the old Latin language lives on in a new form.

Further to the east, from the Rhine onwards, people as a nation would say: 'Well, the scholars in the schools, wearing their wigs, may speak Latin, and anyone wishing to be a priest may as well listen to them.' But the ordinary people kept their language. This has given rise to the difference that Europeans are still finding hard to swallow today, the difference between central and western Europe.

The Trinity. Three forms of Christianity and Islam. The Crusades

The question which has been asked, Gentlemen, is wide-ranging, and we'll need a few sessions to discuss it.

Today I'd like to go into more detail about the later part of the time when Christianity spread. If we look at Christianity today, it has three forms. These have to be considered if we want to find the right way of tracing what really happened because of the Mystery of Golgotha, considering the ideas that are held today.

Let us first of all consider Europe. As I have shown the other day, we have Asia over there, with Europe really a kind of peninsula of Asia. As you know, it looks like this [sketching]. This would be Norway, then Russia over here; this takes us to the north coast of Germany; and here is Denmark. Over here we come to Holland, France, and this would be Spain. Here we have Italy, Greece, the Black Sea, and we then come to Asia. Africa would be down below.

It is difficult to speak about the spread of Christianity in the present day and age because conditions are unusual in this respect. But if we consider Christianity as it was before the World War in these parts of Russia we are able to say: This eastern Christianity still had more of the original religious character that came from Asia. I have spoken of the different forms it took with the Egyptians, Indians and Assyrians. Much of the ritual, the offering ritual, for instance, that was well understood in Asia has flowed into the religion into which Christianity then entered in these eastern parts. When you get to know the religious practices of these parts you get a direct feeling that the ritual is much more important than the teaching. The teaching seeks to express something that belongs to the world of the spirit in human words, or at least as much as human feeling can grasp of that world. It always seeks to address the human intellect. The ritual on the other hand is much more conservative, and religion is conservative by nature in areas where ritual predominates. We may thus say that the eastern religion is conservative by nature, with ritual considered more important in bringing religion, religious life, to human hearts than in areas that lie more to the west.

The second stream in Christianity came from Rome, spreading to the north, and was then strongly influenced by missionaries coming from Ireland. This southern and central European Christianity under the influence of Rome has kept its ritual, but it also put more emphasis on teaching than the eastern religion. People are thus much less aware of the significance of ritual than of the preaching, the teaching. There has been much more dispute about the teaching within the Roman Catholic Church than in the Eastern Church.

There was also another influence. Christianity arose at the beginning of our era, with Islam arising five or six centuries later. I drew Arabia for you the other day. If I draw Asia Minor again, we come to Arabia down here, with India over there. This would be Africa, with Egypt here. Here in Arabia, Islam came through Mohammed.[39] Islam spread with great rapidity in the second half of the first Christian millennium, from Asia initially towards Syria and here to the Black Sea, then through Africa over to Italy, Spain and the west of Europe. The special characteristic of the Islamic religion is that it combines a fantasy element with one that is sober and rational. The main principle of Islam, which spread so rapidly in the seventh to ninth centuries, is that there is only one God, the one proclaimed by Mohammed.

We need to understand what it means in world history that Mohammed insisted on this principle of one God. Why did he stress this point so much? He knew the Christian faith; this does not have three gods, but it has three divine figures. People are no longer conscious of this. They do not realize that Christianity has from its very beginning not had three gods, but three divine figures — Father, Son and 'Holy Ghost'.

What does this mean? You see, the original Latin meaning of 'person' was 'figure, mask, the character represented'. And in the original Christian faith people did not speak of three gods but three figures through whom the one God was revealed. They had a feeling for the true nature of those three figures.

Let us consider what is the real situation with those three figures. Today, we have a science that is distinct from religion, and so we are no longer able to understand this situation. Scholarship has become quite independent of religion, and people do not think of religious life when they speak of the life of scholarship or science. It was different in earlier times, including early Christian times. All scholarship was gained together with religion. They did not have separate priests and scholars, for their priests were also scholars. This was above all the case in the late mysteries I have described to you.

In those mysteries the human being was seen to be part of nature, born from the womb as a physical human being with the aid of natural forces. This, they felt and thought, was where forces of nature were active in the human being. If I consider the way a physical human being comes into existence, I am looking at forces that can also be seen in a growing tree, in evaporating water and in falling rain. These are forces of nature. But in earlier times people perceived spiritual forces behind those forces of nature. Spiritual forces are at work throughout nature. They are at work when a crystal develops in the mountain, and the stone grows, when a plant appears in spring, when water evaporates, clouds form and rain falls. The same spiritual forces are active in the human embryo developing in the womb. They are active in the blood coursing through the veins and the breath going in and out. The ancients saw everything in nature as spiritual and everything in the human being as the Father Principle, calling it the 'Father' because nature study was also religion at the time.

They would say to themselves: 'Someone who has achieved the highest level of enlightenment in the mysteries is an image of this Father Spirit; he knows about everything that exists in nature.' This was the 7th stage in the mysteries.

The next level was that of the Sun Spirit, as I have told you. What did people mean by this Sun Spirit who was later called the Son? As I said, the Christ referred to himself as Sun Spirit. People would say: 'Human beings are born through forces of nature, the same forces that make plants grow, and so on; but they develop during their lives on earth. In the state in which they are born through the forces of nature, we can no more call them good or evil than we can a plant.' You would never dream of calling a deadly nightshade plant evil because it is poisonous to humans. You would say it cannot help it. A deadly nightshade plant does not have a will living in it, whereas a human being does. And when a child is born we cannot say that it may be good or evil because of the forces of nature. It becomes good or evil because the human will gradually develops. In contrast to the forces active in nature, therefore, people would call the principle active in the human will—a principle that may be good or evil—the Son of God or the Sun Spirit. Someone able to reach the 6th stage in the mysteries would merely be a representative of this. All the individual representatives of the 6th level were representatives of the God principle on earth. And people knew the sun to be not merely a body of gas; the sun was giving out not only light and warmth, but also the powers that developed the will. Thus not only light and warmth came from the sun but also the sun spirit. The Son God was also the Sun Spirit. People would say, therefore, that the Father God was to be found everywhere in the natural world, and the Son God wherever human beings developed an independent will.

People then thought of something very strange. They would ask: Does it make a human being worth more or worth less when he develops an independent will? They were still asking themselves this question at the time when Christianity came.

Gentlemen, think of any natural product, even going as high as an animal. Now if a cow has grown old, you may say people pay less for it than when it was young. It would then be worth less than it was when it was young. This is true, but it is not the point, for we realize that the cow has become worth less not because of something active within it as will, but because of a natural event. A human being who does bad things, however, developing his will in a way that is not good, will be worth less than he is by nature. Human beings therefore need a third deity who can guide them to make their will good again, really good, to hallow a will that has grown unsound. And that was the third form of the divine, the Holy Spirit, who was always represented as the 5th level of initiation in the mysteries, and given the name of the nation.

The people of past times thus said the divine principle came to revelation in three ways. You see, they might have said: there is a god of nature, a god of will, and a god of spirit, where the will is hallowed again and made spiritual. They actually did say this, for the old words meant just that. 'Father' was something connected with the origins of the physical world, a natural principle. In the languages we have now, the significance of these words has been lost. But those people of old would add something when they said there is a god of nature, the Father, a god of will, the Son, and a god of spirit, the Holy Ghost who heals all that has grown sick because of the will. They would add: 'These three are one.' Their most important statement, their greatest conviction therefore was this: 'The divine has three forms, but these three are one.'

Something else they would say was: 'If you look at a human being, you see a big difference from the natural world. If you look at a stone, what is active in it? The Father. If you look at a plant, what is active in it? The Father God. If you look at the human being as a physical human being, what is active in it? The Father God. However, if you look at the human being as soul, in his will, what is active in this? The Son God. And if you consider the future of humanity, how it shall be one day when all shall be healthy again in the will—that is where the Spirit God is at work.' All three gods, they would say, are active in the human being. There are three gods or divine forms; but they are one, and they also work as one in the human being.

That was the original Christian belief. Going back to early Christian times we would find people still saying they were convinced of this. They would say: 'Yes, this healing spirit that brings health must act in two ways. In the first place it must act on the physical aspect that comes from the Father, because nature can fall into sickness. And it must act on the principle that comes from the Son, because the will, too, must be healed.' What they said, therefore, was that the Holy Ghost had to act in such a way that it arose from both the Father and the Son. That was the original belief held by Christians.

Mohammed may be said to have grown anxious, as it were. He saw that ancient paganism with its many gods would go into a decline and ruin humanity. He saw Christianity evolve and said to himself that this, too, held the danger of a multiplicity of gods, that is, three gods. He did not realize that these were three forms of the divine and he therefore went into opposition, emphatically saying that there was only one God, proclaimed by Mohammed and that everything else said about the gods was wrong.

This dogma was proclaimed far and wide with great fanaticism, and as a result the thought of three divine figures was completely absent from Islam. They would speak only of the one God whom they felt to be the father of all that exists. The thinking in Islam therefore also was that just as a stone does not grow to be what it is out of its own free will, as a plant does not have its own will but is given yellow or red flowers by nature, so everything in the human being, too, would grow out of nature. This gave rise to a rigid notion of destiny in Islam — we call it fatalism — that human beings have to submit to a wholly unconditional, predetermined fate. If they are happy, this is so because the Father God wills it; if they are unhappy, it is so because the Father God wills it. They have to submit to their fate. That was the religious aspect of Islam.

Mohammed saw everything in the human being to be the same as it is in nature, and this made it much easier for him to accept the whole of the ancient art and the whole of the old way of life than Christianity. Christianity was above all concerned with the healing of the human will. Islam was not concerned with this, seeing no reason for doing so. If it is determined that a person is to be evil, then that is the will of the Father God. Christians would say: 'The pagans of old were mainly concerned with the Father God; we must set up the Son God against this.' Mohammed, and above all his followers, did not say this. They said: 'The pagans of old may have had many gods, but they also venerated nature, and the one God is at work in this.' Much of the old knowledge and art has therefore been preserved in Islam. In the ninth century, for example, Charlemagne,[40] king of the

Franks and later emperor, one of the greatest medieval
rulers in Europe and a well-known historical figure, found
it a great effort to learn his letters and was not yet able to
write. His achievements in the arts and sciences were very
little compared to those made under Harun al-Rashid[41]
who was Caliph of Baghdad at the time. Much of the art and
science from earlier pagan times had been preserved there;
it came to Europe later, from the south, through Spain.

Christianity spread from Rome. We might say that Islam,
coming from Asia, skirted around it. Great battles were also
fought between them. And the followers of Islam did
something very strange. You know that if there is an army
somewhere, much can be gained strategically by secretly
moving around it and attacking from the other side. This is
really what happened with Islam and Christianity. The
followers of Islam skirted around Christian areas in the
south and then attacked from the left flank.

But you see, if this had not happened, if all that had
happened would have been the spread of Christianity, we
would have no science today. The religious element of
Islam was rejected, fought against. But the element that did
not involve religious strife but preserved earlier knowledge
and took it further did come to Europe with Islam. There
the Europeans learned the things that have become part of
modern science. Two things therefore live in the European
soul today: we have the religion that has come with
Christianity and the science that has come with Islam,
though in a roundabout way. And our Christianity has only
been able to develop the way it did because knowledge,
science, has been influenced by Islam.

This aroused an ever greater desire in the European west
to defend Christianity. Where ritual prevails you have less
need to defend religion, for ritual has a great influence on
people. Here the tendency coming from Rome was to make
ritual less important, though it was retained. Dogma pre-

dominated and had to be defended all the time against the Muslim onslaught. The whole of the Middle Ages really passed over these struggles which were fought in the field initially and then in human minds. Everything we call European culture or civilization has gradually evolved in the second half of the Middle Ages. What did evolve there?

Over in the east, all the way to Russia and indeed Greece, Christians could do no other but remain true to the old traditions. This meant to perform outer acts, even if they were purely symbolic by nature. One had to take account of the natural world. And one was much more inclined to put the emphasis on the Father God rather than the Son God. Just as the destiny principle that came to Mohammed was to submit entirely to what the Father God ordained, so this Father God also emerged more strongly in eastern Christianity than the Son, the way the tenor of belief went. The strange shift in thinking that occurred was that the people in the east did hold firmly to the Christ, but they transferred the attributes of the Father God to the Christ. Something of a cloud was cast over it all here; people would speak less of the Son God; they would become Christians, recognizing the Christ to be their God, but they saw in him the attributes of the Father God. The view that evolved in this eastern religion was really: Christ, our Father. This notion of Christ, our Father, is to be found in the whole of the eastern religion.

Over here, in Europe itself, people wanted to fight Islam, the idea of only one God who did not have three forms, and so the concept of the three divine persons took a deep hold.

Well, as you know, gentlemen, you can fight for a time; people may sit down together and be in continual dispute; one says one thing to another person, who then says something else. So they fight. But what is generally the result? They finally separate, each going his own way. The end of the dispute is that people agree to differ. It is extremely rare for agreement to be reached, especially if the dispute is of some magnitude. You'll remember how first there was a socialist party; that had many disputes. There was a right wing and a left wing. In due course the wings became separate party organizations. And that is how it was with the spread of Christianity. It spread. Over in Asia, that is in the East, people thought more of the Father God, though they held to the Christ; in Europe they made more of a distinction between the Father and the Son. They disputed and fought over the issue until the ninth or tenth century. Then came the great split. The eastern Church, called the Orthodox Church today because it has continued with the old, original things, separated from the western Church, the Roman Catholic Church. That was the time when the great division appeared between the eastern Church, eastern Christianity, and western Christianity.

This continued for a time. In the eleventh, twelfth and thirteenth centuries people got used to the idea of an eastern and a western aspect. But then something happened that in some respects upset it all again. It was the Crusades.

Mohammed had originally worked among the Arabs who were the first to take up Islam. The Arab people had a strong nature religion and therefore were prepared to understand the idea of the Father, and recognize the Father God. In the early days of Islam the idea developed of a Father God who worked through nature, including human nature.

Then, however, tribes came from the far regions of Asia. Their descendants today are the Turks. They fought wars against the Arab people. The strange thing about those Mongols, whose descendants are the Turks, is that they did not really have a nature god. Like the people of early civilizations they did not have the eye for nature which the Greeks later developed so strongly. The Turks came from their original homes with no feeling for nature but a tremendous feeling for a spiritual God, a God to be approached in thought only who could never be seen with one's eyes. This particular way of approaching the God-head became part of Islam. The Turks accepted the Muslim religion of the people they conquered but changed it to fit in with their ideas. And whilst Islam had accepted much that came from earlier times, both art and science, the Turks really threw out anything that might be called art or science and really became hostile to art and science. They were the terror of the western peoples, a terror for all who had accepted Christianity.

You see, the region where Christianity arose, in Palestine, with Jerusalem, was particularly sacred to the Christians. Many made pilgrimages there from all parts of the West, which called for great sacrifices. Many people were extremely poor and it was hard for them to get the means together for the journey to Palestine to visit the Holy Sepulchre, as it is called. And they made the journey! When the Turks came, the journey became dangerous, for the Turks extended their rule to Palestine and maltreated the Christian pilgrims. The Europeans then wanted Jerusalem to be freed so that people might go there. They wanted to set up their own European rule in Palestine and therefore undertook those great campaigns called the Crusades. These did not achieve what they were meant to achieve but they reflect the war, the battle, between western Christianity and also eastern Christianity on one hand and Turkish Islam. Christianity was to be saved in the face of a Muslim religion grown Turkish.

Many people then went to Asia to fight. What did they find there? The Crusades started in the twelfth century and continued for some centuries, and so they were in the middle of the Middle Ages. What was the first thing the people who went to Asia as Crusaders would see? They saw that the Turks are fearsome enemies to face. But when a

Crusader looked around a bit on days when there was no fighting, he might find some strange things. He might have met an old man who had withdrawn to his poor hovel somewhere and did not concern himself with Turks, Christians or Arabs but had shown remarkable faithfulness in continuing the culture, the wisdom and religious knowledge of earlier pagan times. The Turks had paid no regard to this. Official civilization had eradicated it; but there were many such people. And so the Europeans got to know much of the old wisdom that no longer existed in Christianity. This they brought with them to Europe on their return.

Imagine how things were at the time. Earlier on, Arabs had come to Europe via Italy and Spain, bringing their art and a scientific thinking that spread and has become our modern science. Now the ancient wisdom from the East was brought back and the two became mixed. As a result, something special developed in Europe.

You see, the Roman Church adopted the ritual, using it less, however, than the eastern Church did. It adopted the ritual but also went strongly into teaching. But in the old Church teaching, religious instruction was connected with the person. It remained such until the time of the Crusades. Instruction consisted in what was proclaimed from the pulpit and approved by the Councils that were held. And apart from this there was also the 'New Testament', as it was called, the Bible. People who were not priests were, however, forbidden to read the Bible, and this was strictly enforced. It was considered a terrible thing for someone to want to read the Bible in those earlier times before the Crusades. It was not permitted. The lay people, the faithful, therefore had only what the priests taught, they did not have access to the Bible.

The science brought by the Arabs and the ancient wisdom of the East made many people feel: 'This is something the priests who are giving instruction do not know. There is a great deal more wisdom than is taught by them.' And a tendency, an intention arose to read the Bible oneself and get to know the New Testament. Protestantism, the third kind of Christianity, developed out of this, with Luther[42] its special representative, though the intention was there even before he came.

Take the areas, for example, where Czechoslovakia, Bohemia and Bavaria are today; take these areas along the Rhine, from Holland down into Germany — I could mention other areas as well. Brotherhoods were developing everywhere in those areas. Here, down the Rhine, the Brotherhood of Communal Life developed, here, more to the east, the Moravian Church or Renewed Church of the Brethren came into being. What were their aims? The brethren would say: 'The Christianity that has come from Rome is not the true Christianity. The Christian faith is something you have to find out of the inner life.' Initially the aim was to find the origins of Christianity in an inward way. Later they would also say that one had to know the Gospels. Both aims came from the same source.

You see, that was the great difference between Huss,[43] who lived and worked in today's Czech region, and Luther. Huss was less concerned with the Gospels; what mattered to him was that Christianity came inwardly alive. Later this took more of an outward form in the study of the Gospels.

The Gospels were, however, written under very different conditions of life. They spoke in images, and those images were no longer understood in later times. Let me give you an example.

A Gospel story tells of the Christ healing the sick. At the time nervous disorders were much more widespread in the areas where he taught than diseases connected with particular organs. Nervous disorders can often be cured by kind words, with the love one human being gives to

another. Most instances we are given of the sick being
healed there are of that kind. But then we read: 'When the
sun had set, the Christ gathered people around him and
healed them.'[44] People do not consider the passage
significant when they read it today; it seems to them that it
merely refers to the time of day. The question is, why is the
time given at this point? Because the writer wanted to say:
'The powers a human being develops when he seeks to heal
others are greater when the sun is not in the heavens above
and its rays come through the earth than they are when the
sun is up above in the heavens.' It is most significant that it
says there: 'When the sun had set, the Christ gathered
people around him and healed them.' People no longer take
note of this. It was meant to say that the Christ used the
natural powers that resided in human beings when he
healed them. The Gospels were thus translated in an age
when it was no longer possible to understand them.
Essentially very, very little of the Gospels is really understood.

It really was true of all these areas, both in eastern
Christianity and in western and Protestant Christianity, and
I have spoken of this on many other occasions. Something
that had originally been well understood continued by
tradition but was then no longer understood. I would say
each of the three forms of Christianity had one main aspect.
Eastern Christianity had the Father God, though he was
called the Christ. The Roman Catholic Church of the west
had the Son God, merely looking up to the Father as an old
man with a long beard who would still appear in their
paintings, but they would not speak much of the Father
God. And Protestant Christianity had the Spirit God. They
would discuss questions such as 'How do we free ourselves
from sin? How can we be healed of sin? How does man
justify himself before God?' and so on. Christianity originally had one God represented in three figures. It fell apart

into three confessions. Each of them has a piece, a genuine piece, of Christianity.

It will not be possible, however, to regain original Christianity by putting the three pieces together. It has to be found again by people finding the right powers in themselves, as I began to show the other day. I wanted to mention this today so that you may see how hard it is to come back to original Christianity. If you ask Christians in the East: 'Which is the true Christianity?' they will say, 'Everything that relates to the Father,' and they will call the Father 'Christ'. If you ask people in the Roman Catholic Church what is the essence of Christianity, they will speak of everything connected with the sinfulness of man, the evils of human nature, and that human beings must be redeemed from their suffering, and so on. They will speak of everything connected with the Son, the Christ. If you ask Protestant Christians about the essential nature of Christianity they will say: 'It all has to do with the principle of gaining health in the will, letting the will be healed, and justification before God.' They speak of the Holy Ghost, calling him the Christ.

This is how everything we have today has come about. People did not think: 'We must now bring together the three different aspects of Christianity.' They said: 'We don't understand any of this any more!' This has created the mood we have today, and the need to find Christianity again.

Next Saturday[45] I would like to talk to you about the Mystery of Golgotha in this way. I hope it will then be possible to finish answering this particular question.

Past and more recent ideas of the Christ

Good morning, gentlemen. Today we shall add something more concerning the question of Christianity. I am sorry I was not able to talk to you last Saturday, when I had to go to Liestal. We have tried to say something about the true nature of Christianity and the elements that entered into it in the course of human evolution. We have spoken of the struggles that arose over Christianity in Europe, struggles that for a long time were essentially due to one party putting the emphasis more on the Father Principle, which would be the Christianity of the East, the other party more on the Son Principle, as the Roman Catholic Church did, and a third party, the Protestant Church, on the Spirit Principle.

It is really difficult to speak about these things because most people ask today: 'Can you really fight over such issues?' Today people fight over other issues in this world, as you know, and it is difficult for them to understand that people once made war on each other in the most terrible way because they put the emphasis on some principle or other. But this is something that needs to be understood, for times will come when people will be unable to understand why there has been strife over the things that are fought over today. This will happen in the not too far distant future. And if you consider this you'll also understand why people in earlier times fought over very different issues than people do today. But we should know what they fought over, for it is still alive among us.

What has survived most strongly as an outer impression of Christianity? For a long time now it has been the dying

Christ — the cross, and on it the dying Christ. If we go back to very early times we find that the most commonly accepted image of Christ Jesus was of a youngish man with a lamb on his shoulders — a shepherd. He was known as the good shepherd. This was really the most widely known image in the first, second and third centuries of the Christian era. The images representing the dead Christ hanging on the cross really only came up in the sixth century — the crucifix, Christ crucified. The early Christians did not really use images of Christ crucified.

Something important lies behind this. You see, the early Christians still believed that the Christ entered into Jesus from the sun, and that the Christ was a spirit from beyond this earth. This was later misunderstood and the whole was made into the dogma of the immaculate conception, saying that Jesus himself was not conceived and born in the ordinary human way. It was only when people no longer understood that Jesus had initially been a human being — though a very special human being — and that the spirit called the Christ only entered into him in his 30th year that the idea came up to show the dead Christ on the cross, the dying Christ, and on the other hand put the time when the Christ entered in the spirit back to the time of the birth. This misunderstanding only arose in the sixth century. It allows us to look deeply into things. Between the time when Christians still saw Jesus Christ as the good shepherd and the time when he was represented as Christ crucified lay a particular event. It was decreed at a Council[46] that the human being consists not of three parts — body, soul and spirit — but only of two parts — body and soul. The soul, they said, had some spiritual qualities.

This is most important, gentlemen. For you see, the trichotomy, the division into three, of the human being was said to be heretical throughout the Middle Ages. No adherent of the true faith was allowed to believe in the threefold nature of the human being. They were not allowed to say: 'The human being also has spirit' but had to say: 'The human being has body and soul, and the soul has some spiritual qualities.' When the spirit was thus got rid of, as it were, the way to the spirit was blocked for humanity. Today knowledge of the spirit has to be regained, restoring to humanity what has been taken from it.

The early Christians knew above all that the Christ who lived in them could not be born, nor could he die. This was not something human. A human being is born and he dies. But the Christ, who entered into Jesus during his life, was not born in a human way, and cannot have been touched by the death of Jesus on the cross. Just as a person may put on another suit and still be the same, so the Christ took another form, a spiritual form. To represent something spiritual — you'll agree we cannot see it with our eyes — we have to use an image. The people at that time wanted to show that the spirit is on guard above the human being, that the spirit is a good counsellor, by representing Christ Jesus as the good shepherd.

Something of this has survived, but people no longer understand it. It happens quite often that only part of an image survives. People will often say 'the Lamb of God' when speaking of the Christ. It appeared in the pictures produced in the early centuries. The part of the picture that showed the lamb, carried on the shoulders of the Christ, remained. In earlier times it was customary to call people by some part. So if someone was called Kappa, or Cappa, that was once a small cap worn on the head, and some people got their name from it. Someone called Eagle would once have had an eagle in his coat of arms, and so on. And the name 'Lamb of God' has remained, having once been a part of the picture.

By the sixth century all understanding of the spirit had

really been lost, and people believed one could only speak of the human destiny of Christ Jesus. They did not see the living Christ, who is spirit, but only Jesus, the mortal human being, and their interpretation was that this was the Christ. The event of his death thus gained real importance from the sixth century onwards.

You see, materialism was already playing a role then. And we can really see materialism develop when we study the evolution of Christianity. Many things that happened in later times would not have happened without this.

As I told you, gentlemen,[47] the knowledge that the Christ is a spirit coming from the sun, a spirit who lived in Jesus, the human being, is reflected in a symbol we can see on every altar today during high mass: the monstrance [Fig. 2] — the sun at the centre and the moon supporting it. This made good sense when people still knew that the Christ

Fig. 2

was a spirit from the sun. What is kept in the monstrance? A wafer made of flour. How did the flour come into existence? It came into existence because the sun's rays reach the earth, the sun lets light and warmth come to the earth, the corn grows and is made into flour. It is therefore a real sun product. We may call it substance created by sunlight. For as long as people knew this, the whole had meaning.

What is more, the moon was shown as a sickle because this seemed the most important aspect. And as I told you, the powers that give human beings their physical form come from the moon. The whole had meaning when people still knew these things to be what they are. But they gradually lost significance. Let me tell you something that will show you the significance that lies in such things.

The Turks, or Muslims, as I told you, considered only the one God, not the three forms. They related everything to the Father God. What sign did they have to use therefore? The moon, of course. The Turks therefore have the half moon for their symbol.

Christendom ought to know that their symbol is the one where the sun gains victory over the moon. And the early Christians had this as their main sign—that the sun gains victory over the moon through the Mystery of Golgotha. What does this mean, however? You see, now everything is topsy-turvy in the life of the spirit. For if you understand what the image of the sun signifies you say to yourself: 'Anyone who knows about this image of the sun assumes that human beings have free will in life, that something can enter into them that has significance for life.' Those who believe only in the moon will think that human beings were given everything at birth and cannot do anything of their own accord. That, of course, is Turkish fatalism. And the Turks still know something of this today. In a way they are wiser than the Europeans, for the Europeans once had the sun for their sign but they have forgotten its significance.

If you consider that people really no longer knew anything of the spiritual Christ you will understand why in
medieval times—around the tenth, eleventh, twelfth, thirteenth centuries—disputes suddenly arose about the
meaning of the eucharist. It has meaning only for those able
to see an image of a spiritual quality. This they were no
longer able to do and so they fell into dispute. Some would
say: 'The bread truly changes into the body of Christ on the
church altar.' Others could not believe this, for they could
not imagine the bread to have become flesh, seeing it looked
just the way it did before. Disputes thus arose in the Middle
Ages that were to have dreadful consequences. Those who
said it did not matter whether the thing could be understood or not, but they believed that the bread had indeed
become flesh, later became the Roman Catholics. Those
who said they could not believe this and that the whole
could at most have symbolic meaning later became
Protestants.

All the religious wars of medieval times really were over
this issue, culminating in the dreadful Thirty Years War
from 1618 to 1648. This started because Catholics and Protestants could not agree. As you know, it began with the
event called the Defenestration of Prague. Two governors
were thrown from a window by the opposition. It was only
from the second floor and they fell on a dung heap and
therefore were not harmed. The dung heap was not made of
cow dung or horse manure but bits of paper and so on, for it
was the order of the day in Prague simply to throw bits of
paper, envelopes and so on out of the window. It served
well, however, for when governors Martinitz and Slavata
together with private secretary Fabricius were thrown from
the window—this was quite common in those days and far
from unusual—all three were saved. But it started the
Thirty Years War.

You must not think, of course, that the whole of that war

was over religious disputes. In that case it probably would have ended sooner. But added to this were disputes among the princes. They made use of the strife between people. One joined one side, another the other, and they pursued their own aims under the pretence of religious disputes, with the result that the war lasted 30 years. But it really started with the event I have told you about.

Now people were fighting over such issues until the Thirty Years War, that is until the seventeenth century, which is not that long ago. And the Protestant Church may be said to have developed out of this dispute.

You will say, 'Yes, but if the spirit had been got rid off, how can you say that the Protestant Church adopted the spirit, which was one of the three forms of the divine?' The answer has to be that the Protestants did not actually know they were venerating the spirit, which after all had been got rid off. They were not aware of it. But as I have said to you on other occasions, people may not know about something but it can nevertheless exist. And a spiritual principle, though not exactly a major spiritual principle, was active in the Protestant Church, even if they did not know it. You see, if everything professors do not know, for instance, did not exist, what would there be in this world? The point is, gentlemen, you have to understand that it is possible to speak of something people do even when they are not aware of it. And speaking of the origins of Protestantism we may indeed say that the element that mattered was the third form, the spirit.

But you can literally see materialism arise. The earliest Christians did not have to dispute over flat flour cakes being physically transformed into real flesh, for it would never have occurred to them to think about such a thing. It was only when people wanted to think in material terms that this matter, too, became material. This is altogether rather interesting. Materialism has two forms. Initially everything spiritual was seen in material terms, and then the spirit was denied. That is the route people follow in materialism.

It is interesting to see that later on, even after the sixth century, people had a much more spiritual view in central Europe than later. Christianity first became materialistic in the south. In central Europe, we have two beautiful poetic works. One was Otfried's Gospel Harmony, written in Alsace in the ninth century.[48] The other, called the *Heliand*, The Saviour, came from the area where Saxony is today.[49] Reading the *Heliand* you will discover that the monk – a monk of peasant origin – wrote of Christ Jesus in a special way, describing him the way the Germans would describe a prince of earlier times who rides at the head of his army, fighting and overcoming his enemies. You feel yourself to be in Germany and not at all in Palestine. The work relates the events that are told in the Gospels, but in a style as if Christ Jesus had been a German prince. The things Jesus did are also told in that style.

We have to ask ourselves what this means. It means that the outer circumstances, the things one would have seen with one's eyes in Palestine of old were of no interest to the writer; he was not intending to give a faithful description of them. The external situation was immaterial to him. He wanted to speak of the spiritual Christ and felt it did not matter if he moved around the world as a German prince or a Palestinian Jew. People really still believed in the spiritual Christ at that time in central Europe; they had not yet become materialists. In the south, this had happened; the Romance and the Greek peoples had already become materialists. But in central Europe people still had a feeling for the spiritual, and the Saxon monk who wrote the *Heliand* was speaking of the Christ, but in the image of a German prince. You can see from this that it is possible to prove that here in central Europe the Christ was originally seen in a wholly spiritual way, in fact as the Sun Spirit I have described.

If we then study the character given to the Christ in the *Heliand* we find that the main point is that the Saviour, the Christ, is shown to be a 'free man' in this book, meaning that he has the sun principle in him and not only the moon principle, which makes him a free man.

It is really true that the whole connection the Christ had with the world beyond this earth has been completely forgotten and is no longer perceived today.

There is something else I want to tell you. If you go back to the ancient mysteries of which I have spoken, which were centres of education, religion and art, you find that festivals relating to the seasons of the year were celebrated there. In the spring they would always have the festival of resurrection, as they called it. Nature does rise again at Eastertime. People would say to themselves: 'The human soul can celebrate its resurrection just as nature can. Nature has the Father. In spring its forces are renewed. In the human being, if he takes the right care and works on himself, the powers of the soul are renewed.' The main aim in the ancient mysteries—the aim of those who really knew, the people said to have wisdom—was for the soul to gain a kind of spring experience in human life. This was a spring experience where one might say of oneself: 'Everything I have known before is really nothing. Now I am as if new-born.' It can happen in one's life that a moment comes when one feels as if new-born, born again out of the spirit. Now this may sound strange to you, but throughout the East, in Asia, people were divided into those born once and those born twice. Everyone would speak of the twice-born. Once-born people were born through the powers of the moon and remained like that all their lives. The others, the twice-born, had been instructed in the mysteries, had learned something and knew that human beings can make themselves free, they can act out of their own powers. This would be shown in image form.

Now you can go back a very long way. Everywhere there would be a festival at springtime where it would be shown in the mysteries that a god, who had human form, died, was buried and rose again after three days. This was a real ceremony performed in the spring in the ancient mysteries. People would gather. There would be this image of the god in human form. It was shown how the god died and the image would be buried. After three days the image would be taken from the grave again and carried around the area in solemn procession, with everyone shouting: 'The saviour has risen for us again!' During the three days when the saviour image lay in the grave they had a kind of mourning feast and this would be followed by a joyful feast.

You see, gentlemen, this means a great deal; it signifies that the event which happened on Golgotha had been celebrated in image form year after year in the ancient mysteries.

When the Gospels tell us of the cross on Golgotha on which Christ died, this is a historical event. But the image of it had existed throughout antiquity. For the early Christians the actual event was thus the fulfilment of a prophecy. And they would say: 'The people of the ancient mysteries were prophets of what happened in the Mystery of Golgotha.'

One of the most important saints in the Roman Catholic Church is St Augustine, who lived in the fourth and fifth centuries.[50] Initially pagan, he converted to Christianity and became one of the most renowned priests and saints in the Roman Catholic Church. He wrote a strange thing, saying that Christianity existed before the coming of Christ Jesus; the wise people of old had been Christians, though they were not yet called such. It is tremendously significant that it was admitted that Christ Jesus openly revealed a Christianity that had already existed in the ancient mysteries at a time when the mysteries no longer survived. It thus had to be an event that happened once and for all for the whole earth. Awareness of the fact that Christianity had been part of ancient paganism has also been lost. Materialism simply destroyed many things which humanity had already discovered.

The wise initiate of old saw his own destiny reflected in the image that every spring represented the resurrection of the human god who had died. He would say: 'That is what I must become; I must develop a wisdom within me that allows me to say that death only has significance for the part of me that has come into being through forces of nature and not for the part of me that arose in me on a later occasion, something I have gained through my own human powers.'

In early Christianity people still said to themselves: 'To be immortal, human beings must awaken the soul in themselves; then they will truly be immortal.' A false view cannot go against this, of course. But there was a false view that did fight against it. In the early centuries the people who spread Christianity would say: 'We must nurture the human soul so that it does not die.' Later the Church preached a different view. Instead of letting human beings care for their souls it wanted to do this for them. The Church was to take on the care of human souls. This also meant that people could no longer see that to care for the soul in the right way meant to let the spirit, the sun principle, be reborn in it. I think you'll agree that we cannot take care of the sun principle in a materialistic way. How would one take care of the sun principle in a materialistic way? Well, perhaps by organizing an expedition to the sun so that one might collect from there whatever people were to be given. This, of course, cannot be done. And so the whole of it was falsely presented.

You see, gentlemen, everything I have to tell you in this respect shows that materialism gradually took hold more and more, with the spiritual element in man no longer understood. Today we have a situation where the principle according to which human souls must not care for themselves but be cared for by the Church has taken the life of the human soul. If this principle were to continue it would not take long before souls would die with their bodies. Today, human souls are still alive; they can still be woken up if there is the right knowledge of the spirit. In a century or two this will no longer be possible unless there is a science of the spirit.

What would happen if materialism continued? Well, you see, this materialism would gradually and inevitably make itself ridiculous. Even education has to be out of mind and spirit. You cannot teach and educate without speaking of mind and spirit. But if things were really to go that far — and we can already see it in some places — materialism will either have to make itself ridiculous when speaking of mind and spirit, or it will have to become honest.

When I myself and some anthroposophical friends had spoken at the congress held in Vienna in 1922, an article[51] was published afterwards in which the author said: 'We wage war against the spirit!' He wanted to dispose of us with these words. The question is, what would happen if the war against the spirit was waged honestly? People honestly wanting to educate a 6-year-old child would have to say: 'Confound it! This is actually matter, and it actually presupposes the spirit! Perhaps we should give the child a pill or something similar so that his matter is changed; this will make him clever, and then he'll know things.' This is what you get when materialism is honest. Children would enter school and just as today we vaccinate them against smallpox, for instance, we would have to vaccinate each in turn with cleverness. If cleverness is a material thing it must be possible to inoculate it. Human children would thus have to be inoculated with cleverness. And materialism would then be honest. For if someone says he thinks with his brain, not with his soul and spirit, then it must be possible also to make the brain clever in a material way and not through mind and spirit. That is the kind of terrible contradiction in which materialism would get itself caught up.

The only salvation is to gain knowledge of the spirit again. It has indeed been necessary for a science of the spirit to come in this day and age. For otherwise human souls would die.

Easter

Good morning, gentlemen. Next week I'll have to be in Bern and therefore won't be able to meet with you. Today I'd really like to speak of something else connected with our discussion of the Easter festival. Or do you have another question, something that is important right now?

Mr Burle: I would have a question, but it is not connected with Easter. There has been a newspaper article recently from Paris in which it says that it is possible to read, to see, with the skin. Could Dr Steiner say something about this? I was really surprised to hear this.

Rudolf Steiner: One has to be careful when something is presented in the form one gets in a newspaper article. It needs to be checked. It it said that some people — though the man says anyone — can be made to see with their skin, to read with some area of their skin.

This is something that has been known for a long time. It can be done with some people by training them to develop the ability to read with their skin, any area of skin. I'd like to use this opportunity to say that we should not be greatly surprised by such things. You have to remember that people do not learn everything they are capable of; they do not develop it. And it is possible to develop some things very quickly if one concentrates on them. It would of course be possible to train all children to read with their fingers by first of all taking individual letters and letting the children feel the paper. The paper is quite different in the parts where there is no letter than in the part where the letter has been put. Imagine that letters, which tend to be slightly raised, have been scraped out of the paper. Surely there is no reason why one should then not be able to read them quite easily! You can also read letters cut from wood with your eyes closed, and all one has to do is to refine the talent a little.

You see, when I was a boy I practised something that few people practise – to write with a pencil held between the big toe and its neighbour. You can learn to do that. We are able to learn all these things which otherwise we do not learn, and this develops certain abilities; these are refined and lead to something people think they ought to be amazed at. But it is not at all amazing. It is merely a matter of developing the sense of touch. We are able to use the sense of touch with any part of the body. And just as we are able to perceive the prick of a needle so are we able to perceive the fine scratches that make the letters. This, then, is the method for developing such things.

It does not, however, quite meet the case, for the man maintains that he is able to develop the ability to read with the skin in anybody. The way the article is written does not allow us to check every detail. Once a scientific basis has been given it will be easier to say if it is true that you can read a page in a book someone has put on your belly. We have to find out if it is a matter of developing extremely subtle perception, a subtle sense of touch, or if the man made it all up. The article does not show what lies behind it. I did not feel all that surprised at the matter, for I can imagine that it would be possible. What did surprise me was the silly remark the journalists have added, which is that if this were really true it should have been discovered long ago. Can you imagine anyone saying, for instance when the telephone was invented: 'If it were really true someone would have discovered it long ago and humanity would have known about it for a long time'? I've been more surprised that people could say such a thing than I have been about the matter itself. That is not all that amazing, for human beings can learn a great deal where their organs of touch and sensation are concerned. People simply do not notice what happens, and that is because they are able to focus their eyes on something in forming an opinion about objects. It is possible, for example, to train one's fingers and make them able to gain subtle perceptions of all kinds of things.

A genuine scientific approach has to be used to judge if when the man says that he can make any part of the body able to see this needs years of training or not. I have read German, English and French newspaper reports on this and it is impossible to say if the man is mad, telling stories or taking a genuinely scientific approach. That is the situation.

Now there is something else I want to tell you about Easter. Easter relates so well to what we have been saying about the Mystery of Golgotha because, as you know, it is a movable feast. It is celebrated at a different time each year. It fluctuates. Why does it do so? Because the date is set according to cosmic rather than earthly standards. It is set by asking oneself the date of the first day of spring, which, of course, is always on the 21st of March. Easter is never put before that date. One waits for the next full moon and the first Sunday after this. That will be the date set for Easter. The first full moon may be on the 22nd of March, and in that case the following Sunday will be Easter Sunday, which would be very early. The next full moon may, however, also be 29 days after the 21st of March. If we have a full moon on the 19th of March, for instance, the first day of spring follows this, and the next full moon will be 28 days later. The next Sunday four weeks later will then be Easter Sunday, taking us well into April. Easter may thus fall on any date between the 21st of March and the end of April.

The question is, gentlemen, why is the date of Easter set by heavenly standards? It is because, as I have told you, people knew in the past that moon and sun have an influence on everything on earth.

Consider a plant growing in the soil. If this is the soil [Fig. 3] and you want to have a plant, you take a tiny seed and put it in the soil. The whole plant, the whole life of the plant is concentrated in this tiny seed. What becomes of the seed? First of all the root. The whole of life expands into the root. Then it contracts again and grows in contracted form, becoming a stem. It then expands again and leaves develop. The flower follows. And then it contracts again in the seed which will wait for the following year. We thus have expansion, contraction, expansion, contraction, expansion, contraction in the plant.

Every time the plant expands it is the sun which draws forth a leaf, for instance. Every time the plant contracts, being either seed or stem, it is the moon which causes the contraction. The moon is thus active there, between the leaves. If we have a plant therefore where the leaves have spread and the root has spread we can say it is first, in the seed, the moon, then the sun; moon again, sun again, moon again, sun and in conclusion moon. We can thus see sun

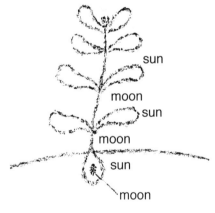

Fig. 3

actions alternating with moon actions, powers of sun and powers of moon. Looking at the field full of growing plants all around us we thus see the actions of sun and moon. As I have told you, when human beings come into the world, the configuration of their physical bodies depends on the moon; their inner powers, the capacity to change themselves, depend on the sun. I spoke of this in connection with the Mystery of Golgotha.

You see, this is something people would have known in the past, but it has been forgotten. People would say to themselves: 'When do we have the most powerful activity going on in the spring that enables plants to thrive and grow to be most beneficial for humanity?' 'When sun and moon work together in the right way.' This is the case when the full moon sends all its rays to the earth for the first time, supporting the sun's rays. This is when sun and moon come together and work together most effectively, the sun having its greatest power in the spring and the moon at its greatest power every four weeks. Easter thus came on the Sunday dedicated to the sun, after the first full moon in spring. The people who set the date for Easter in the past knew that this was something to be fixed as the beginning of spring after the winter solstice.

Easter does not have its origin in Christian times but in an ancient pagan festival, a festival I have mentioned to you before and which I'll now describe more fully. It was the feast of Adonis. It was celebrated in the art, educational and religious centres I have spoken of as the mysteries. Adonis was a kind of image people had of the element in man that is soul and spirit. And people would say that this element of soul and spirit in human beings was also in accord with the whole world. We have to note, however, that the pagans, who still took account of the whole situation in the realm of the spirit, originally celebrated the feast in the autumn.

This autumn feast of Adonis would be celebrated as follows. The image of this eternal, immortal aspect of the human being, of the human soul and spirit, would be immersed in a pond — or in the sea if it was on the coast — and left there for three days. People would sing laments and dirges as the image was lowered into the water. This was a solemn moment, as solemn as the occasions when people had seen a member of their family or a friend die — a real celebration of death. This was always on a day that we would call Friday today. The term used in German, *Karfreitag*, only came up when Christianity reached central Europe; it is based on *chara*, which is to lament. The English call the day Good Friday.[52] If there was no body of water in the region they would make an artificial one into which they would lower the image, which was a statue, lifting it out again after three days, that is, after the Sunday. So you see, gentlemen, it was a real feast of death.

When the statue was raised again hymns of joy would be sung. For three days, emotions of deepest mourning had lived in human souls, and after three days the greatest joy. Those hymns of joy would always be about the god having risen again.

The question is, gentlemen, what was the meaning of this feast? I must stress again that originally it was celebrated in the autumn.

I have told you on other occasions that when human beings die they put aside their physical body. Family and friends will mourn and, depending on the prevailing mood, the mourning feast would naturally come to be like the one when the Adonis statue was lowered into the water. Another aspect of it was missing, however. I have told you that a human being looks back on his life on earth for three days after death. He has put aside his physical body but he still has an ether body. This grows bigger and bigger and finally evaporates in the world. After that the human being is only in his astral body and his I.

The people who created the feast of Adonis said to themselves: 'People should know that a human being does not merely die when his physical body dies but rises again in the world of the spirit after three days.' The feast of Adonis was created to remind people of this year after year. When it was celebrated in the autumn, they would say: 'You see, nature is dying. The trees are dropping their leaves; the earth is covered with snow; it grows cold and sharp winds come; the earth loses its fertility; it looks just as a human being does when he dies.' When it is the earth, however, we must wait until spring for it to rise again, whereas the human being rises again in soul and spirit after three days. This had to come to awareness, and therefore the feast of death was followed immediately by the feast of resurrection, but in autumn, when it would be possible to show that human beings are the opposite of nature. Nature has to submit and remains dead throughout the winter, for it is but nature. The human being lives on in the world of the spirit after death, which is the opposite of nature. When the leaves drop, snow is falling and the cold winds blow, people must be made aware that they are different from nature, for when they die they rise again after three days.

It was a lovely feast which was celebrated throughout antiquity. People would gather at the mystery centres and remain there for the whole period of their Easter. They would join in the lamentations and on the third day they would know: Every soul, every I and every astral body rises again in the world of the spirit three days after death. Taking part in the feast they would enter into the world of the spirit, turning away from the physical world during Easter. This was possible then, for the times were different from the way they are now. Now people celebrate Easter in spring, and if they are country people they are also busy with other things. The old Easter festival, the feast of Adonis, was celebrated when the crops had all been gathered, the grapes had been picked and people were going to have a rest through the winter. This was a time when they wanted to wake up in the spirit. And so they celebrated the feast of Adonis. Adonis would have different names in different places, but the feast was celebrated in all areas where people had the old religions. For this was how all the old religions spoke to people of the soul's immortality.

In the early Christian centuries Easter, too, was not celebrated the way we do now. It slowly changed to what it is today in the third and fourth centuries. Then people no longer understood anything; all they wanted to do was look at nature. They were only concerned with the natural world. And then they said: 'How can we celebrate the resurrection in the autumn? Nothing is resurrected at that time!' They no longer knew that man rises again and so they said to themselves: 'Nothing rises in autumn, when snow covers everything; all things rise in spring, so let us have the Easter festival in spring.' This is one of the fruits of materialism, though a materialism in which people still looked up to the heavens and set the date of Easter according to sun and moon. Materialism had already developed in the third and fourth centuries, but a materialism where people still looked out into the cosmos, not the earthworm materialism where people look only at the soil. It is an earthworm materialism because earthworms are always underground, emerging only when it rains.

Modern people look only at the things that are of the earth. In the early times materialism was still of a kind that people did believe the millions of stars to have an influence on the human being. But this, too, has been forgotten from the fifteenth century onwards. Easter then became a spring festival. Christians were concerned to get rid of all the old truths. I mentioned this when I spoke of the Mystery of Golgotha. They desired to get rid of the old truths. In the eighth and ninth centuries people then no longer knew that the coming of the Christ had anything to do with the sun.

You see, it is rather interesting to consider two Roman emperors of the fourth century. Constantine I,[53] a vain man, founded Constantinople. He had a treasure that had originally been taken from Troy to Rome, carried from Rome to Constantinople and buried in the ground. Above it he built a column that supported a statue of the ancient pagan god Apollo. He sent to the Orient for wood — said to be taken from the cross on which Christ died — and had a radiant halo made of it. And people were supposed to see Constantine in that halo. From then on Constantine was venerated as the figure on the column built over the greatest jewel Rome possessed. He arranged things in an outer way so that people would no longer know of the secrets of the cosmos, or that the Christ was connected with the sun.

The other emperor, Julian,[54] had been trained in the mysteries which still existed at that time, though they found it difficult to survive. Struggling to survive for centuries, they were later eradicated by the emperor Justinian.[55] They were no longer wanted; Christians hated them like poison. Julian had still been trained in the mysteries, however, and therefore knew that there was not just one sun but that there were three suns. People were enraged to hear him say there were three suns, for that was a secret belonging to the ancient mysteries.

You see, the sun is first of all the yellow or white physical body you see. But it has a soul, and that is the second sun. A third sun also exists — the sun of the spirit. Just as human beings have body, soul and spirit, so does the sun have body, soul and spirit. Julian spoke of three suns, wanting it to be recognized in Christianity that the Christ came from the sun and entered into the human being called Jesus.

The Church did not want people to know this. Churchmen did not want people to know about Christ Jesus, but only the things they decreed. Julian was therefore murdered during a campaign in Asia, so as to get rid of him. He was always called Julian the Apostate, which means dissenter or heretic. He wanted people to see the link that existed between Christianity and the old wisdom, believing that Christianity would fare better if it had wisdom and not only the decrees of priests.

At the time when Easter was moved to the spring, people still knew it had to do with a resurrection. They no longer knew about the resurrection of the human being, but they celebrated the resurrection that occurred in nature. Gradually this, too, was forgotten in places were Easter was still celebrated though people no longer knew its significance. Today we have reached a point where people ask themselves: 'Why does the date of Easter have to be set by the sun, moon and stars? It should simply be the first Sunday in April, for that would make bookkeeping much easier.' People would like to set the date on a commercial basis. The people who want to do this are really more honest than those who set the date according to the cosmos though they no longer know why. It is more honest to say, if that is your point of view: 'We can do without the date being set this way.' The sad thing is that we can only be honest because no one knows the real situation any more. Today it is our task to make people aware again that the spirit is the major influence in everything.

In earlier times, therefore, people would wait for the first full moon in autumn and celebrate the feast of Adonis on the following Sunday. The date of the feast was thus set by the moon and other heavenly bodies. And people knew that when the heavens sent snow — the feast of Adonis was always celebrated between the end of September and the end of October — this was the best time to think of the resurrection of the human being. They did not need a resurrection in nature. In the early days of holding the Easter festival it was at least still known that the feast celebrated death and resurrection. This, too, has been lost.

We have to say, therefore, that it really is necessary for us to remember the original meaning of the festivals when we celebrate them, for we need to find the spirit again. To find the spirit it will not do to celebrate Christmas and Easter in an unthinking way. We have to see clearly that they must have real meaning.

We can't turn the world upside down, of course. People would not be keen to celebrate Easter in the autumn. But we can see that it has meaning if people remember: 'Human beings lay aside their physical body when they go through death and look back on their life on earth. They then lay aside the ether body and are pure spirit and soul in the world of the spirit, having their resurrection in that world. This also gives the Mystery of Golgotha deeper meaning. It showed in outer reality what had always been shown in image form in the feast of Adonis. The ancients had an image. The Christians have the historical event. But the historical event took the same course as the old image cult. At the feast of Adonis, the image would be lowered into the water and resurrected after three days. It was a true Easter festival. Then, however, the event always presented as an image became reality. The Christ was in the man Jesus, who died. He rose again in the way I have told you. And this is what we should remember today; this is the Easter festival we should celebrate year by year.

This would have been exactly right to begin with. For why did people always have an image at the ancient feast of Adonis? Because they needed something they could perceive with the senses. It was exactly at the time when the world was still seen in the spirit that people wanted to have an image they could perceive with the senses. But when the Christ had gone through the Mystery of Golgotha, they thought there was no longer any need for an image. It was then considered right to remember what had happened there in mind and spirit only. Easter should be celebrated more in mind and spirit. People should not produce a pagan image but remember in heart and mind only. This, it was thought—and the mysteries still continued at the time of Christ Jesus—would make the Easter festival spiritual.

After all, what was the ancient feast of Adonis really about? You see, as Europeans you cannot really get a clear picture of how the pagans of old celebrated their feasts. If such a feast were to be celebrated in your area you would say: 'But it is only an image, and indeed an image for people initiated in the mysteries; but the statue would be fetched out and immersed every year for the populace at large.' This has led to something called fetishism. A statue like that was a fetish, a statue with a god inside; veneration of such an object would be called fetishism. This was, of course, something that should be given up. Something of this has, however, survived in Christianity. For the monstrance which I drew for you the last time, with the holy of holies placed on it, is venerated as Christ in person in the Roman Catholic Church. They say that bread and wine change physically into the body and blood of Christ. This is something left over not from enlightened paganism, where people would see the spirit behind everything, but from a paganism that had deteriorated, with people taking the statue for the god.

You see, gentlemen, I say you have no idea of this, for today one has to have real inner experience of such things if one is to really see how strong people grow in their belief in such an idol. I knew a very clever professor once—you still get clever people in the academic world; they are really all of them clever, but modern science does not help them to find the spirit. This man was a Russian travelling from the East, from Japan, through Siberia. In the middle of Siberia he began to feel rather uncomfortable. He felt lonely and abandoned. So what did he do? Something I am sure you or anyone living in the West would never do, but he was half Asiatic, however learned he might be. He made himself a wooden idol which he took with him as he continued on his travels, and he truly venerated it. When I got to know him he was terribly anxious and twitchy. This was because of the wooden idol. You simply cannot imagine what it means to venerate such a wooden idol.

The mysteries that still existed at the time when Christianity began were designed to help people come closer to the spirit. Things that had previously happened before people's eyes at the feast of Adonis were now to come alive only as memories, through prayer.

Instead of becoming spiritual, the whole unfortunately became highly materialistic; it became superficial and a matter of form. During the third and fourth centuries it gradually evolved that the priests would pray on Good Friday, and the people would be put in all kinds of moods. And at three in the afternoon, the time when the Christ was said to have died, the bells would cease ringing. All was quiet. And then the crucifix would be lowered into the water, again an external act, just like the old feast of Adonis; later they would merely cover it with something. Three days later Easter would be the resurrection festival. It is the same, however, as the old feast of Adonis. The very way in which it is celebrated has gradually brought it about that souls were governed from Rome. In some areas, for instance where I was born—I don't know if the same thing is done here as well—it is like this. On Good Friday, when the Christ lies on his bier, the young men go around carrying rattles, which are instruments used instead of bells, swinging their rattles and saying:

We swing our rattles, here by the dome.
The bells are going to Rome.

It is thus particularly at Easter that everyone can clearly see how everything tends towards Rome.

Today it is our task to leave materialism behind and learn to see things in the spirit again, see Easter, too, in terms of the spirit. For you see, why do we celebrate Easter? Every year we are able to remember at Easter that when a human being goes through death the *chara*, the lament for the dead, is sung to remind people that the individual is leaving the physical world. But he only looks back to this world for three days; then he lays aside his second body, the ether body, and rises again in the world of the spirit as an I and astral body. This must also be remembered. It would be bleak, brutal, if people were to break into joyful song three days after someone has died. But we can remember those hymns of joy when we think in general terms of the immortality of the human soul which is resurrected in the world of the spirit after three days.

Many strange things have evolved from this. You see, Easter is connected with every single human death because of this. And we should really say to ourselves of every such occasion: 'We mourn; but Easter is coming. Then we shall remember that every human being rises again in the world of the spirit after death.' You will know, I am sure, that today the festival of remembrance of all who have died is celebrated as All Souls in the autumn. All Saints was made to precede it when people no longer knew that Easter was part of it. These things go together. They have been torn apart and are more than six months apart now. The way the year is organized today one can no longer understand what really lies behind it all.

You see the situation is that everything on earth does not go by the earth but by the heavens. We are surprised if it snows at Easter, for there really shouldn't be any more snow at that time and the plants should be sprouting from the ground, for we know that Easter is intended to be a festival for remembering the resurrection and man's immortality.

Seen in this light, Easter will again be a festival celebrated in our hearts and minds, with people remembering that it relates to something connected with the human being. Easter will then be a festival of strength and people will know why they need it so that they may remember. Today we only know that man relates to the seasons because he must put on winter clothes in winter and summer clothes in summer, that he feels hot in summer and cold in winter. This is only the material aspect. People do not know that when spring comes spiritual powers draw the plants from the soil and that it is also spiritual powers that destroy everything in autumn. When this is understood, people will find life everywhere in nature, they will find the whole of it full of life. Most people talk nonsense about the natural world today. They will tear a plant from the ground and botanize, knowing nothing about it. It would be a nonsense to tear out a hair and describe it, for a hair can only grow on an animal or a human being; it does not arise by itself. You can't put something on a lifeless piece of rock and say a hair is to grow there. It needs a basis in life. Plants are the hairs of the earth, for the earth is a living organism. And just as human beings need air to live, so does the earth need the spiritual light of the stars. It inhales this in order to live. And just as a person walks around on the earth, so does the earth move around in the cosmos. It lives in the whole of the universe. The earth is a living entity.

We may say, therefore, that the least we can achieve when it comes to Easter is to realize the earth itself is a living entity. It grows young when it lets plants sprout, just as a child is young when the baby hair grows. An old man loses his hair, just as the earth loses its plants in autumn. That is a life which merely has a different rhythm, youth in spring, old age in autumn, youth again, and old age again. It merely takes longer in human beings. And everything in the cosmos really lives like this. Thinking of Easter, think that this festival can be something for us—at least at the present time—where we say to ourselves as we see nature coming alive again: 'It is not true that all of it is dead. It is merely that life forms must go through death. Life is the primal element and always conquers death. Easter exists to remind us of life's victory over death and thus gives us strength.' If people are able to gain strength again in this way, they will also be able to use common sense and improve external conditions. Not the way it is generally done today. But we must first of all have this spiritual quality in the science of the spirit, so that we may be in harmony again with the world of the spirit which is also alive and not dead.

Let me then wish you a truly beautiful Easter, gentlemen, hoping it will be as beautiful in your hearts as the spring flowers that grow from the soil. After Easter we'll return to scientific questions.

What we should feel about Easter is this, therefore. Human beings can take up their work again joyfully and with renewed zest. I think it is often not possible for people to look forward to their work, but perhaps this is a place where we can. Here we may have occasion to look forward even to our work! I very much wanted to see you again, gentlemen, to tell you this and to wish you a truly beautiful Easter in the spirit that can be gained from the science of the spirit. I'll see you again after Easter.

How scars develop. The mummy

Questions. *The first question was why a wound, a cut, for example, heals up completely, but when you cut away a piece of flesh a scar remains. The questioner has had no sensation in such a skin area for 30 or 40 years. He wanted to know why that is so, because it is said that the body renews itself every seven years.*

The second question was about archaeological finds in Egypt. It had been reported that a mummy, a grave, had been found and that two engineers, the leaders of the group, had died from poisoning on opening the grave or on working their way into the passage. The first one was thought to have died of a heart attack or the like, and then the other one also died. The papers said poisons might have been used to embalm the mummy to prevent people reaching the burial places. The speaker said he could not believe that poisons would persist for so long. Or was it perhaps that gases evolved in the inner chambers, causing death within a short time? Or was it possible that the poisons they had in Egypt would keep for so long?

Clothing found in the burial chambers had fallen to dust as soon as they were brought outside. Chemicals were used to treat the clothing so that it might be preserved for posterity.

Cereal grains had also been found in the tombs of the Pharaohs. They had been there for thousands of years but still germinated when put in the soil.

The questioner wanted to know if any of this would have been possible under normal conditions.

It said in the papers that it took 80 days to cope with the main stone. But it was as if the mountain had collapsed, and the gravestone, a large stone, had been rolled on top. Or as if everything had later collapsed by being blown up, and it had been difficult to reach the burial chamber. How had this been possible?

Rudolf Steiner: First of all, as far as the healing of wounds is concerned—if we answer the questions in sequence. Cuts made during operations heal more or less well. This is important to remember. You can see that these cuts sometimes heal extraordinarily well, so that one has to look carefully later on to discover the scar. Other cuts—and you are not only thinking of surgical wounds but of when one cuts oneself, is that right?—do not heal at all well. The scar is thick and it may often also be hard.

As a boy I often carved wood. It was a foible of mine that I always had to have a pocket-knife—it was a long way to school, and one has to have such things, you know. But I would always lose my pocket-knife and therefore needed many new ones. I was doing a great deal of whittling and would cut myself quite badly every now and then, which is the way these things go. You'd have to look very carefully, however, to see the traces of this; it has healed over almost completely. If you look closely you can see this cut, which had been a gaping wound and bled a great deal. But it is hardly visible now. With some cuts, however, the edges, the thick scars, can be seen for a long time. The question is, how do thick scars develop? You see, the human body is entirely developed from inside; you'll remember how I described the development of the human body. I also told you that everything the human body produces has to be produced from inside, all the way to the skin surface.

Now, how do colds develop? This is something else we spoke of. Colds develop when external heat or cold act on us, so that we are more or less treated by the environment as if we were a log of wood. We are soon cold and get chilled, and we experience the coldness as a stimulus that goes against something coming from inside us. All this is foreign to the human body, which will fight it.

When you cut yourself, be it because you're clumsy, in an accident, or in an operation, you have a foreign instrument in a place where only the human body should be active. The knife enters into the space where really blood, nerve, muscle and so on should be active. A lively struggle develops in that place between the powers you have inside the body and the forces that enter from outside. These are invaders. To fend them off, the inner physical matter of the human body gathers itself together and creates a scar. It comes together to prevent those forces getting in. A scar is therefore in the first place a protective covering created to stop the foreign forces getting in. Initially you always get a scar.

Now let us assume you are young, very young, for example, as I was when I did my whittling; I was 10, 11 or 12 at the time. When you are as young as that the ether body is extraordinarily active. And when it is as strong as it is in early youth, the scar will gradually heal completely once the physical matter has dropped away, with the physical tissues appropriately organized. Then let us assume you are older; the ether body is less powerful then, especially in the place where the scar is; it is not strong enough to overcome it. It tries again, being unable to overcome the material that has collected in the scar. It always depends on the strength or weakness of the ether body if a scar develops or is gradually got rid of. Injuries suffered in childhood will always leave less severe scarring than injuries one sustains later. But people differ. Some have an extraordinarily powerful ether body all their lives and in that case scars will be more easily overcome than in others whose ether bodies may be weaker.

A farmer who is always working in the open air and not so much in an atmosphere full of carbon dioxide has a stronger ether body. He may be in that atmosphere in winter, when he is not working, so that he alternates between open air in summer and bad air in winter. We thus cannot say that he is always in the open air. There is a saying. Why is the air so good in the country? Because the farmers do not open their windows! The air would not be so good if they did open their windows. But that is by the way. People who live in the country experience marked alternation between air with high oxygen levels and air with much carbon dioxide in it. These are much healthier conditions. The effect can be seen not only in the way scars form but also in other ways. Out in the country people walk barefoot, without their boots, in the summer. It is quite common for someone to get a rusty nail in their foot, but it does not signify much. They pull out the nail, wipe off the blood with a dirty finger—everything is dirty; the nail is dirty and so is the blood they wipe off—there'll be a bit of pus developing but it all heals up in a short time. It is not much of a problem.

Townspeople have much more sensitive ether bodies. Someone may have a small pimple; he shaves, cuts himself—and dies! I am telling you something that is really true. Someone with a small pimple hurt himself shaving and died of that small pimple because he immediately developed blood poisoning. This happened because the ether body was weak. It was no longer strong enough to remove the poisons, the foreign matter that got in, quickly enough. This needs a robust, vital ether body. Farmers have such ether bodies. Nowadays they are getting weaker, but if you went out into the country in my young days it was a great pleasure to see the farmers' brimming ether bodies. When they reach the appropriate age, of course, farmers in particular tend to collapse, for the ether body goes down fast and the astral body is not so strong in farmers. But their ether bodies are very strong and that is why everything heals much more quickly than in city people. Working on the soil is tremendously healthy.

It is possible to know these things but under present-day social conditions we cannot change them. They must first be made more widely known. I think it is not difficult to understand that scars develop more or less strongly depending on whether the ether body acts more strongly or more weakly, and this also affects the body coping with things that do not belong in it. A knife is an external substance, for instance, and so is dirt getting in; the body must immediately defend itself. Knowing this, one is not surprised to learn that some wounds do not heal at all because the people concerned have emaciated, eaten-up ether bodies. This is the case particularly where the work people do is no longer in harmony with nature. It is not so much due to the carbon dioxide in the air but simply to the fact that people are no longer connected so much with nature. When people are in an office or on a shop floor all day long, the work they do has nothing to do with nature any more. Our unbelievable civilization which has gradually evolved cuts people off completely from the natural world, creating substances that are increasingly more harmful, increasingly more foreign to the natural state.

This has brought a sudden great change in recent times. People do not usually consider these things from the spiritual point of view, but they need to consider them from that point of view. Just consider this. In the past people would write. Today they work for the typewriter. What is important for health when we write, apart from movement and so on? I would say one of the less obvious things to affect our health when we are writing is the smell of the ink. With the kind of ink manufactured in the past, the smell was not harmful but in a sense acted as a corrective. When people had worn themselves down by being in an unnatural position, putting strain on their writing hand, the old-style ink made from oak apples would restore the balance. The smell of the substances obtained from oak apples was such that it actually strengthened the ether body — not much, but a little. When aniline dyes came to be used, so that one no longer drew on nature but made synthetic ink, as chemists call it, the human being was completely closed off. Aniline ink has a smell that is literally the opposite of the effect the smell of ink used to have. Today many people have changed to using a typewriter. The movements that are required for this and the rattle of the keys — there are typewriters now that write quietly, but that is a very new design — are not the worst part of it. The worst thing is the dirt used to make the ink for the letters. This completely ruins the human ether body, going so far that people develop heart disease from typing, for the heart is mainly activated by the ether body. Civilization is, of course, making progress in this area, but this is never balanced out by the knowledge which people should have about what is really involved. It is a fact that people today are increasingly resisting progress. That should not be so, but there is a certain instinct that makes people notice, though they don't know exactly why, that things are getting increasingly more harmful as advances are made into the future. These things go together. It is how things are.

Concerning your other question, why such highly dangerous things occur when access is gained to burial chambers, we must note that this applies not only to the ancient burial chambers where mummies lie but for example also where you do not have mummies, as in Egypt, but where the burial places are well secured and are rock tombs. On entering these for the first time one has air coming towards one, if I may put it like this, that is extraordinarily poisonous and harmful. Why should this be so?

You may find it strange, gentlemen, that I have to go a long way round to explain the matter, but this will be necessary if you are to understand it. You see, human beings do not only live once on this earth but have repeated lives on earth; they return over and over again. I have briefly spoken of this before. But when they come back they are different from the way they were before. You would probably be utterly amazed if a painter were to come along who knew the science of the spirit so well that he could paint a picture of the whole group of people sitting here the way they were in an earlier life on earth. You would be amazed to see each of you looking very different indeed from the way you look now. It would certainly be interesting! You see, you will return. When your present life is at an end and you have gone through death and the world of the spirit, you will return to earth. The power in us out of which the next body will be created — our bodies come not only from our mothers and fathers but also by the principle that now lives in us and is taken through death into the world of the spirit — continues to act. The principle that was active in earlier bodies on earth is preserved.

Now you may well ask if human beings really have the power to transform something that is in them today and is wholly connected with their present bodies in such a way that it will be a completely different body. No one would be able today to transform the spiritual powers in his body to such effect that another body can be created. But you also cannot die and be born again right away. There has to be an interval of time, quite a long interval of time. This has to exist between lives. And there all the powers are transformed. Under normal conditions, unless one has been a criminal or something similar, the time between death and a new birth is quite long. Now when do we return to earth? We return to earth when the conditions under which we have lived have changed completely. Yes, some people return to previous conditions, and that is very painful. Normally, however, we only return to earth when conditions have changed completely. So we are not born into the same situation again.

The question is, what makes conditions change so completely? You see we must never merely fantasize but stick to reality. The powers we have when we are not living on earth but between death and a new birth are such that they also have an influence here on earth. They come to us from all the stars and from everywhere out there. They are in fact our own powers. It is just that we are not on earth during that time. When we are on earth, these powers we have act from the earth; when we are not on earth they act from cosmic space. These are powers of destruction. They destroy the conditions under which we have been living.

It is easy to understand this when it comes to external circumstances. But it goes further, gentlemen, right into the natural world that is around us!

Think of someone being cremated or buried under present-day conditions. After a time you have an awareness that hardly anything remains of this person. And if you go to the cemeteries 50 or 60 years later and see what you can find in the place where you know one of your forebears was buried in the past, the most you will find are a few bits of bone; but these, too, gradually dissolve. Nothing remains, therefore, of the things that need to be destroyed. Our whole body must have been destroyed by the time we are born again. Yet although nothing remains to be seen of the body, much is still there, a great deal of us. Someone who is able to perceive more subtle forms of matter will find that something remains for a long time of a person in the place where they were buried, or even if they were cremated. All this must first be destroyed.

The ancient Egyptians had a particular purpose when they bound up mummies. Basically they wanted to prevent human beings having to return to earth again.[56] They did not want this to happen, and if you embalm a body you prevent it coming down again. They wanted the individuals concerned to have the convenience of remaining in the world of the spirit. They therefore not only preserved the mummies but used materials—they had great skill and knowledge in this field — so that the dead bodies retained their physical conformation so well that we can still have them in our museums today. They are an exact copy of what the person has once been.

Now, gentlemen, in the first place it is inevitably true that anything that has survived through thousands of years is like poison, for it is destructive. It really belongs to the powers of destruction. A mummy holds tremendous powers of destruction. It is truly the case that if you look at a mummy and dust comes from it, those are powers of destruction coming out. These powers of destruction exist because, as I have said, the human being who is beyond this earth really wants to destroy everything that has been, including the form. So there it is, and the individual has sent powers of destruction into it. So it really does have powers of destruction in it.

Secondly, the Egyptians used special materials to pre-serve the mummies. These materials are extremely hostile to destruction. And they will within a short time create a poison atmosphere. You always have a poison atmosphere around a mummy. This arose from the religious views held by the ancient Egyptians.

There is something else as well. How did the Egyptians get hold of substances that they themselves were able to work with quite easily but which turned to poison within a relatively short time? You see, today people have no idea of the power of speech. The power of speech was enormous in earlier times, and also in Egyptian times. Imagine you have a fire that produces a lot of smoke. If you blow into it you change the shape of the smoke cloud [drawing]. Blowing lightly you can make it rotate. So you are able to change the shape. Just blowing will not do much. But if you start to whistle a tune, which means continuous blowing, you shape the smoke and flames according to the content of the tune. The ancients knew that matter changes if you speak into it in some way, and especially if you use particular words. They had spices with which to embalm their mummies and they did not work with them the way we would today. They would always be saying something as they did their embalming. It was something like: 'Whoever approaches my body shall suffer death.' They would use an intonation and a choice of words that made matter obey, and this power therefore entered into the material of the spices they used in embalming. This lives in there. People cannot believe this today, but it is true. If you have a mummy and come close to its substance, the words 'Whoever approaches my body shall suffer death' are still in it. Another reason is that the material has since absorbed the power of those words.

Today only remnants remain of all this. If you go to a Roman Catholic Church the priest no longer has the power to bend embalming spices to his will with words, but he uses a lesser power, which is to create smoke from incense. The whole procedure would be completely harmless if he would first do what is necessary, then light the incense and speak certain prayers or send particular thoughts into the incense. This does not happen, however, but they burn incense and say specific words into the smoke. These are then in the smoke and affect the people who are in the incense atmosphere. The smell of incense is thus an important medium for getting sinners to repent, and this is a last remnant of all the things that were done in the past.

Embalming was a religious ceremony in which matter was changed. I know a man who went to Asian tombs — the Egyptian tombs are most characteristic of these things, but Asian tombs have them as well. He found that one cannot approach those tombs beyond a certain point, realizing that if one goes any further one will lose consciousness or die. The poison atmosphere keeps people at a distance and this is because the destructive word that will cause harm has been implanted in the materials used to treat the dead bodies.

Something else is the following. You see, if a person has been on earth ten centuries, that is a thousand years ago, his powers change. He passes through the period between death and a new birth and returns. He then has the powers to build himself a new body. He only has these powers because he is able, in the spirit, to overcome all powers of destruction. The power acting out of the seed is thus increased. Otherwise people would not be able to shape a human seed into the body they want; it would merely become the body again that existed centuries ago. The power in any seed must also be old; it must come from earlier times. The power we have now does not allow us to influence any kind of seed. For a plant seed to be active and produce a plant the following year it must be withdrawn from the forces that come from outside and be given up to the inner forces of the earth for a whole winter. These forces are destructive for anything that is by nature external.

The cereal grains in the tombs of the Egyptian Pharaohs were really buried together with those powers of destruction. Whereas everything that is body at the moment when the human being takes his body towards the powers of destruction is destroyed, the situation is the opposite for the principle that lies in the seed, for its vitality is strengthened. It may happen, therefore—not with all seeds but with many—that the process occurs which normally occurs in winter. The plant seeds come together with the powers of destruction that exist in the dead body and their powers are actually preserved. They will then be as active as fresh grain, even after a very long time.

It is particularly when we consider things like these, therefore, that we have to understand that things happen in life that cannot be explained in terms of materialistic science, because spiritual forces are involved. These spiritual forces immediately become actively involved once a certain time has passed in earth evolution.

Let us assume the following. I can only tell you this, of course, but it is possible for a person to look back on earlier lives on earth, both for himself and for other people who shared those lives. Those people will have become spirit, however. Nothing remains of what they once were. So if someone has lived in ancient Greece, let us say, is born again and has great wisdom today, and then looks back at the form he had when he walked about in ancient Greece, he sees that form in the spirit, truly in the spirit. If for some reason — I do not know how, let us say through a devil — the form he sees in the spirit were to be transformed into an actual person, so that he would meet himself in the flesh, he would die. You cannot meet the past in the flesh. If you did you would die. Anyone seeing a past incarnation the way it really was would also come face to face with the powers that seek to make the future element die, really make it die. That is how it is. This would of course produce completely unnatural conditions. You see, the people whose bodies lie mummified in Egypt, so that their form still lies there, have long since returned to earth. So they have been living or are still living, and their earlier forms lie over there. These preserved forms act not only on the people who have returned; when such an individual has returned they also have a destructive effect on other people who come close to such a preserved form. Every mummy is thus hostile to human life. It cannot be any other way. Enmity comes from them for human life. People take no note of this. And so it may, of course, also happen that mummies that once belonged to particularly ambitious people who held great power, and into which much has been secretly put, so that they may be preserved for a long time and have a harmful effect, may indeed have such a bad effect on occasion that someone coming close to them will fall ill or perhaps even die. This is why these inexplicable things happen that we hear of.

The third point was that we are told it is extraordinarily difficult to reach these tombs today. That is indeed the case. When we hear of the ancient mysteries today—one often hears about them—we may also ask: Where were those mysteries? We would have to dig deep down into rocks and there we would find caves and in them all kinds of signs written which would be most interesting if we could decipher them. Basically all of it lies deep down under rocks that have joined so closely that anyone taking a superficial view will not notice that those rocks did not get there in a natural way but were worked by human hands. The Egyptians wanted the tombs to be protected. They therefore put them deep down in the rocks and put artificial constructions on top. These have gradually changed over thousands of years and now look like natural rock formations.

Only one question remains, but this will help you to understand many aspects of history that otherwise cannot be understood. You see, I'd like to know how it would be possible for people today, however great their number, to find the strength that must have been needed to build those things. Even just to destroy them needs a lot of time, as you said. The Pharaohs—that's what Egyptian kings were called—had great spiritual powers that enabled them to influence people. If you are able to influence matter you will certainly also be able to influence people by using the power of the word. Those ancient Pharaohs had enormous powers that enabled them to have enormous influence on people's energies, the energy they needed for work. You also need to consider another phenomenon. You see, normal people can lift things, move them, and so on. But perhaps you have also seen someone who was off his head and the enormous strength such a person would have. It is amazing to see the energy a person gains to lift things which he would not normally be able to lift, to carry things which he would not normally be able to carry. And think of the strength he develops when he fights you! You may have been able to beat him easily when he was not yet off his head; but when he is, he'll have you on your back in no time. People's strength grows enormously when they go mad.

The Egyptians were not mad. Yet they also were not as rational as we are today. They lived as in a dream and had the strength of giants. People are quite unable to grasp today how few people it took to move a huge rock, taking it to a place that might be very high up, in ancient Egypt. It is impossible for us to understand that there have been times when five people would take an enormous rock and transport it over a long distance and raise it to a great height. People had tremendous powers in ancient Egypt. The only way of achieving this was to develop such strength in them by practically making them slaves. That was not the only purpose why slavery existed. This became clear when humanity had grown weak and the intellect had woken in them. In the period which followed the Egyptian period, strength grew less as the intellect developed. Slavery was then such that people merely wanted to keep it going and demanded the right to keep it going. It was different before that, for in earlier times the whole of human nature was made to remain dull, dumb and dreamlike, as this would increase people's physical strength. This artificially produced physical strength was used to create such things as the royal tombs where it takes such tremendous effort today just to destroy them.

You see, completely wrong ideas are presented about all this today because it is usually the most materialistically inclined people who go there. They cannot understand what these things really are. Someone opens up a royal tomb—and he must die. People are amazed for they do not know that this was really intended by the ancient Egyptians. They had the means to make things happen at a much later time.

Think of this. Imagine you are in Basel and have a wireless telegraph. Someone in Berlin records the telegram; he hears what you say by wireless telegraphy. That is a long way away. Why is it possible? Because we overcome distances with our wireless telegraphy and are able to have an effect through space. The telegram is sent, it passes through space, and comes alive in another place. Now imagine you sent a telegram that says 'Whoever hears these words will die!' And perhaps the person in Berlin is an anxious individual, someone who is easily influenced. He hears the message—he'd have to be an extremely anxious individual, of course—and he dies from the shock, especially if the person who sent the message is a madman. The forces that live in the speech of a mad person are much more powerful than those of a sensible individual. So if you have a madman speaking in one place and someone else hearing his words elsewhere, he may die.

The Egyptians had the facilities to preserve such things in their tombs, to put such words in there. These act through time rather than space. And if an Englishman sticks his nose in, he does not know that the words put into the embalming spices are still active in the odour that reaches his nose.

The anxious individual who hears the madman's wireless message would at least die of shock. The other individual dies without hearing anything, because of an odour. The 'wireless message' has been magicked into it, and in the things done by the ancient Egyptians one is dealing with a kind of time telegraphy. They intended to kill anyone who stuck in his nose. And it actually happens because they had the skill that enabled them to speak words into the spices that would have an effect.

You see, if you consider the things that may be known in the spirit you will no longer be amazed at such things. The strange thing is that when people go to all sorts of places today and make their investigations, they sometimes have their noses rubbed in the way the spirit works in a highly unpleasant way. Those who are most affected by the spirit, in that it kills them, would certainly tell the truth if they were able to share their wisdom after death. This is not possible, and so we ourselves must speak out about the decrees made in the world of the spirit.

10.   *Discussion of 5 May 1924*

Creating an astronomy based on the science of the spirit

Good morning, gentlemen! Has anyone thought of something for today?

Mr Erbsmehl: I wanted to ask why it is that people look at the starry heavens the way they do today when the ancient Babylonians looked at it in a very different way.

Rudolf Steiner: This question makes it possible to say something about the great change that has come in the way we look at the world. Dr Vreede[57] is giving a course on astronomy here, and one can see how difficult it really is to cope with all the calculations and the mathematics.

To get clear about these things we must first of all realize that the people who lived in earlier times really were much more spiritual still than people are today. For quite a long time people still knew about effects that occur in nature that are really quite unknown today. I'll speak about a few things that go in this direction. It is impossible to understand what the ancient Babylonians and Assyrians sought to achieve with their science of the stars unless we know certain things that really are quite unknown today.

Rousseau still told the following story, for instance.[58] He said that in Egypt, which does of course have a warmer climate, and we have heard strange things about it at our last meeting, he was able to make toads be immobile by looking at them in a certain way, staring into their eyes, so that they could not move at all. They were paralysed. This is something people have always been able to do in warmer climates such as Egypt. Rousseau was able to paralyse the toads and also kill them. He later wanted to do the same thing in Lyons. A toad was coming towards him. He looked at it, stared at it, and lo and behold! he himself was paralysed. He could no longer move his eye and was paralysed as though dead. People came and called a physician and he was given viper venom, a snake venom which got him out of the seizure, so that he was saved. The tables had been turned. You see, you only have to go from Egypt to Lyons and influences that come from creatures simply turn into their opposite.

We are thus able to say that there are influences connected with the human will, for what we had there was the activation of the human will. There are such influences, and these powers exist. For you see, something that existed a century ago still exists today and will continue to exist for as long as the earth continues. People no longer want to know about these things, however, and take no interest in them.

But you see, gentlemen, this also relates to other things. To understand certain things we must take account of the place where they are done. It means we must consider the geography, in a sense. This is not the ordinary geography of today, for that only refers to ordinary things and not to influences going to and fro between toads and human beings.

Let me give you another example that goes in this direction. You see, van Helmont, a scientist living in the seventeenth century,[59] still knew many of the things people used to know in the past. That earlier knowledge really only came to be lost completely in the nineteenth century. In the seventeenth century it was still quite strong, with the decline starting in the eighteenth century. Nineteenth-century people thought they were the first to be really clever!

Van Helmont was wondering how one might get to know more than is possible with the ordinary human intellect. Nowadays people do not give any thought to how one might know more than is possible with the ordinary human intellect, for they believe the human intellect can know everything. But van Helmont, who was a physician, did not think much of this human intellect. He wanted spiritual knowledge.

At the time, however, it was not yet possible to gain spiritual knowledge by developing mind and spirit the way we now try to do in anthroposophy. Humanity had not yet got that far. Van Helmont therefore used even earlier methods, and he did the following, though I would not advise anyone to copy him. You can't. And it would no longer have the effect it had in those times. Van Helmont did still do it, however.

You see he took a plant, a poisonous, medicinal plant.[60] It is prescribed for certain diseases. He took it. Being a physician, he knew that this plant cannot be eaten, for it would kill one. But he took a quick lick at the root tip, the lower part of the root. He described the state he got into as follows. He said he felt as if his head had been completely cut out, as if he'd grown headless. He had completely lost his head. Of course, his head did not fall off, but he could no longer feel it being there. He was then no longer able to have the knowledge that came through the head. But his belly region began to function as if it were a head. And lo and behold, he received great enlightenment in the form of images, something we call imaginations in anthroposophy today, taking the form of images coming from the world of the spirit. This suddenly changed the whole of his life, a terrific change, for now he knew: It is possible not just to say things about the world of the spirit out of the intellect but really and truly to see the world of the spirit. It was not that he was not thinking by means of the nervous system which is present in the human limbs and metabolism; no, he saw, truly saw, the world of the spirit. He thus received imaginations of the world of the spirit.

This lasted for two hours. After those two hours he felt a little dizzy. Then he was well again. As you can imagine, this changed his life significantly; from this time onwards he knew that it is possible to see the world of the spirit. He also knew something else. He knew that the head with its thinking is an obstacle to seeing the world of the spirit.

We don't do what van Helmont did, which is to take a lick at a plant root—though there are some people who think we do, which, of course, is nonsense—but mental exercises are used to turn off the head way of thinking. The head is there only to receive what is perceived, seen, with the rest of the human organism. The same process is therefore brought about by using one's mind which van Helmont brought about by very ancient methods.

Now I won't tell you everything that would be required to tell you once again about training in the science of the spirit. That can be done on another occasion. But I am telling you this because of the question Mr Erbsmehl has asked. The two things I have told you about are connected with the influence of the stars. Today people completely refuse to believe that the stars have any influence, and no attention is therefore paid to these things.

Van Helmont found his life completely changed. He had enjoyed the experience and therefore wanted to repeat it, and he took several more licks at the tip of this plant root. But he did not achieve the same result.

What does it mean, that he did not succeed again? You see, it means that on the later occasions van Helmont did something or other that was not quite the same as before. Van Helmont himself could not explain it. Now I cannot, of course, tell you—read van Helmont yourselves and you'll find what I am going to tell you now—when it was that van Helmont took that first lick at the plant root, for he did not give the date. But in the light of what we know, through the science of the spirit, it is possible to say the following.

You see, the first time van Helmont took a lick at that root tip there must have been a full moon. And he did not take note of this. Later he did not take his licks at full moon, and then it did not succeed. Something stayed with him from that first time; he was again and again able to get a glimpse of the world of the spirit. But he never again experienced that enormous sudden change.

Being a seventeenth-century person, he no longer knew that this depends on the moon. He thought it was entirely due to the plant root. But in earlier times people knew this very well. And because of this people of earlier times were very much aware that the stars have a definite influence on the lives of people, animals and plants.

To investigate how such things happen we would have to say to ourselves: We may not eat poisonous plants, but we do eat plants, and also the roots of plants. And whereas poisonous plants can only be used medicinally, the other plants, which are not poisonous, are used for food. You see, gentlemen, it is like this. When you eat the root of a plant, this is under the influence of the moon just as much as a poisonous root is. The moon influences the growth of plant roots. This is also why certain plant roots are very important for people with a particular constitution. As you know, there are creatures living in the intestines, in the digestive organs; these are worms, a serious nuisance. Beetroot is a good food for people who easily get worms. When the beetroot gets to the intestine the worms get upset; they are paralysed and are then eliminated in the stools. You can see, therefore, that the root definitely has an influence on the life of these lower animals, the worms. Beetroot does not poison us but it poisons the worms. And again the situation is, and you can find this out, that plant roots eaten at full moon have greater power to drive out worms. This is certainly something that should be taken into account.

Now you see, we might say: When we study the root of a

plant, the situation is that the plants give us something that has a powerful effect on the system of metabolism and limbs. People who have certain illnesses may even be helped a great deal by giving them a root diet, arranging things in such a way that the diet is taken at the time of the full moon and not at the time of the new moon.

Now you see, everything we are thus able to observe in plants also has importance for human beings, for human reproduction and growth. Children who have a tendency to stay small could also be brought on a bit with such a root diet, so that they'd grow better; only it needs to be done when they are young enough, between birth and the seventh year of life. Moon forces have a powerful influence on everything in the plant world and on anything connected with reproduction and growth in the animal world and the human world. But we need to study the moon not just by looking at it through a telescope but by studying what it brings about here on earth. People of learning among the ancient Babylonians and Assyrians—they were called initiates then—knew exactly: this plant is under the influence of the moon in such a way, this one in another way, and so on. They would not speak of the moon as a mere spherical body of ice up there in cosmic space. They saw the moon's influence everywhere. And the moon's influence is mainly apparent on the earth's surface. It does not go deeper. It goes just far enough to stimulate the roots of plants. It is not down in the earth itself.

You can find proof that the moon forces do not go down into the earth if you talk to people who go for a swim in the moonlight, for instance. They'll soon come out of the water again, for they feel as if they are sinking. The water is pitch black. The moonlight does not enter into the water, it does not go in more deeply anywhere, it does not connect with the earth. And so you see that the situation is such that animals and plants are under an influence of the moonlight that does not act from the earth but only from its outermost surface and as far as the roots of plants. This gives you your first information about the starry heavens. Let us now move on to the example I gave of Rousseau who was able to paralyse and indeed kill toads in a hot climate but was himself paralysed in the temperate region, in Lyons. What was behind this?

Well, gentlemen, you only have to consider this. When the sun shines on the earth, which is a sphere, or almost a sphere, the sun's rays are almost vertical in the hot region. Their effect is different there from the way it is in the temperate region where they come in at an angle, a very different angle. And just as growth and reproduction in plants and humans are under the influence of the moon, so are man's inner animal forces, which come to expression in the look of the eyes, under the influence of the sun. These animal forces, which are actions, depend on the sun. The sun's powers thus make it possible that people can easily fascinate, paralyse and indeed kill toads in Egypt, whilst they have to submit to the influence of the toads in the temperate regions. This therefore depends on the powers of the sun.

And you will also know that it is sometimes harder to think, that the whole inner life gets harder at times, and sometimes it gets easier. That is due to Saturn, depending on its position at the time.

The stars thus influence everything that happens in human, animal and plant life. Only minerals are the result of earth activities. A science that limits itself to the earth therefore cannot give real understanding of the human being. Nor can we know what the stars do if we do not look at their activities.

Just imagine—it is no longer so bad today, but it could happen in the past—that someone is a great statesman, if you like. One might have asked the people living in the same house, people who cooked his meals, like the cook, for instance, what the man did. The cook, who had no interest in the skills of statesmanship might well have said: 'He eats breakfast, eats his midday meal and his evening meal; otherwise he does nothing at all; he goes away the rest of the time, and apart from that he does not do anything.' She simply would not have known what else the man did.

Modern scientists also speak only of things they can calculate with regard to the stars. That is all they know. People of earlier times were interested in what else the stars were doing. And they therefore had such knowledge of the stars. They knew that the moon had a connection with the plant element in man, the sun to the animal part of man, and Saturn to the part of man that is wholly human. And so they would go on.

They would say to themselves: The sun therefore has a relationship to the animal in man. When the sun shines down vertically, people are able to have a strong influence on animals in the hot region.

Now you see, people in Europe have a strong relationship to horses, for example; but it can never be as close in Europe as it is with the Arabs, that is in the hot region, for you cannot have that relationship between people and animals in Europe. It has to do with the sun's rays coming down vertically, with the sun's actions.

Take this further, gentlemen. In Babylonia and Assyria people knew that certain influences, certain effects came from the sun. And they would observe the sun [drawing]. They said to themselves, there is the Lion constellation, and there, let us say, the Scorpion. Now there is a time of the year when the sun is in the Lion, that is, it covers it up, and one sees the Lion behind the sun. At another time the sun covers up the Scorpion, or the Archer, or some other group of stars.

The Babylonians and Assyrians knew that the effects

people have on animals are strongest when the sun is in front of the Lion; they grow weaker as the sun moves on and is in the Virgin or the Scorpion. So they knew not only that the planets relate to what human beings do, but also that there was a relationship to the position of the sun — in front of the Lion or the Scorpion — for then these things would change.

What do people do today? They simply calculate: The sun is in the Ram within the zodiac, in the Bull, in the Twins, in the Crab, the Lion, the Virgin, the Scales, the Fishes and so on. They calculate the length of time when it is in that sign of the zodiac, and so on. They know that the sun is in the Fishes on 21 March but they do not know any more than that. The ancient Babylonians and Assyrians still knew, for example, that the human head is most free when Saturn is in a constellation called the Pleiades. They knew all this. They could easily judge it, for they lived in a hotter region than we do and developed a science through which they understood the whole human being in terms of the heavens.

So if we are able to say that this science was of that kind, that related to the human being — well, that science has gradually been forgotten. They would look at the planetary system, and also the fixed stars. They knew that depending on whether a star was in this or that position this would mean one thing or another for human life. They knew that when the sun was in the Lion it would have the strongest influence on the human heart.

The thing is like this. People then tried to see how it was with the minerals. They said to themselves: Only the earth acts on the minerals. But the minerals in the earth have not simply come into existence now; they have developed much earlier, and in earlier times they, too, were plants. You know that coal has come from plants. But not only coal but all other minerals have once been plants. Then the moon had an influence on them, and in even earlier times also the sun, and before that also Saturn. And when they wanted to know which mineral had in earlier times been under the influence of the sun they would test the effect minerals had on people. They found, for instance, that when the sun is in the Lion and has that powerful effect on the heart, you get the same heart action as if you give someone gold to take. They concluded from this that the sun once had a great influence on gold. Or when Saturn was in the constellation of the Pleiades, the biggest influence was on the human head. It came free. And they then tried to find out which mineral once, when it was still animal — for minerals were animals before they were plants — was most under the influence of Saturn. They found that this was lead. And so they discovered that lead also has the effect of making the human head more free. So if someone gets dull in the head, and this is because certain digestive processes that really should no longer happen in the head are done with the head, because of an illness, one must give him lead.

And so you have a metal for every planet. And the Babylonians and Assyrians would use this sign for the sun: ☉. And they also used this sign for gold. They knew, therefore, that now that we have the earth, the stars no longer influence the minerals, but they did do so in the past. They wrote the sun and gold like this: ☉. They would not write 'lead' either, but use the sign: ♄, which means both Saturn and lead. No one would have dreamt of writing 'Saturn' or 'lead' in ordinary letters in those old times. If they wanted to write it, they would put this sign: ☽. To write 'silver' they would put this sign: ☽. It meant both moon and silver. Thus the earth, in so far as it is metallic, was also seen in relation to the stars.

Well you see, gentlemen, that we really do not know very much about the human being and his relationship to the universe unless we are able to consider such things.

Let us move on. These things were generally known in

antiquity. The thing is like this. When Christianity first spread, that knowledge existed also in the more southern parts of Europe. A book about the natural world still exists that comes from the early Christian centuries. It says many of these things. Today we have to know it properly again, otherwise we cannot sort out the confusing statements, for it is already fairly confused. But there is still much of the old wisdom. Then came the time when Christianity became a matter for the intellect only, giving up all else in favour of dogma. It was the time when all the old knowledge was eradicated in Europe. Between the fifth and the eleventh or twelfth centuries, everything was done to eradicate the old knowledge. And that has been largely successful. For, you see, it was like this. People who worked with the old knowledge in ancient Greece, Rome, Spain, that is, in southern regions, were already quite ruined in soul and body. The history of Rome at that time is really quite terrible. People's morals had completely deteriorated. They still had the old knowledge, but were no longer able to remain human beings, and we have the figures of absolute rulers like Nero or Commodus.[61]

Commodus was a Roman emperor of whom I can tell you the following. Like all Roman emperors he was an initiate. The question is, what does 'initiate' mean in this case? It was like a title given to someone today. Every Roman emperor was automatically considered to be an initiate, because he was an emperor. This does show that knowledge was highly esteemed in those days. Only, except for Augustus,[62] the Roman emperors did not actually have that knowledge. But they did enter into the mysteries; they were even able to initiate others. At a certain level of initiation, the person to be initiated had to be struck on the head. This was a symbolic act. Emperor Commodus struck someone so hard that the individual fell down dead. This could not be punished, since it had been the emperor Commodus who did it. And the way they were as 'initiates', so they were also as human beings.

Further to the north lived peoples who were still completely uncivilized at the time, though later they developed the central European culture. But the ancient Germans later conquered Italy, Greece and Spain. Only those who worked with pure logic, using only the intellect, were able to keep their end up. That alone was to be dogma. The rest was to be disregarded. Thinking was limited to the most superficial level. And so it happened that the old knowledge was eradicated in schools and monasteries everywhere. And we can see how something of that Babylonian knowledge only reached Europe surreptitiously, as contraband, as it were. But it did not get far. In Babylonia that knowledge was still retained for a relatively long time.

Greek imperialism continued right into the Middle Ages in Constantinople. And you see, gentlemen, strange figures would often appear there. We sometimes see Polish Jews here with their caftans and ancient scrolls. They are not always well regarded but are profoundly learned in Judaism. Such figures would also arrive in Constantinople at the time when all knowledge was being eradicated. They would bring mightily large parchment scrolls on which many things were written. Now you see those parchment scrolls were taken from them in Constantinople and opened up. And so everything that came from Babylonia and Assyria was stored in Constantinople. No one paid any heed to it. And in Europe everything was eradicated. It was only when the empire perished in the twelfth and thirteenth centuries and later in medieval times that the parchments became available again, and all kinds of people would pinch them. They would then move around Europe. This is the source of everything people deciphered in those scrolls—not scholars at that time, but people of no great learning.

And so a little bit of knowledge spread abroad again in the Middle Ages. This little bit of knowledge served as a stimulus for others, and there could not have been a van Helmont, a Paracelsus,[63] and so on, if those people had not pinched the parchment scrolls, brought them to Europe and sold them for large sums of money. In this way, some things did reach Europe again. And quite a few secret societies still live on these things today. There are all kinds of orders — Freemasons, Odd Fellows, and so on. They would not have any knowledge if some had not come to Europe with the parchment scrolls which were sold for large sums of money at that time.

But people did not think much of that knowledge. A learned canon such as Copernicus[64] would not go to the people who had those scrolls. That was not done. You would have lost respect. And because of this the old knowledge also lost all respect. People like Copernicus then established the body of knowledge that is our modern science.

But something very odd happened then, gentlemen. The cream of the jest is that Copernicus established a particular science of astronomy, and it was a fact that he no longer knew the things people had known before, just as people do not know them today, but the people of later times were unable to understand even what he had said. Two of his theses were understood, the third was no longer understood. If one understands the two theses of Copernicus, one believes the sun to be at the centre, with Venus, Mercury, the earth and so on moving around it. That is taught in every school today. But if you understand the whole of Copernicus it is not like that at all, for Copernicus himself pointed out that there you have the sun [drawing], behind it Mercury, Venus, here the earth, and so on. In reality all of this moves through the universe in this kind of spiral movement. You can read about this in the works of

Copernicus if you wish. So we have the strange situation that whilst Copernicus showed contempt for the old knowledge, people of more recent times did not understand him either. Some are now beginning to understand Copernicus, that is, they realize that he had three and not two theses. The third was difficult for people to understand. And so astronomy has gradually become what it is today — mere sums and calculations.

Now as you can imagine, the knowledge that remains from the past was not gained the way we want to gain knowledge today. We have to gain it in full clarity of soul today. The ancients had more instinctive ways. And it is really no longer clear what the ancients meant by knowledge.

An interesting example happened a few years ago. A Swedish scientist[65] was reading an old book on alchemy. It said all kinds of things about lead, about silver — if you put together lead and silver, this happens, if you add gold, this happens, and so on. What did the scientist do? He said: 'This is what it says. Let's try it.' And he repeated these things in his laboratory, taking lead the way it is today, silver the way it is today, processing them with fire, as the book said — and nothing came of it! Nothing could come of it, for what he read were those symbols. He thought: 'The symbol ☉ means gold; so I'll take some gold and process it chemically. This sign ♄ means lead; so I'll take some lead and process it chemically.'

Now the terrible thing was that the man, the alchemist whose book the Swedish scientist was reading, did not mean the metals in this case but the planets. He thought if one mixed sun forces with Saturn forces and moon forces — he was referring to the human embryo at this point — if sun and moon forces acted on the child in the womb, particular things would happen.

The Swedish scientist was therefore trying to do in a

retort with the physical metals something which in the work of the old alchemist referred to the developing embryo in the womb. And that could not work out, of course, for he should have been considering development in the womb. Then he might have discovered what it was about. So you see how little the true nature of that old knowledge is understood today.

All this will show you how Mr Erbsmehl's question needs to be answered. The way of answering is really that we realize that whilst everything in modern science is good and right and proper, so that one can exactly calculate the position of a star and its distance from another star, one can look through a spectroscope, see the colours in the rays of light and draw conclusions as to the chemical composition of the stars, we have to study again how the stars influence life on earth. And it would be wrong to do it the way many people do today, simply taking the old books. It would of course be easy just to take those old books and find out from them what people no longer know today. But it does not serve, not even in the case of Paracelsus, for people do not understand him any longer if they read his works with present-day eyes. Instead we must learn to discover again how the stars influence human beings. And this is only possible through the science of the spirit, anthroposophical science of the spirit.

There one comes to study again not only the position of the moon but how the moon relates to the whole human being. You come to see that in 10 lunar months, 10 times 4 weeks, the child in the womb experiences the influence of the moon, experiencing it in such a way that the full moon is experienced 8 or 9 times during this period. The child is floating in the waters, and is therefore quite a different kind of creature before it is born, protected from the forces of the earth. This is the most important thing, that it is protected from the earth's forces and is above all under the influence of the moon. It is of course also under the influence of the other stars.

You see, that is what should happen, that at our universities and schools, even at primary schools in so far as it is possible, things are studied in a very different way, that above all the human being is studied, the human heart, human head, and in conjunction with this the stars. And at the universities one should first of all give a description of how the very tiny human seed develops into an embryo in the 1st, 2nd, 3rd, 4th, 5th week and so on. This we have, this description exists, but not the other description, of what the moon is doing during this time. We can only have a science of physical human development if on the one hand we describe what happens in the womb and on the other hand describe the doings of the moon.

And again, we can only properly understand the changing of the teeth, for example, in around the 7th year, if we not only describe how there is a milk tooth, with the other tooth growing beneath it, pushing up behind it, but have a sun science again; for this depends on the sun's forces.

Again, today people only refer to purely physical processes as human beings gain sexual maturity. But those processes depend on Saturn; we need a Saturn science. And so it is not possible today to describe each thing by itself the way it is done today. Then you get what happened in a hospital in a large European city. Someone came to this university hospital thinking he had a disease of the spleen. So he asked: 'Which department should I go to with a disease of the spleen?' He was told to go to some department or other. Unfortunately he also mentioned in passing that he had a liver disease, and he was told: 'You can't have that here, you need to go to another hospital, which is for people with liver diseases; we only have patients with diseases of the spleen.' He thus found himself between the two piles of hay, like the ass in the well-known story. The two piles were the same size, looking exactly the same. This is a famous picture logicians have produced for freedom of will. They said: What does an ass do when it finds itself between two piles of hay that are the same size and have the same scent? About to decide for the one on the left he thinks: the one on the right tastes just as good. About to decide for the one on the right he thinks: the one on the left tastes just as good. And so he goes to and fro and finally dies of hunger! That was the situation of the man with two illnesses. He did not know where to go and might well have died in trying to decide whether he belonged to the department for liver diseases or the department for diseases of the spleen.

I am just mentioning this in order to show that today everyone knows only about a very small piece of the world. But that means one cannot really know things today. If you want to know something about the moon you have to go to an observatory and ask the people there. But they know nothing about embryonic development. There you have to ask a gynaecologist, an expert in women's diseases. Yet he'll know nothing of the stars. The two things go together, however.

This is the great misery with modern knowledge, that each knows a piece of the world and no one knows the whole. This is also why science is so terribly boring when it is presented in public lectures. It has to be boring, of course, gentlemen, if people tell you only a little bit about something.

Let us assume you want to know what a chair looks like that is not here where you are, and someone tells you about the wood; but you want to know how the chair is made. You'll get bored when someone just tells you about the wood. And it is boring when you study anthropology today, which is the science of the physical human being, because nothing is said about what really matters. And if it ever is mentioned, it does not relate at all.

The science of the stars will only be as it should be when we combine it with knowledge of the human being. And that is the crux of the matter. This is the way in which I can answer your question properly today. It really is true that one needs to understand such important things as those I have told you about Rousseau and van Helmont, things that exist and cannot be at all understood in earthly terms. People have become materialistic even in the use of words. What did people call it when they spoke of someone being able to paralyse animals by looking at them? They called it magnetism. Yes, but later the word magnetism was only applied to iron, to the magnet. And when people speak as scientists today they say one should limit the word 'magnetism' to iron, and not abuse it. Charlatans will still speak of magnetizing people; but they have no real idea of what they are talking about. You need a science of the spirit to be able to see through such things.

The Sephiroth Tree

Mr Dollinger: What does the Sephiroth Tree mean to the Jewish people?
Rudolf Steiner: The Jews of ancient times really put all their most sublime wisdom into this Sephiroth Tree.[66] It would be fair to say that they have put into it their knowledge of man's relationship to the world. We have often said quite clearly that man is not only the part we see with our eyes but also has other, supersensible aspects. We have called these the ether body, the astral body, the I or the I-organization. People knew this instinctively in earlier times, not the way we know it today. This ancient knowledge has been lost, and today people think that something like the Jewish Tree of Life, the Sephiroth Tree, is simply fantasy. But it is not.

Today we'll consider what the ancient Jews really meant with their Sephiroth Tree. You see, they saw it like this. The human being is here in this world, and the forces of the world influence him from all directions. If we look at the human being as he is here in this world [Fig. 4], we may imagine it to be like this, shown in schematic form. Let us consider the material human being in this world like this. The ancient Jews saw the forces of the world influencing him from all around. I put an arrow here that enters into the heart—the forces of the world acting on the human being; down here is the force of the earth [Fig. 5].

The ancient Jews said: In the first place, three forces act on the human head—I have shown this by the three arrows 1, 2 and 3 in the drawing—three forces on the human middle, on the chest, mainly on man's breathing and the circulation of the blood [arrows 4, 5 and 6]. Three more forces act on the

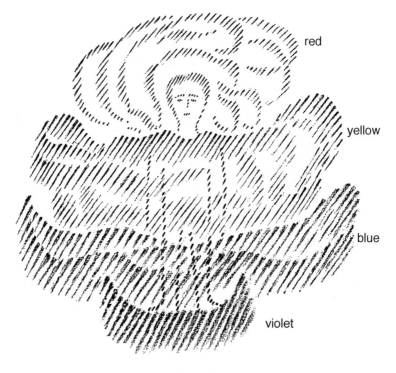

red

yellow

blue

violet

Fig. 4

human limbs [7, 8 and 9], and a tenth acts from the earth [10, from below]. Ten forces, the ancient Hebrews thought, influence the human being from outside.

Let us first of all consider the three forces that may be said to come from the most faraway parts, the most distant parts of the universe and act on the human head, really making the human head round, an image of the whole spherical universe. These three forces, 1, 2 and 3, are the most noble; using a later term, a Greek term, for example, they come from the highest heavens. They shape the human head, making it a spherical image of the whole spherical universe.

Now we must right away develop an idea that might

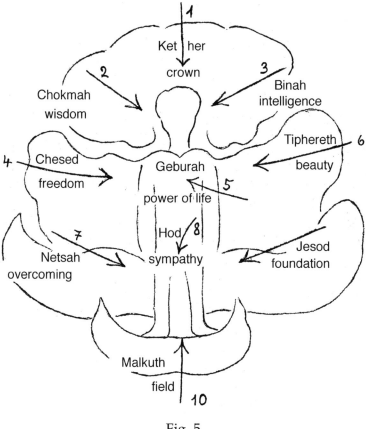

Fig. 5

upset you if I were simply to tell you what it is. For, you see, the first of these ten concepts, the one the Jews made the first and foremost in their wisdom, was later most dreadfully misused. At a later time people who managed to gain power by force drew the signs of this power and the words for this power down into the external realm of power. And individuals who gained power over nations and passed this on to their descendants laid claim to what we call a crown. In earlier times 'crown' was the word for the highest spirituality that can be given to man. And only someone who had become an initiate in the way I have told you, and had therefore gained the most sublime wisdom, was entitled to wear the crown. It was a sign of sublime wisdom. I have explained to you that medals and orders originally all had special meaning and were later worn for vanity and no longer had meaning. Above all, however, we must pay regard to this when we use the word 'crown'. To the ancients, 'crown' was the quintessence of everything that is greater than human and must come down into human beings from the world of the spirit. No wonder then that kings had themselves crowned. As you know, they were not always wise and did not always combine in them the most sublime gifts of heaven, but they wore the sign on their heads. And when such terms are used according to ancient custom we must not confuse this with the misuse that has developed. The most sublime, the greatest gifts of the universe and of the spirit that can come down to man, which he is able to unite with his head if he has great knowledge, were called *kether*, the crown, by the ancient Hebrews.

And this human head also needed two other powers. These two other powers came to him from the right and from the left. The ancients thought that the highest came from above, with the other two forces, two cosmic forces that are present throughout the universe, coming from the right and the left. The one that came in through the right ear, as it were, was called *chokmah*, wisdom. If we wanted to translate the word today we would say 'wisdom'. And on the other side *binah* came in from the universe. We would call this intelligence today (2 and 3 in Fig. 5). The ancient Jews distinguished between wisdom and intelligence. Today any intelligent person is also thought to be wise. But that is not the case. You can be intelligent and think the most foolish things. The most foolish things are thought out in the most intelligent ways today. Thus if we look at many things in modern science we have to say that it is really intelligent in every respect, but it is definitely not wise. The ancient Jews distinguished between *chokmah* and *binah*, the wisdom and intelligence of old.

The human head, and really everything that belongs to the system of the senses in us, including the nerves that spread in the sphere of the senses, was referred to by the three terms *kether*, *chokmah* and *binah* — crown, wisdom, intelligence.

This is how the ancient Jews saw the human head being developed out of the universe. They thus were very much aware — otherwise they would not have taught this — that man is part of the whole universe. We might consider the human body, for instance, and ask what the situation is with the liver. Well, the liver has its blood vessels from the blood circulation; it has its energies from the human environment. In the same way the ancient Jews would say: Man receives the powers from the surrounding universe which then — initially in the womb and also later — bring about the development of his head.

Three other powers [4, 5 and 6 in Fig. 5] act more on the middle human being, on the human being where the heart and the lungs are. They act on the middle human being, coming less from above but living more in the environment. They live in the sunlight that moves around on earth, they live in wind and weather. These three powers were called *chesed*, *geburah* and *tiphereth* by the ancient Jews. In present-day terms we would speak of freedom, energy and beauty.

Let us above all consider the middle power, *geburah*. I told you I would draw the arrow so that it entered the heart. The power human beings have, the heart quality that is both power of soul and physical strength, is indicated by the human heart. The Jews saw it like this. When the breath enters into the human being, when the breath goes into the heart, it is not only physical forces coming into him from outside but also the spiritual power of *geburah* which is connected with the breath. So to put it more accurately we would speak of the power of life, the power which also enables him to do things = *geburah*. But to one side of *geburah* we have the power they called *chesed*, human freedom. And on the other side *tiphereth*, beauty. The human form is indeed the most beautiful thing on earth! The ancient Jews would say: Hearing the heartbeat I perceive the power of life as it enters into the human being. Putting out my right hand I perceive that I am an independent human being; as the muscles extend, the power of freedom enters. The left hand, moving more gently, able to take hold more gently, brings the element which man creates in beauty.

These three powers — *chesed* = freedom, *geburah* = power of life, *tiphereth* = beauty — thus relate to everything connected with the breath and the blood circulation in man, everything that is in motion and always repeats itself. This also includes the movement of sleep, alternating between day and night. This, too, is an element of movement; man also relates to this.

Man is however also a creature able to change his position in space, able to walk about, who does not have to stay in one place like a plant. Animals are of course also able to walk about. This is something humans have in common with animals. Animals do not have *chokmah*, nor *tiphereth*, nor as yet *chesed*, but they do have *geburah* — power of life. And human beings only have the three I have just shown in common with the animals because they have those others.

The ancient Hebrews called this aspect — that we are able to walk about, that we are not tied to a place — *netsah*, indicating that the fixed state of the earth is overcome and we move [arrow No. 7 in Fig. 5]. *Netsah* is 'overcoming'. And the principle that acts more on the middle of the human being, where his centre of gravity is—it is really interesting, you know—that is a point which is about here; it is a little higher up when we are awake and moves down during sleep, which also confirms that something is outside us when we sleep—the principle that is active in the middle of the body, that is also responsible for human reproduction and therefore connected with sexuality—this the ancient Jews called *hod*. Today we would use a term such as 'sympathy' for this. You see, the terms are getting more human. *Netsah* thus means movement in the outside world—we go out into space—and *hod* means inner feeling, inner movement, inner sympathy with the outside world. All this is *hod* [arrow No. 8]. Then, under 9: *jesod*. This is the foundation, the basis on which the human being actually stands. There man feels himself connected with the earth. The fact that he is able to stand on the earth is the basis, is *jesod*. Man has such a foundation also because those powers come to him from outside.

And then the forces of the earth itself act on him [arrow No. 10]. Not only forces from the outer environment act on him, but also the forces of the earth. This was called *malkuth*. Today we would call it the field in which the human being is active, the earthly environment. *Malkuth*—the field. It is difficult to find a suitable term for this *malkuth*. We may say realm, field. But all things have really been misused and present-day terms no longer express what the ancient Hebrew would feel: that this was where the earth actually influenced him.

We only have to visualize that this would be the middle of the human being. There is a thigh bone, on both sides of the human being, and this goes down to the knee, so this would be the kneecaps [drawing]. All these forces also act on this bone; but that it is hollowed out like this, a hollow long bone, is due to the fact that the earth forces enter into it. And everything where the earth forces enter would be called *malkuth*, the field, by the ancient Jews.

So you see we have to consider the human being if we want to speak of this Sephiroth Tree. All ten together— *kether, chokmah, binah, chesed, geburah, tiphereth, netsah, hod, jesod, malkuth*—were called the ten *sephiroth* by the ancient Hebrews. These ten forces are the actual connection between man and the higher, spiritual world, though the tenth force, *malkuth*, is placed within the earth. Basically, therefore, we have here the physical human being (pointing to the drawing) and around him is the spiritual human being, down below first of all as the earth forces, and then as forces that come closer to the earth but act out of the environment—*netsah, hod, jesod*. Spiritually the way these forces influence him is part of the human being. Then the forces that act on his blood circulation and breathing— *chesed, geburah, tiphereth*. And then the noblest powers to influence the human being, acting on his head system— *kether, chokmah, binah*. So that the Jews really saw the human being connected with the world in every direction, as I have shown here in colour [Fig. 4]. Man really is made in such a way that he also has supersensible aspects. And they saw these supersensible aspects in this way.

We may now ask: What else did the Hebrews want to achieve with their ten *sephiroth*, apart from insight into man's relationship to the world. Every student of Judaism had to learn the ten *sephiroth*, not just to list them. You would be quite wrong to think that the instructions given in the ancient Jewish establishments were such that the essential aspect was the diagram I have drawn for you. Simply to answer the question as to what the Sephiroth Tree was would have taken no time at all; you could have learned that in an instant. Today people are satisfied if you ask: What is the Sephiroth Tree? 'There is this and that written in it, as I have just shown you.' But that does not relate to the human being! One simply gives ten words and all kinds of fantastic explanations of them. But in relationship to the human being it is correct the way I have told you. That was not the end of it in those schools, however, for the Jewish student who was to gain knowledge, as it was then seen, had to learn a great deal more about it.

Imagine, gentlemen, you had merely been taught what the alphabet is, and if someone asked you what A, B, C, D and so on was, you would know the letters A, B, C, D and so on. You would have learned to give the 22 or 23 letters one after the other. One could not do much with this! If someone was only able to recite the 23 letters, he would not be able to do much with them, would he? And that is how an ancient Hebrew would have been regarded who would only have been able to say: *kether, chokmah, binah, chesed, geburah, tiphereth, netsah, hod, jesod, malkuth,* that is, been able to recite the ten *sephiroth.* Someone giving that as an answer would have seemed to the ancient Hebrews like someone able to say A, B, C, D, E, F, G, H and so on. You have to learn more than just the alphabet, don't you? You have to learn to use the alphabet to be able to read, using the letters to read. Now just think, gentlemen, how few letters there are and how much you have read in your lives! Just think on this. Take any book, let us say Karl Marx's *Capital*, for instance, and look at it. There is nothing in those pages but the 22 letters; nothing else. Only the letters are written in the book. But it says a great deal in there, and this is all brought about by jumbling up the 22 letters. A sometimes comes before B, then before M, then M before A, L before I, and so on, and this creates the whole complicated content of the book. Someone who only knows the alphabet will pick up the book and perhaps say: 'It is perfectly clear to me what this book contains. It says A, B, C, only in different order; I know everything it says in the book.' But he is unable to read the real inner content and get the meaning of the book; he does not know this. You see, you have to learn to read, using the letters such as they are. You must really be able to jumble up the letters in your head and mind in such a way that they gain meaning. And the ancient Hebrews had to learn the ten *sephiroth* in this way. They were their letters. You'll say: Ah, but they are words. But in earlier times letters were referred to by using words. Humanity only lost this when the letters came to Europe; it was lost in Greece.

You see, something highly significant happened when Greek gave way to Roman civilization. The Greeks did not call their A 'A', but 'alpha'. Alpha really means the spiritual human being. And they did not call their B 'B' but 'beta', which is something like 'house'. Every letter thus had a name. And a Greek could not have imagined a letter to be anything else but something to which you give a name. When the transition was made from Greek to Roman civilization people no longer said alpha, beta, gamma, delta, and so on, with each name indicating what the letter meant, but they said A, B, C, D and so on, and the whole thing became abstract. At the time when Greek civilization went into decline, becoming Roman civilization, a great cultural diarrhoea developed in Europe. The spirit was lost in a massive diarrhoea on the road from Greek to Roman civilization.

And you see this is where Judaism showed particular greatness. When they wrote down their aleph, their first letter, they meant the human being. That is aleph. They knew that wherever they put this letter to be perceived in the world of the senses, whatever they brought to expression in this letter must be in accord with the nature of man. And so every letter used to give expression of the world of the senses had a name. And these names here — *kether, chokmah, binah, chesed, geburah, tiphereth, netsah, hod, jesod, malkuth* — were the names for the letters of the spirit, for things that needed to be learned to be able to read in the world of the spirit. And so the Jews had an alphabet—aleph, beth, gimel and so on—for the outer, physical world, and they also had the other alphabet, with just ten letters, ten *sephiroth*, for the world of the spirit.

You see, gentlemen, if I give you the names like this: *kether, chokmah, binah, chesed* and so on, that is like A, B, C, D and so on. But just as we jumble up our letters, so an ancient Hebrew would have known to say: *kether, chesed, binah*. And if he had said *kether, chesed, binah*, jumbling up the *sephiroth* in this way, he would have said: In the world of the spirit the most sublime spiritual power uses freedom to bring about intelligence. He would have been referring to the higher spirits that do not have a physical body and among whom the most sublime power of heaven uses freedom to bring about intelligence.

Or he would have said: *chokmah, geburah, malkuth*. That would have meant: Out of wisdom the gods create the power of life through which they have an influence on earth. He knew how to jumble up all these things just as we do letters. The students of ancient Judaism understood the science of the spirit in their own way with these ten letters of the spirit. This Sephiroth Tree was to them what the Alphabet Tree is to us with its 23 letters. Developments took a strange turn in this area, you see. In the first two centuries after the coming of Christianity people knew of all this. But when the Jews scattered over the whole world, this way of knowing things with the ten *sephiroth* was lost. Individual students of Judaism—you may know they were called *chachamim* when they became pupils of a rabbi—still learned these things; but even then people really no longer knew exactly how to read by means of these ten *sephiroth*. In the twelfth century, for example, a major dispute arose over two sentences. The first was '*hod, chesed, binah*'. It was posited by Maimonides.[67] His opponent would maintain: *chesed, kether, binah*. So they did have disputes over those sentences. You have to know that they come from the Sephiroth Tree; one person would read it one way, someone else another way. But towards the Middle Ages this reading skill had really been lost. And the interesting thing is that later on, in the middle of the Middle Ages, a man appeared — Raymond Lully, a most interesting person, this Raymond Lully![68]

You see, gentlemen, to get to know such a person is really extraordinarily interesting. Let us imagine there is someone among you who is extremely curious. This individual would say to himself: 'I have heard Raymond Lully mentioned. I'll go and look him up!' So you first of all take an encyclopaedia, and then some books where it says something about Lully. Well, if you read what it says about Raymond Lully in books today you can split your sides laughing, for that would have been the most ridiculous person you can think of! People say: Raymond Lully wrote ten words on bits of paper and then he took the kind of thing you have for playing hazard, a kind of roulette, which you turn, jumbling things up, and he would write down what came out of this, and that was his universal wisdom. Well, if you read something like this, that words were simply written on ten bits of paper and jumbled up, and that the man wanted to discover something special in this way, you'll split your sides laughing, for that would indeed be a ridiculous person.

But of course that was not the way it was with Raymond Lully. What he really said was this. You may search and study far and wide with the knowledge given by your earthly alphabet, but you'll not find the truth. And he then said: Your ordinary heads are not able to find the truth. This ordinary head is like a game of roulette where you turn and there is nothing inside, and so nothing can be selected from it that will make you win. Lully told people in his day that they had really all got hollow heads, with nothing inside them any more. And he said they would need to put ideas like the ten *sephiroth* into their heads; then they must learn to turn their heads from one *sephira* to the next until you learn to use the letters. This is what Raymond Lully told them. It is also written in his books. He merely used a picture, and the philosophers took the picture literally and thought he really meant a kind of roulette, which you turn to jumble things up, yet his roulette was meant to be supersensible perception in the head.

This Tree of Life, the Sephiroth Tree, is therefore the spiritual alphabet. People who were more to the west, in Greece, had a spiritual alphabet in ancient times. And when Alexander the Great[69] lived, and Aristotle,[70] ten concepts would be given in the Greek way. You still find them in all schools of logic today: existence, quality, relationship, and so on—again ten terms, except that they were different, being more suited to the West. But in the West people understood those ten Greek letters of the spiritual alphabet just as little as those we have been speaking of.

But you see, it is really an interesting development in human history. Over there in Asia, people who still had some knowledge learned to read in the world of the spirit using the Sephiroth Tree. And in the early Christian centuries people who still knew something of the world of the spirit learned to read using the Aristotelian tree of life—over in Greece, in Rome, and so on. Bit by bit, however, all of them—those of the Sephiroth Tree and those of the Aristotle tree—forgot what these things really were for, and were only able to list the ten terms. And we now simply have to use these things to learn to read in the world of the spirit, otherwise we shall gradually cease to know anything whatsoever about the human being. You see, a most interesting statement is the following. If such a Jewish sage wrote or said: *geburah, netsah, hod*, we would today have to translate it into the words: 'The power of life hatches out the dreams in the kidneys'. But if we were to say 'The power of life hatches out the dreams in the kidneys' today we would speak of physical forces, physical effects. Yet the Hebrew of old, saying *geburah, netsah, hod*, would have meant: 'The principle which is the spiritual human being in the human being is bringing about something that appears in dreams.' It always was a spiritual statement given expression by jumbling those letters.

It really is true that today we can only gain insight into these things through the science of the spirit. For no one will tell you today that those ten *sephiroth* were such letters for the world of the spirit. You'll not hear this said anywhere else, and no one really knows this today. So that we may say that the situation is such that modern science no longer knows most of the things that people did know in the past. They have to be regained.

Take just this letter here [drawing]: aleph א. What does this aleph mean in the world of the senses? Well, there stands man. Thus he stands, sending out his power. That is this line. He raises his right hand—this line—and he extends the other hand downwards—this line. So that this first letter aleph represents the human being. And every letter represented something, in Greek, too, just as this first letter represents 'man'.

You see, gentlemen, people simply have no feeling any longer for the way these things hang together. The ancient Hebrews called the first letter, representing man, aleph, the Greeks called it alpha, and they meant it for the spirit that moves in man, the spiritual principle behind the human being. Now we have an old German word that is used primarily when people have particular dreams. When a spiritual human being oppresses them, this is called the *Alp*. People say something comes and possesses a person. Later *Alp* became *Elp*, and then elf—those spirits the elves. Man is merely a condensed elf. This word elf, deriving from *Alp*, may still remind you of the Greek alpha. You only need to leave off the a at the end and you have Alph, ph is the same as our f, something spiritual. Because the f has been put, one says: the aleph in man, the *Alp* in man. If you leave off the vowels, as is customary in Hebrew, you actually get alph — elf — for the first letter. Human beings say elf to speak of this spiritual entity. We talk about elves. Of course, people will now say that these were invented by the ancients, a product of their imagination, and that we no longer believe in them today. But the ancients would say: 'You only have to look at the human being and you have the alph, only that the alph is inside the body and is not a subtle etheric entity in man but a dense, physical one.' But people have long since forgotten how to consider the human being.

You come across the funniest things, gentlemen. Just think, the following became fashionable in the second half of the nineteenth century — I am not going to say anything against it, such things may happen. There would be a table, with people sitting around it, let us say eight people. They put their hands on the table in such a way that they would touch on their outer edges, and then the table would begin to dance. They would count the number of dance steps the table took, and make words out of them, words out of letters. Those were spiritualist seances. What were these people thinking? They thought: 'Well, if we sit and think, no real insight will come; true insight must somehow come to us.' Now the truth is that people who say this might well say this of themselves, for they are usually rather thoughtless. They do not want to sit and think; they would prefer the truth to come to them from somewhere without any effort on their part. So eight of them would sit around a table, and they would let the table rap — one rap A, two raps B, then C, and so on, and make words out of this, and those would be spiritual revelations. So you see, wisdom came to them of its own accord; they did not struggle to gain it.

But you see, what should one really say to such people? They wanted to gain insight into the world of the spirit; it was their honest intention to gain insight into the world of the spirit. The spirits cannot be looked at; we do not see or hear them, for they do not have bodies. Those people therefore thought they might use the table as a body, and this would make it possible to communicate in some way. By the way, the results tended to be rather general; they could be interpreted in one way or another. But we would certainly have to say to these people: 'There you sit, eight people, around the table; you want a spirit to come and make itself heard. But surely you are spirits yourselves, you who sit there! Look at yourselves and look for the spirit that is in you. Then you will be able to find a spirit that is much greater. You would not suppose that you can only be seen if you make a table rap, but by using your limbs, your voices and above all your powers of thought in a proper human way!' And it is indeed the case, we need not doubt it, that if eight people sit down around a table, the table will begin to dance, for unconscious powers act on the table. It is indeed the case, but it does not lead to anything that would not emerge in a much higher sense if people were to make an effort with their own alpha or aleph that is in them.

But when Greek civilization gave way to Roman civilization humanity forgot its aleph. The first letter is A today. Well, to think that the first letter is merely A is to stand and gape. Just like that, you'll get nowhere. A wife once got tired of her husband always giving lectures based on science. He had learned a great deal and was always holding forth. This went very much against the grain with her. And one day she said to him: 'You always want to hold forth. If you want to hold something, just hold your tongue!' Yes, the content has really been lost completely. The Greeks did not think A, or alpha, without thinking of the human being. They would immediately be reminded of the human being. And they did not have a beta without thinking of a house in which the human being lives. Alpha is always the human being. They thought of something like the human being. And with beta they thought of something around the human being. So the Jewish beth and the Greek beta became the form enveloping the alpha, which is still inside as a spiritual entity. And so the body, too, would be beth, beta, and alpha would be the spirit in it. And today we speak of the 'alphabet', which to the Greeks meant 'man in his house', or also 'man in his body', in something that envelops him.

Well, gentlemen, it is really very amusing. If you take an encyclopaedia today, you read the whole wisdom of humanity in the alphabet. If someone were to start with A and end with Z — you won't do that — he would have the whole wisdom. But how should this wisdom be arranged in the human being? According to the alphabet, according to what can be known about man. It is most interesting. Human beings have managed to spread all wisdom because they no longer knew that it really points to what comes from the alphabet. If we translate 'alphabet', we get, putting it a bit differently: 'human wisdom, human knowledge'. Using a Greek word this would be 'anthroposophy, wisdom of man'. And this is what every encyclopaedia says. Anthroposophy should be written in every lexicon, for it is only arranged according to the alphabet, according to human wisdom, 'man in his body'. It is very amusing. Every encyclopaedia is really a bony skeleton, where the ancient wisdom has vanished in the alphabetically arranged knowledge. All flesh and blood has gone, all muscles and nerves have dropped away. Today you consult an encyclopaedia, and in it you find only the dead skeleton of the ancient knowledge.

We need a new science now that is not just a skeleton, like the encyclopaedia, but really has everything in it again of the human being—flesh and blood and so on. And that is anthroposophy! So one would really like to say all those encyclopaedias can go to the devil—although we do need them today—because they are the dead skeleton of an ancient knowledge. New science must be created.

You see, gentlemen, that is something we can learn, especially also from the Sephiroth Tree if we understand it rightly. It has been very useful that Mr Dollinger asked this question, for it has taken us a bit deeper again into anthroposophy.

The next time, then, at 9 o'clock on Wednesday.

Kant, Schopenhauer and Eduard von Hartmann

Mr Burle: We've had the (200th) anniversary of Kant's birth-day.[71] *May I ask Dr Steiner to tell us something about Kant's teaching, what would be its opposites, and if it might today be an anthroposophical teaching?*

Rudolf Steiner: Well, gentlemen, if I am to answer this question you'll have to follow me a little bit into a region that is hard to understand. Mr Burle, who also asked about the theory of relativity, always asks such difficult questions! And so you may have to accept that things won't be as easy to understand today as the things I usually discuss. But you see, it is not possible to speak of Kant in a way that is easy to understand because the man himself is not easy to understand. The situation is that all the world talks about Kant today as of something that is of tremendous importance for the world, though people are not really interested in such things; they merely pretend to be. And you know that a whole number of articles have been written on this 200th anniversary, to show the world the tremendous importance Immanuel Kant had for the whole intellectual life.

You see, even as a boy I would often hear my history teacher[72] at school say: Immanuel Kant was the emperor of literary Germany! I once said king of literary Germany by mistake and he immediately corrected me, saying: the emperor of literary Germany!

Well, I have studied Kant extensively and—I have described this in the story of my life[73]—for a time we had a history teacher who really never did anything but read aloud from other people's books. I thought I might as well read that for myself at home. And once when he'd left the room I had a look to see what he was reading to us and got hold of a copy myself. That was much better. I had also got myself a copy of Kant's *Critique of Pure Reason* from Reclam's Universal Library;[74] this I had divided up and put between the pages of the school-book I had before me during the lessons. And so I would read Kant whilst the teacher was teaching history. I therefore also felt perfectly confident to speak about Kant, of whom people really always say when something to do with mind and spirit comes up: 'Yes, but Kant said...' Just as theologians will always say: 'Yes, but it says in the Bible...' And many of the enlightened will say: 'Yes, but Kant said...' It is now 24 years ago that I gave some lectures at which I got to know a man who always sat in the hall and slept, always heard the lectures sleeping. Sometimes, when I raised my voice a little, he would wake up, and especially also at the end. I also said something about mind and spirit at the time. Then he would wake up, jump up like a jack-in-the-box and shout: 'But Kant said!' And so it is true that people go on a great deal about Kant.

Now let us consider how this man Kant really saw the world. He said, with some justification, that everything we see, we touch, in short, perceive through the senses, that is, the whole world of nature outside us, is not real but only seems to exist as phenomena. But how does it come into existence? Well, it comes into existence—this is where it gets difficult, you'll need to pay careful attention—because something he called the 'thing in itself', something unknown of which we know nothing, makes an impression on us; and it is this impression we perceive, not the thing in itself.

So you see, gentlemen, if I draw this for you it is like this [drawing]. This is the human being—one could just as well do it with hearing or touch, but let us do it with seeing—and somewhere out there is the thing in itself. But we do not know anything about it; it is quite unknown. But this thing in itself makes an impression on the eye. One still knows nothing about it, but an impression is made on the eye. And in there, in the human being, a phenomenon arises, and we puff this up and make the whole world out of it [pointing to the drawing]. We know nothing of the red thing, only of the phenomenon we now have—I'll draw this in violet. And so the whole world is really, according to Kant, made by man. You see a tree. You do not know anything about the tree in itself; the tree merely makes an impression on you. This means something unknown makes an impression on you and you make it into a tree, putting the tree there in your sensory perceptions. Consider therefore, gentlemen. Here is a chair, a seat—a thing in itself. We do not know what it really is; but this thing which is there makes an impression on me. And I actually put the chair there. So if I sit down on a chair I do not know what kind of thing I am sitting on. The thing in itself, the item I sit on, is something I myself have put there.

You see, Kant speaks of the limits of human knowledge in such a way that one can never know what the thing in itself is, for everything is really only a man-made world. It is extremely difficult to make this clear in any real way. And when people ask one about Kant it is indeed true that to really describe him, characterize him, one has to say very strange things. For looking at the true Kant it is really difficult to believe someone who says it is like that. But the thing is that Kant insists, on the basis of theory, of his thoughts: No one knows about the thing in itself, and the whole world is merely made of the impression we have of things.

I once said that if we do not know what the thing is in itself, it may be all kinds of things; it could for instance be made of pinheads. And that is how it is with Kant. It is fair to say that according to him, the thing in itself may be made of anything. But now there is something else. If we stop at this theory, then all of you here, as I see you, are merely something that presents itself to me; I have put you all on these chairs, and I do not know what lies behind each of you as a thing in itself. And again, as I stand here, you, too, do not know what kind of thing in itself that is, but see a phenomenon which you put there yourselves. And anything I say is something you yourselves create by hearing it. So none of you know what I am really doing here—the thing in itself, what it really does. But this thing makes an impression on you. You project the impression to this point; and basically you are listening to something you produce yourselves.

Now if we take this particular example, then, speaking in Kantian terms, we might say something like this: You are sitting out there for your morning break and say: 'Right, let's go into the hall and hear one thing or another for an hour. We cannot know what this thing in itself is that we hear; but we'll use our eyes to put that man Steiner there so that—at least for an hour—we have this phenomenon, and then we'll put the things we want to hear there so that they may be heard.' This, in the first place, is what Kant says when he insists that one can never know the thing in itself.

You see, one of Kant's successors, Schopenhauer,[75] found this so clear that he said: 'You simply cannot doubt it!' He said it was quite definite that if he saw blue, it was not that something out there was blue but that the blue was created by him when a thing in itself made an impression on him. And when he heard someone complaining of pain out there, the pain and the complaining did not come from him but from Schopenhauer himself! This, he said, was really perfectly clear. And when people close their eyes and go to sleep, the whole world is dark and silent; then there is nothing there for them.

Now, gentlemen, according to this theory it will be the

simplest thing to create the world and put it aside again. You go to sleep, the world has gone; you wake up again and you have once again made the whole world — at least the world you see. Apart from this there is only the thing in itself, of which you know nothing. Yes, Schopenhauer found this perfectly clear. But he did feel a bit funny. He was not quite comfortable with the thesis. He therefore said: 'There is at least something out there — blue and red, and all the cold and heat are not out there; if I feel cold I produce the cold myself. But what is out there is the will. Will lives in everything. And the will is a completely independent demonic power. But it lives in all things.'

So he put a little something into 'the thing in itself'. Everything we see before our mind's eye was to him also mere phenomenon, something we produce ourselves. But he did at least furnish the thing in itself with the will. There have been many people, and there are many people to this day, who do not really consider the consequences of Kant's theories. I once knew a person who was really full of Kant's teaching — which is what one should be if one has a dogma. This man said to himself: 'I have actually made everything myself — mountains, clouds, stars, everything altogether, and I have also created humanity; I have made everything there is in the world. But now I don't like it. I want to get rid of it.' And he then said he started to kill a few people — he was demented; he said he started to kill a few people in order to manage this, to get rid of something he himself had created. I told him he should think about the difference which exists. He had a pair of boots; according to Kant's teaching he had made them, too. But he should consider what the shoemaker had done, apart from what he himself created as a phenomenon relating to his boots.

You see, that's how it is. The greatest nonsense may be found in things that are most highly regarded in the world. And people will cling to the worst kind of nonsense with the greatest possible stubbornness. And oddly enough it is exactly the most enlightened who cling to it.

These things which I have put to you in a few words, difficult enough to understand as it is, have to be found by reading many books if one reads Kant. For he teased it apart in long, long theories. He started his book *Critique of Pure Reason*, as he called it, for example, by first of all proving that space is not out there in the world; I make it myself, I spin it for myself. In the first place, therefore, space is a phenomenon. Secondly, time is also a phenomenon. For he said: There was a man called Aristotle once, but I myself have put him into time, for I create the whole of time myself.

He wrote this major work called *Critique of Pure Reason*. It does make quite an impression. So if a real philistine, a smug middle-class person, comes along and picks up a big volume called *Critique of Pure Reason*, he'll lick his chops, for this is something terribly clever, *Critique of Pure Reason*; if you read something like this you'll yourself be a kind of Lord God here on earth! The introduction is followed by Part 1: Transcendental aesthetics. Well, now, that's what it says: Transcendental aesthetics. If someone opens my *Philosophy of Spiritual Activity* the chapter heading might be no more than 'Man and world'.[76] Oh, man and world, that is so common, one does not bother to read it. But transcendental aesthetics! When a philistine opens such a book, then this is something that must be really tremendous. As to what transcendental aesthetics may be, this is something he does not usually consider; but that suits him fine. It is a word he really has to get his tongue round. So that is the main title.

Now comes the subtitle. Section one. Transcendental deduction of space. You can't think of anything better for a philistine but to have such a chapter. And it then starts in such a way that he does not really understand any of it. But everyone has been calling Kant a great man for more than a hundred years, and reading the book our philistine gets a little bit of something, and a little bit of a delusion of grandeur.

Now comes the second section: Transcendental deduction of time. Having battled through the transcendental deduction of space and of time one comes to the second major part: transcendental analysis. And transcendental analysis mainly offers proof that man has transcendental apperception.

Well, gentlemen, the question has been asked, and so I must tell you these things, this business of transcendental apperception. You have to read hundreds of pages to take in the learned statements concocted in this chapter on transcendental apperception. Transcendental apperception means that a person develops ideas and that these ideas have a certain coherence. So if everything is merely idea, the whole world, then it must be that the whole world is a tissue created out of the nothingness of one's own nature by means of transcendental apperception. Yes, that is more or less the way this is put in those books.

We now realize that in his chapter on transcendental apperception Kant creates the whole world, with all its trees, clouds, stars, and so on, out of himself. But in reality he is creating a tissue that one keeps battling with in the whole of this vast chapter which in reality offers the same ideas, only translated into the thinking of a later age, as I wrote into the Sephiroth Tree for you the other day, though only as a mere alphabet, not in a way that enables one to read, to know something. What is more, it was something very real in the past. But Kant makes a tissue where he says: 'The world thus is 1) quantity, 2) quality, 3) relation, 4) modality.' Each of these concepts has three subsumptions; quantity for example has unity, multiplicity, totality. Quality has reality, negation, limitation, and so on. Those were twelve subsumptions, 3 times 4 being 12, and you can create the whole world with them. Good old Kant did not in fact create the world with them; he only thought up twelve terms with his transcendental apperception. He thus only created twelve concepts and not the world.

Now if there were anything in this, we should get somewhere with it. But the philistines do not notice that nothing comes of it, only twelve concepts. They go about with full stomachs and Kantian philosophy and say: Nothing can be understood! Well, we can understand this in the case of philistines who like being told that the lack of understanding is not theirs but is due to the whole world. You are right to think you know nothing; but this is not because you are incapable but because the whole world is unable to know anything. And so you get these twelve concepts. That is transcendental analysis.

Now we come to the really difficult chapters. First a big chapter with the title: About transcendental paralogisms. And that is how it goes on. You get title after title in Kant's *Critique of Pure Reason*. He wrote that some people say space is infinite. He proves it the way people prove things who are able to see that space is infinite. But there are others who say that space is finite. This is also proved, the way people do prove it. You therefore find the following in the *Critique of Pure Reason* — in the later chapters it always presents two opposite aspects. On the one hand it is shown that space is infinite, on the other that it is finite. Then you get proof that time is infinite, is eternity, followed by proof that time had a beginning and will have an end. And that is the way Kant did it, gentlemen. Then he gave proof that man is free, and again that he is unfree.

What did Kant want to say by giving proof of two opposite statements? He wanted to say that we actually cannot prove anything! We may just as well say space is infinite or finite; time goes on for ever or time will come to an end. In the same way we may say man is free or he is unfree. It all goes to show that in modern times we have to say: Think about things whichever way you want; you'll not find the truth, for it is all the same for you human beings.

One is also shown how to think in this way, taught transcendental methodology. And so one can first of all go through one of Kant's books. We may ask ourselves why Kant went to all that trouble. And we then discover what he really intended. You see, until Kant came, people who were philosophers may not have known much, but they did at least say that some things can be known about the world. On the other hand there was the thinking that had come from medieval times — I have shown you how ancient knowledge was lost in the Middle Ages — that one can only know something of things perceived by the senses and nothing of the things of the spirit. This was something that had to be believed. And so the idea came up through the Middle Ages and up to Kant's time that you cannot know anything about the spirit; things of the spirit can only be believed.

The Churches do of course do very well out of this dogma that one cannot know anything of the spirit, for this makes it possible for them to dictate what people should believe about things of the spirit.

Now, as I said, there were philosophers — Leibniz,[77] Wolff,[78] and so on — who said, until Kant came, that it is possible to know something, from mere common sense or reason, about the spiritual aspects of the world. Kant said it was nonsense to believe that it was possible to know anything about the spirit, and that things of the spirit were a matter of belief. For the spiritual aspect lies in the 'thing in itself'. And you cannot know anything of the 'thing in itself'. One therefore has to believe when it comes to matters of the spirit.

Kant actually betrayed himself when he wrote the second edition of his *Critique of Pure Reason*. This second edition contains a curious statement: 'I had to let knowledge go to make room for faith.' That is indeed a confession, gentlemen. It is the thing which led to the unknown thing in itself. It is because of this that Kant called his book *Critique of Pure Reason*. Reason itself was to be criticized for not knowing anything. And in this statement 'I had to let knowledge go to make room for faith' lies the truth of Kant's philosophy. And that leaves the door open to all faith and belief. And Kant might indeed have referred to all positive religion. But people who do not want to know anything may also refer to Kant, saying: 'Why do we not know anything? Because one cannot know anything.' So you see, Kant's teaching has really come to support belief. It was quite natural in the light of this that I myself had to reject Kant's teaching from the very beginning. I may have read the whole of Kant as a schoolboy, but I always had to reject his teaching, for the simple reason that one would then have had to stick with the belief people had concerning the world of the spirit, and there could never have been any real knowledge of the spirit. Kant was therefore the man who excluded knowledge of the spirit more than anyone, only accepting some degree of belief.

Kant thus wrote this first book called *Critique of Pure Reason*. It was shown in this book that one knows nothing of the thing in itself; one can only have belief in what the 'thing in itself' is.

He then wrote a second book called *Critique of Practical Reason*, and a third called *Critique of Judgement*, but that was less important. *Critique of Practical Reason*, then, was his second book. There he evolved his own belief. So he wrote firstly a book of knowledge: *Critique of Pure Reason*, where he showed that one cannot know anything. The philistine can now put it aside, for he has been given proof that one cannot know anything. Then Kant wrote his *Critique of Practical Reason*, in which he developed his faith. How did he develop his faith? He said: Looking at himself in the world, man is an imperfect creature; but it is not really human to be so imperfect. So there must be a greater perfection of human nature somewhere. We do not know anything about it, but let us believe that greater perfection exists somewhere in this world; let us believe in immortality.

Well, you see, gentlemen, this is a big difference from what I tell you about the aspect of man that continues after death, based on knowledge. Kant did not want such knowledge; he simply wanted to prove that humanity should believe in immortality because of man's imperfection.

He then proved in the same way that one should only believe, being unable to know anything about freedom, that man is free; for if he were not free, he would not be responsible for his actions. One therefore believes him to be free in order that he may be responsible for his actions.

Kant's teaching about freedom has often reminded me of the statement with which a professor of law always started his lectures. He would say: 'Gentlemen, there are people who say man is not free. But, gentlemen, if man were not free, he would not be responsible for his actions, and then there could also be no punishment. If there is no punishment, you also cannot have penology, which is in fact the subject on which I speak, and then you also would not have me. But I am here, and therefore penology exists, hence also a penal system, hence also freedom. I have thus proved to you that freedom exists.' The things Kant said about freedom remind me very much of those words spoken by the professor. And Kant would also speak of God in this way. He would say: We cannot know anything of any power as such. But I am unable to make an elephant. I believe therefore that someone else can make it who is better able to do so than I am. I thus believe in a God.

In his second book, *Critique of Practical Reason*, Kant said that as human beings we should believe in God, freedom and immortality. We cannot know anything about these but we should believe in them. Now just think how inhuman this really is. First, proof is given that knowledge is really nothing, and secondly it is said that one should believe in God, of whom one can know nothing, in freedom and immortality. Essentially, therefore, Kant was the greatest reactionary. People create apt terms. They have called him 'the crusher'. Yes, he crushed all knowledge, but only the way one crushes a plaything. For the world was still there! And with this he really gave quite considerable support to faith and belief.

This continued for the whole of the nineteenth century and right into the present century, and today people everywhere are referring to the 200th anniversary of Kant. In reality Kant is the perfect example of how little people really think. For what I have just told you has been Kant's teaching in its pure form. But the things people say—that Kant was the greatest of all philosophers, that he cannot be refuted, and so on—well, you see, if we take this example we really see that it is indeed Kant to whom the opponents of spiritual science can always refer. Simply because they are then able to say to themselves: Yes, we do not base ourselves on religion but on the most enlightened of all philosophers. But it is indeed true that the most dogmatic of religion teachers may base himself on Kant just as much as some enlightened individual.

Kant also wrote other works, in one of which he more or less considered how metaphysics may be a science in the future.[79] Here he was really proving once again that it is impossible, and so on. We really have to say that the whole of nineteenth-century science sickened because of Kant; basically Kant was a sickness of science.

So the right way to take Kant is as an example of the

nonsense sometimes produced by human minds. But you will then also say to yourselves: One really has to watch out when it comes to gaining insight, for the world is terribly keen to produce the greatest possible nonsense exactly when it comes to gaining insight. And you can imagine the difficult position one is in as a representative of spiritual science. Not only does one have the representatives of the religions against one but also those other people, all the philosophers and people who have caught their ideas, and so on. Every philistine comes along and says: You say this about the world of the spirit; Kant has proved — so they say — that one cannot know anything about it. That is really the best general objection anyone can raise. A person can say: I don't want to hear anything of what that man Steiner says, for Kant has proved that one cannot know anything about these things.

Does this satisfy you?

Mr Burle said he had mainly wanted to hear what Kant had said. As Dr Steiner said, you hear a lot about Kant but nothing positive. It did, however, take quite some effort to understand it.

Rudolf Steiner: There were consequences. In 1869 someone who had taken up Kant's ideas published *The Philosophy of the Unconscious*, a book that caused a sensation. And Eduard von Hartmann[80] was a very intelligent man. If he had lived before Kant, if Kant had not had such an influence on him, he would probably have done much better. But he could not overcome this enormous prejudice, which came from Kant. Like Schopenhauer before him, Eduard von Hartmann realized that one does not know anything of the world except for one's own ideas of it, something one puts out there oneself. But he also took up Schopenhauer's idea that the thing in itself must be furnished with will. So now we have the will everywhere inside it. I once wrote an article on Eduard von Hartmann in which I also mentioned Schopenhauer.[81] Schopenhauer said that one knows nothing of the thing in itself; one only has ideas of it. Ideas are clever, the will is dumb. So that really all one knows by oneself is no more than dumb will.

In the article in which I mentioned Schopenhauer I wrote: 'According to Schopenhauer everything that is intelligent in the world is the work of man; for man brings everything into the world; and behind it lies the dumb will. The world is thus the dumbness of the Godhead.' But this was impounded at the time. It was to have been published in Austria.

The thing is like this. Eduard von Hartmann had assumed that the thing in itself had to be furnished with the will; but the will is really dumb, and this is why things are so bad in the world. He therefore became a pessimist, as one says. He held the view that the world was not good, but essentially bad, very bad. And not only what people did but everything there was in the world was bad. He said: 'You can work it out that the world is bad. Just put on one side of the balance sheet, the debit side, everything one has in life by way of good fortune, pleasure and so on, and on the other side everything you have by way of suffering and so on. It is always more on the other side and the balance is always in the negative. Therefore the whole world is bad.' This is why Hartmann became a pessimist.

But you see in the first place Eduard von Hartmann was an intelligent man and secondly he was someone who also drew the consequences. He said: 'Why do people go on living? Why don't they rather kill themselves? If everything is bad, it would be much wiser to fix a day when the whole of humanity commits suicide. Then everything that is created there would be gone.' But Eduard von Hartmann also said: 'No, one will never be able to do this, to fix a day for general human suicide. And even if we did — humans have evolved from animals; the animals would never kill themselves; and then human beings would again evolve

from animals! So we'll not be able to do it this way.' He then
thought of something else. He said to himself: 'If one really
wants to eradicate everything that exists as earthly world,
one cannot do it by means of human suicide but has to
thoroughly eradicate the whole earth. We do not yet have
the machines for this today; but people have invented all
kinds of machines so far; all wisdom must therefore be
directed towards inventing a machine that enables one to
drill deep enough into the earth and which will then blow
the earth up, using dynamite or the like, so that the frag-
ments fly out into the world and turn to dust. Then the right
goal will have been achieved.'

This is no joke, gentlemen! It is a fact that Eduard von
Hartmann said a machine should be invented to blow up
the whole earth, reducing it to dust and rubble.[82]

Comment: *In America they want to build cannon to shoot down
the moon!*

Rudolf Steiner: But what I have told you was genuine
philosophical teaching in the nineteenth century.

Now you'll say: There was such an intelligent man—but
how can this be? He must have been dumb, stupid, the man
who said this. No, indeed, Eduard von Hartmann was not
stupid but more intelligent than anyone else. I'll prove this
to you in a minute. But it was exactly because he was more
intelligent than the teaching that originated with Kant that
this stupid notion of the machine arose which might be
used to throw the world into nothingness. This was seriously put forward by a highly intelligent man who had
been thoroughly thrown off course by Kant.

So he wrote this *Philosophy of the Unconscious.* In it he said:
'Yes, it is true that human beings have evolved from
animals, but spiritual powers played a role in this. These
spiritual powers are powers of will, which means they are
not intelligent but dumb.' And he put this very intelligently,
and in this way contradicted Darwinism.

So at that time — in the 1860s — there was this intelligent work by Hartmann, *Philosophy of the Unconscious*, and there was Darwinism, supported by Haeckel,[83] Oscar Schmidt[84] and others, which was the cleverest thing there was in the eyes of other people. The *Philosophy of the Unconscious* contradicted it, however. So all those stubborn Darwinists came and said: 'This Eduard von Hartmann needs to be thoroughly refuted; he does not know anything about science.' And what did Hartmann do? What he did at that time is evident from the following. When the others had done shouting — on paper, in print, of course — a book appeared that had the title 'The Unconscious from the Point of View of Darwinism'.[85] It was not known who had written it, however.

Well, gentlemen, this pleased the scientists no end, for it said things that thoroughly refuted Eduard von Hartmann. Even Haeckel said: 'The individual who has written this book against Hartmann should make himself known to us, and we consider him to be one of us, a naturalist of the first order!' And indeed, the book sold out quickly and a second edition appeared.[86] This time the author gave his name — it was Eduard von Hartmann himself! He had written against himself. Then they stopped praising him. The matter did not become widely known. He thus proved that he was cleverer than all the rest. But you see, the news given to people never says anything about these things. It is, however, a piece of academic history that should be told. You can see that Eduard von Hartmann was someone who had been led astray by Kant but was highly intelligent.

Now when I tell you he wanted to blow up the world with a huge machine that was to be invented — you may well say that this man Eduard von Hartmann may have been terribly intelligent, but to us, who have not yet studied Kant, it nevertheless seems a dumb thing. And you may well think that however intelligent I told you von Hartmann was, he was nevertheless stupid. You may easily think so. But then you must also tell this last bit, and see that the others were even more stupid. I'll leave it at that, if you like. But it is perfectly possible to provide historical evidence that the others were even more stupid than the person who proved that the earth should be blown apart.

It is important to know such things; for today we still have this strange adulation of anything that appears in print. And since Kant has been published by Reclam — it was only because of this that I was able to read him then, otherwise I could not have afforded it at the time; but it was cheap, even though they were thick volumes — since then the fat is in the fire worse than ever where Kant is concerned, for everyone is reading him. I mean, they read the first page, but they do not understand any of it. They then hear that Kant is 'the emperor of literary Germany' and think: Wow, we know something of his work, and so we are clever people, too! And most of them are prepared to admit: 'I clearly must say I understand Kant, or other people will say I am stupid if I don't understand Kant.' In reality people do not understand any of it, but they won't admit it; they say: 'I have to understand Kant, for he is very clever. So when I say I understand Kant I am saying I understand something very clever and people will be impressed.'

In truth, gentlemen, it has been difficult to present this matter in a more popular form, but I am glad the question was asked, for we can see from it what goes on in academic life, as it is called, and how careful one really has to be when such things influence one, even going so far that now there is a lot of brouhaha in the papers about the 200th anniversary of Kant's birth. I am not saying that Kant should not be celebrated — others are also celebrated — but the truth of the matter is the way I have shown you.

We'll continue at 9 o'clock next Saturday.

Comets and the solar system, the zodiac and the rest of the fixed stars

Mr Erbsmehl: What do the comets mean that appear from time to time? And how is the zodiac different from other stars?
Rudolf Steiner: This question can help us to gain some understanding of astronomy. You are attending lectures on astronomy, and it may be quite a good thing to discuss this particular issue from a particular point of view.

Looking at the starry heavens [drawing], we see the moon as the largest star, which is also closest to us. The moon's influence on human beings on earth is therefore also most easily apparent. And you'll no doubt have heard people say how the moon stimulates people's imagination. This is something everyone knows. But I have told you of other influences the moon has, on reproduction, too, and so on. Then we see other heavenly bodies that behave in a similar way to the moon. The moon moves — you can see it move — and other stars, which are similar to it, also move. These stars, which also move, we call wandering stars or planets.

Now the sun also appears to move. And it does indeed move. But relative to our earth it does not move. It is always at about the same distance and it does not orbit the earth. The sun is therefore called a fixed star. And all other stars, except for those that clearly change their position, are also fixed stars.

Looking at the starry heavens we see more or less what we see when we look at them every night — especially on moonlit nights. But there are changes in the heavens. During certain weeks in summer in particular you can see one star after the other — seemingly — moving swiftly across the sky and disappearing: falling stars. They also appear in the sky on other occasions, but are particularly visible in some weeks during the summer when swarms of such small stars light up, pass rapidly across the sky and vanish.

Apart from them there are the stars to which Mr Erbsmehl referred in his question — the comets. These comets appear less often; they also differ from other stars in their form. Their shape is something like this [drawing]. They have a kind of nucleus and then a tail which follows behind. Sometimes they also appear to have two such tails behind them. If we look at the other stars that move we find their movements to be fairly regular, and we always know that they appear at certain times and at other times are beneath the earth and do not appear. But with these stars, the comets, one sees them coming and going without really ever knowing where they are going. Their movements are therefore irregular, as it were, among the other stars.

Now these comets have always been regarded as something different from other stars by people, and they have played a big role above all among superstitious people. These superstitious people thought that the appearance of a comet signalled disaster.

This should not surprise us, for anything that is irregular causes amazement and surprise. We need not take it too seriously, for people will also consider it to mean something special when objects that normally behave in one way behave differently. If you drop a knife, for example, it will not normally stick in the ground but fall flat. This does not signify anything, for we are used to it. But if the knife sticks in the ground, superstitious people will think this means something. When the moon appears it is something people are used to and it does not mean anything special. But when such a star appears, and what is more, has a special shape, well, then it does mean something special! So there's no need to get excited when superstitious people think things mean something.

We have to consider the matter in a scientific way. And above all the following is true. In times not that long ago, people went by what they saw in the heavens, and said the earth was the centre of the world — I am merely telling you how people saw it — and that the moon, Mercury, Venus, the sun and so on moved around the earth, and that the whole of the starry heavens — as one also can see now, every star rises and sets[87] — was moving. So you see the starry heavens in motion. If you stay outside long enough you'd see the so-called fixed stars move across the sky. People took it the way they saw it in earlier times.

Now, as you know, Copernicus came along in the fifteenth, sixteenth century and said: 'No such thing! The earth is not the centre. The sun is the centre, and Mercury, Venus, earth and so on move around the sun.' [drawing] So the earth itself became a planet. A completely different system, a new way of looking at space, came up. And like the sun, so the other fixed stars were now said to be stationary. Their movements would thus only be apparent movements.

You see, gentlemen, the matter is like this. I spoke of this before, when Mr Burle asked about the theory of relativity, wanting to know if those theories were correct and also some other things that were said. Another theory was established by a man called Tycho Brahe,[88] for instance. He said: 'Yes, the sun is standing still, but the earth is also standing still,' and so on. So there were also other systems. But we'll look at these two, the old one, mainly based on Ptolemy,[89] the Ptolemaic system, and then the Copernican system, which goes back to Copernicus. So there we have two systems of the universe. Each is right in some way. Above all we cannot tell, if we go into these things in detail, if the one is right or the other.

The thing is this, gentlemen. I told you before that some people cannot say, when I drive a car from the Villa Hansi up to the Goetheanum, if the car is moving or the Goetheanum is coming to meet it. Well, it is certainly something you cannot tell by just looking, but only by the fact that the car gets worn, the car uses up petrol, and the Goetheanum does not. You can tell the difference by things that are internal. In the same way you can tell, if you walk to Basel, if Basel is coming towards you or you are going there because you get tired. So it is internal things that tell the difference.

This is only to show you that really every system of the universe is such that in one respect it may be correct and in another it may be wrong. You cannot tell with absolute certainty. That is how it is. You really cannot say which system of the universe is completely right and which is completely wrong. Ah, you'll say, these things are worked out by calculations! Well, you see, those calculations are made, but the calculations that are made are never entirely correct. If you calculate the rate at which a star moves, for example, you'll know that after a certain time it must be in a particular position in the heavens. So you work out where a star should be at a given time, and you turn your telescope in that direction—now it should appear in the telescope. Often it does not, and then the formula has to be corrected; and so one finds that one's calculations are never quite right. The thing with the universe is that none of our calculations are ever exactly right.

Why is that? Imagine you know someone quite well. You'll say to yourself that if he promises something you can definitely rely on it. Let us assume you know someone pretty well. He has promised to be in a particular place at 5 in the afternoon on the 20th of May. You will also be there. You'll be quite sure he'll be there, because you know him. But it may happen after all that he does not turn up. And that is how it is with the system of the universe. Looking at minor things one may say: You can rely on it that things will happen the way you know they will. So if I make a fire in a stove, it will, according to the laws of nature, bring warmth to the room. It is not very probable that a fire will not make a room warm. But this is no longer so, gentlemen, when we get to large-scale events in the universe. The matter then becomes as certain as it is with an individual person, and it also becomes as uncertain as it is with an individual person. So that everything one calculates always has a flaw in it somewhere. And where does this flaw come from? The flaw is not only because these solar systems do not exist on their own. Let us assume the person saw something he really liked as he was on his way to meet you. He was held up. If these planetary systems were such that nothing could happen with them but what sun, moon and stars are doing, we would also be able to calculate them. We would know exactly where a star will be at a particular time, to the thousandth of a second, for calculations can be extremely accurate. But, as I said, there is a flaw. This is simply due to the fact that these systems are not permitted to be entirely free and easy amongst themselves in the universe, for the comets come in, passing right through. And with these comets coming in from the universe, the universe is giving the planetary system something that is rather like what we are given when we eat. The comet is a kind of food for the planetary systems! And it is like this. When such a comet comes in, small changes occur in the movements, and so one never gets an entirely regular movement. So that is the situation, gentlemen. The comets bring irregularity into the state of motion or of rest in our whole planetary system.

Now as to the comets themselves. You see, people will say: 'Yes, such a comet, it comes from so far away that you do not see it at first; you begin to see it when it comes closer to the solar system [drawing]. So there you see it. Now it moves on; you still see it, then you see it a little, and then it vanishes.' So what are people saying? They are saying: 'Well that is above the earth, and one can see it. But then the comet moves over there, becomes invisible, and comes back again there after a number of years.' That is what they say.

If I draw the solar system for you, we have here the sun; here the planets. People imagine that the comet comes from far away, from beyond the solar system, and enters the sphere of the sun; and there you no longer see it, when it is down below. There it comes back again. So they imagine the planets move in short ellipses, and the comet in a tremendously long ellipse. And when it comes and we have it above us, so that one can look up, it is visible; otherwise it is invisible and then comes back again. Halley's comet, called after the man who discovered it,[90] appears every 76 years.

Now, gentlemen, this is something where the science of the spirit cannot agree, because of observations made in it. For it is not true that the comet moves like this. The real truth is that the comet only comes into existence here, and it sunders matter together[91] from the universe; matter from the universe gathers. There it comes into existence [pointing to the drawing], moves on like this, and here it vanishes again, dissolving. This line [ellipse] here, actually does not exist. So we are dealing with a structure that develops some distance away and passes out of existence again at some distance. So what is really going on here?

Now one gets to the point where one says: It is not true that the sun is standing still. It is standing still in relation to the earth, but it moves at tremendous speed in relation to space. The whole planetary system is rushing through cosmic space, moving forward. The sun is moving towards the constellation of Hercules. Now you may ask how people know that the sun is moving towards Hercules. You know that if you go down an avenue and stand at one end, the trees near you seem further apart, and then they come closer and closer. You know, if you look down an avenue, the trees seem to be closer and closer together; but when you walk in this direction it seems as if they move apart. The distance you see between trees keeps growing. Now imagine this here is Hercules [Drawing], the stars in that constellation are at some distance from one another. If our solar system were standing still, those distances would always be the same. But if the sun were moving towards it, the stars in Hercules would grow bigger and bigger and would appear to move apart. And this is what they actually do! It has been observed through the centuries that the distances in Hercules are getting bigger and bigger. This shows that the sun is truly moving in the direction of Hercules. And just as it is possible to calculate things here, using ranging instruments, how close we are when walking past and how fast we are walking—when someone walks faster, the distance increases faster than it does for someone else—so it is possible to calculate how the sun moves. The calculations are always very accurately done. Our whole planetary system is thus rushing towards the constellation of Hercules.

This rushing pace affects the planetary system just as work does you. Working, you lose some of your substance and need to replace it. And as the planetary system rushes through cosmic space it is also all the time losing some of its substance. This needs to be replaced. So you have the comets moving around. They gather the substance, and it is captured again as the comet passes through the planetary system. Comets thus replace substance for which the planetary system no longer has any use and which it has eliminated. But the comets also cause irregularities as they enter into the planetary system, so that it is in fact not possible to calculate the movements.

This also shows that if you go far enough, things come alive for you in cosmic space. Such a planetary system is really a form of life; it needs to eat. And the comets are eaten!

What do these comets essentially consist of? The most important substance they contain is carbon and nitrogen, which is indeed something needed in the planetary system and has to come from the heavens. We need nitrogen in the air, and it has to be renewed all the time; we need carbon because all plants need it. And so the earth does truly get its substances from the universe. They are always replaced.

But there's more to this. You know that when you have a meal you eat things that are still quite large when they are on your plate. You reduce them in size by biting. First of all you cut them up. And you have to do this, for if it were possible for you to swallow a goose whole, this would not be good for you! You need to cut it up. You also can't swallow a whole calf's head; only snakes can do that, people cannot. It needs to be cut up. The planetary system also does this with its food. Comets may sometimes—not every one of them, but some can sometimes be swallowed whole, snake-fashion. But other comets are broken up when they enter the system. The comet then breaks up, just as a shower of meteors has broken up into lots of small stars. These meteors are tiny parts of comets that rush down. And so you see not only how cosmic food enters into the solar system but also how this cosmic food is consumed by the earth. We are thus able to get a clear idea of the role that comets, which appear at irregular intervals, play for the earth.

Now you see, the thing is like this—we must leave aside all superstition. The comet coming from beyond the earth has an influence on everything that happens on the earth, and this is something we can see. It is certainly a strange thing. As you know, there are good and bad years for wine. But the good years really come because the earth has got hungry. It then leaves its fertility more to the sun, and the sun gives the wine its quality. Now when the earth has had a good wine year, you can be pretty certain that a comet will appear soon after, for the earth has been hungry and needs food again for the other things. You then get poor wine years. If there's another good wine year, a comet will follow. The earth's state concerning its substance is definitely connected with the way in which comets appear or do not appear.

The other question was how the zodiac differs from other fixed stars.

You know, if we simply look out into the distant universe we see countless stars. They seem to be irregularly placed. But one can always distinguish groups of them, and these are called constellations.

Now the stars we see are further away from the moon or closer to it. Looking at the stars we see the moon pass through the starry heavens like this [drawing], don't we? But whilst some constellations are positioned in such a way that the moon always passes through them, it does not pass through others. So if you consider Hercules, for instance, the moon does not pass through. But if you look at the Lion, then the moon always passes through the Lion at given intervals. Twelve constellations have the special characteristic that they form the path, as it were, taken by the moon and also by the sun. We may say, therefore, that the twelve constellations Ram, Bull, Twins, Crab, Lion, Virgin, Scales, Scorpion, Archer, Goat, Water Carrier and Fishes mark the path of the moon. It always passes through them and not through the other constellations. We are thus always able to say that at any particular time the moon, if it is in the sky, is in one constellation or another, but only a constellation that is part of the zodiac.

Now I want you to consider, gentlemen, that everything there is by way of stars in the sky has a definite influence on the earth as a whole and specifically also on man. Man truly depends not only on what exists here on earth but also on the stars that are there in the heavens.

Think of some star or constellation up there. It rises in the evening, as we say, and sets in the morning. It is there all the time, and always influences the human being. But think of another constellation, the Twins, let us say, or the Lion. The moon passes that way. The moment it passes that way it covers up the Twins or the Lion. I see only the moon and not the Twins. At that moment they cannot influence the earth, because their influence is blocked. And so we have stars everywhere in the sky that are never blocked out, neither by the sun nor by the moon, and always have an influence on the earth. And we have stars which the moon passes, and the sun seemingly also passes them. These are covered up from time to time and their influence then stops. We are therefore able to say that the Lion is a constellation in the zodiac and has a particular influence on man. It does not have this influence if the moon is in front of it. At that time the human being is free of the Lion influence, the Lion's influence does not affect him.

Now just imagine you are terribly lazy and won't walk but someone gives you a push from behind, and you have to walk. He drives you on, and that is his influence. But imagine I do not permit him to influence you; he cannot give you a push. Then you are not subject to the influence; and if you want to walk you have to do it yourself.

Human beings need these influences. And how does this go, gentlemen? Let us hold fast to this: The Lion constellation has a particular influence on man. It has this influence for as long as it is not covered up by the moon or the sun. But let us take this further. Again consider an analogy from life. Let us say you want to know something. Imagine you have a governess or a private tutor — he usually knows everything. When you are a little boy you don't want to think for yourself, you ask your tutor and he'll tell you. He'll also do your homework for you. But if the tutor has gone out, so that you do not have your tutor available at the moment and have to do your homework, then you have to find the power in yourself. You have to recall things for yourself.

The Lion continually influences human beings except when it is covered by the moon. Then the influence is not there. When the moon blocks the Lion's influence, man must develop using his own resources. Someone able to develop his own strong Lion influence when the moon covers the constellation may thus be called a Lion person. Someone able to develop particularly the influence in the constellation of the Crab when this is covered up is a Crab person. People develop the one or the other more strongly depending on their inner constitution.

You see, therefore, that the constellations of the zodiac are special, for with them, the influence is sometimes there and sometimes not. The moon, passing through the constellations at four-week intervals, brings it about that there is always a time in a four-week period when some constellation of the zodiac does not have an influence. With other constellations the influence is always the same. In earlier times people took these influences that came from the heavens very seriously. The zodiac was therefore more important to them than other constellations. The others have a continuous influence which does not change. But with the zodiac we may say that the influence changes depending on whether one of its constellations is covered over or not. Because of this, the influence of the zodiac on the earth has always been the subject of special study. And so you see why the zodiac is more important when we study the starry heavens than other stars are.

You will see from all this that mere calculations cannot really give us all the knowledge we want of the heavens, as I told you before. We certainly have to consider things like those I have been speaking of.

Talking about such things one is still thought to be a dreamer today, something of a fool, for people say: 'If you want to know something about the stars you should go to the astronomers at the observatory. They know everything!' As you know, there is a saying—because conditions like gout also depend on all kinds of external influences, some people will tell someone with gout to go to the observatory and have the matter sorted there. But when you want to speak of these things out of the spirit today, people think you are something of a fool. But the following kind of thing happens. Having gained knowledge through the science of the spirit, I was able to say the following in a series of lectures I gave in Paris in 1906.[92] If everyting is like this with the comets, if they really exist to perform this function, then they must contain a compound of carbon and nitrogen. This was something people did not know before. Carbon and nitrogen combine to form cyanide, prussic acid. Carbon and nitrogen would thus have to be found also in comets. I said this in Paris in 1906. People who did not acknowledge the science of the spirit did not need to believe it at the time. But a short time after this I was on a lecture tour in Sweden and all the papers brought the surprising news that spectroscopic analysis had shown comets to contain cyanide.

You see, people are always saying that if anthroposophists know something they should say so, so that it may later be confirmed. There have been many such instances. Honestly, I predicted the discovery of cyanide in comets in 1906! It was made soon after. You can see, therefore, that these things are correct, for the truth will be confirmed in due course, if one sets about it in the right way. But of course, when this kind of thing happens again people do not mention it, they hush it up because it does not suit them. But it is true nevertheless. Spiritual perception thus enables us to say things about the comets, including their chemical composition, and this will be confirmed in due course. This is one such example.

So I am not afraid to say things that may seem utterly foolish to people: that the comets come into existence here and pass out of existence again there, gather matter here and vanish again here as they leave the planetary system. Spiritual observation shows this, and in due course physical observation will confirm it. Today one is only able to state it on the basis of spiritual observation.

Many things said in materialistic science today are utterly fantastic. People imagine the sun to be a kind of gaseous sphere, for instance. It is not a gaseous sphere, but really something quite different. You see, gentlemen, if you have a bottle of carbonated water you get those small beads in there. So one might think: Right, that is carbonated water, and in it are small beads — things that float in it. But that is not how it really is, for there you have your carbonated water, and there it is hollow [drawing]. You have less in there than in the rest of the water. It is of course carbon dioxide gas, with water all around it, but the gas is thinner than the water. With reference to the water, you have a hollow space in there, and compared to water you merely have the subtle nature of the gas. The sun, too, is a hollow space in the universe; but this is thinner than any gas; it is extremely thin in the place where the sun is. And what is more, gentlemen, when you move around in this world you are in space. But space is also hollow where the sun is. What does it mean: 'space is hollow'? You can see from the following what it means when we say space is hollow.

If you create a vacuum with a vacuum pump, removing all the air [drawing], and then make an opening here, the air rushes in with a tremendous hissing sound. The situation with the sun is that what you have there is definitely above all a hollow space; empty not only of air but also of heat. It is above all a hollow space. The nature of this hollow space is such that it is spiritually closed off all around, and something can rush in only at intervals through the sun spots. Astronomers would get a big surprise if they were to go there in a space car or space ship — it could not be an airship, of course, for the air does not go as far as that. The astronomers would expect that when they got up there and arrived at the sun they would enter such a nebula, for the sun, they think, is red-hot gas. And they would expect this red-hot gas to burn them up, that they would perish in flames, for they believe they would find a temperature of many thousands of degrees. But you do not get the opportunity to burst into flames, for the sun is hollow also as far as heat is concerned. There is no heat either! One would be able to tolerate all this. One would also be able to tolerate the temperature if one went to the sun in a giant space ship. But something else could not be tolerated. The situation would be similar to the air rushing in with a hiss — rushing in, not out — and you would immediately be drawn into the sun and would instantly turn to dust, for the sun is a hollow space that sucks in everything. You would be completely absorbed. It would be the most certain way of disappearing.

The sun is thus seen entirely in the wrong light by materialistic scientists. It is a hollow space with regard to anything else; and this really makes it the lightest person among all the stars nearest to us out there in space, lightest of all. The moon is relatively heavy, for it once came away from the earth, taking with it the heavy substances for which the earth had no use. It would be lighter than the earth, of course, if we were to weigh it, being much smaller, but relatively speaking, in terms of what we call the specific gravity, it is heavier. It follows that spirituality comes from the sun, for it is the lightest body in cosmic space. This is why I was able to say, when Mr Dollinger asked about the

Christ, that the greatest spirituality comes from the sun when we are born, for the sun is the most spiritual entity. The moon is the most material entity. And if the moon is the most material body, its influence on human beings goes beyond the ordinary in material terms. You see, all the other stars apart from the moon also have an influence, of course. They have an influence on material processes. But if you imagine you're eating a piece of bread, the bread is gradually transformed into blood; something is transformed into something else. Part of the human being is created, blood is created, when you transform bread in the metabolic process. If you put salt in your bread, the salt goes into the bones; it is transformed. It is always a part that is produced, for these materials relate only to parts of the human being. All things on earth can only create part of the human being; and whatever is produced must remain in the human being. The moon itself has a powerful material influence on reproduction, but in that case it is not part of the human being that is produced but a whole human being. The sun influences the most spiritual part, the moon, being material itself, the material aspect. Man thus creates himself, or an image of himself, under the influence of the moon. That is the difference. Sun actions may be said to recreate our thoughts, our powers of will all the time. The moon's influence is that it recreates the material forces, reproducing the material human being. And between the sun and the moon we have the other stars which bring about parts of the other things that happen in man.

We can understand all this. But you must include the human being whenever you consider astronomy. You see, an astronomer will say: 'What I see with my naked eye does not impress me; I have to use a telescope. I rely on my telescope; it is my instrument.' The spiritual scientist will say: 'Why bother with telescopes! Of course you'll see a great deal, and we acknowledge this. But the best instrument you can use to gain insight into the universe is man himself.' You perceive everything through the human being. Man is the best instrument, for everything becomes apparent in him. What happens up there in the Lion is apparent in the circulation of the blood. And when the moon is in front of the Ram, our hair grows more slowly, and so on. It is always possible to see in man what happens in the universe. When someone gets jaundice, for instance, we must of course primarily consider the cause in the body in medicine. But why, in the final instance, does a person get jaundice? Because he has a special disposition to develop the powers of the Goat from his own resources when the moon covers up the constellation of the Goat.

We can thus always see that man is the instrument by which all may be perceived. When a person is no longer open, for instance, to the Water Carrier influence, that is if the Water Carrier is covered up by the moon and the individual is unable to develop his own Water Carrier powers, he'll get corns. And so we can always use the human being as an instrument to see what is happening in the universe. We have to do it scientifically, however, and not from superstition. And so, in this way, it is a proper scientific method used in the science of the spirit. Of course, it is vague the way many people think it, and then one cannot see anything from what they are thinking. This is where the old maxim applies: When the cock on the midden crows, the weather will change or stay as it was. It is indeed exactly the way many people think about the world: When the cock on the midden crows, the weather will change or stay as it was.

But when we really go into the matter, that is no longer the case. Through the human being, the most perfect instrument you can have, you perceive things more perfectly than through anything else in the universe. So it is not a matter of simply inventing things, but you study what goes on in the human being. You need to know, of course, how it is with corns, how they develop out of the skin, and so on, and only then can you see what happens when the Water Carrier is covered up. Studying the matter through the human being, we can study the whole universe through the human being.

Our next meeting will be on Wednesday, then.

Moses. Decadent Atlantean civilization in Tibet. Dalai Lama. How can Europe spread its culture in Asia? British and Germans as colonial powers

Good morning, gentlemen. Maybe one of you has thought of something for today's session?

Question: What should one think about the miracles told in connection with Moses in the Bible – the sea standing still?

Rudolf Steiner: Now you see, this was less a matter of there being a sudden miracle than of Moses[93] having a great deal of knowledge. He was not just the person presented in the Bible but had in fact studied at the Egyptian universities, which were the mysteries. At those schools students were taught not only about the world of the spirit but from a certain point of view also about the natural world. Now in the oceans we have ebb and flood, with the waters rising and falling again, and the point was that Moses knew how to arrange the passage across the Red Sea in such a way that he took the people across at a time when the sea had receded, exposing a sandbank that could be used. The miracle therefore was not that Moses held back the Red Sea and fought it, but that he really did know more than others and was able to choose the right moment. The others did not know this. Moses had worked it all out so that he got there at the right time. He knew how long it would take, or rather that they had to be quick, so that the sea would not take them by surprise. All this did, of course, seem like a miracle to the others. With such things we must always realize that they are based on knowledge, not some other kind of thing, but knowledge.

That is how it is with most things we are told of earlier

times. The people were amazed because they did not understand the matter; they did not know. But if one knows that in those early times, too, there were some very clever people, one can find the explanation. Otherwise there is not much to explain here.

Maybe someone else has another question?

Question: Can the culture that streams from Tibet into the rest of Asia still be adequate for those people, or is it getting completely decadent?

Rudolf Steiner: Now you see, the culture of Tibet is very ancient; it really still comes from ancient Atlantean times. You just have to realize that there was a time once when Europe was largely submerged, with the water only getting less towards Asia. On the other hand you had land where the Atlantic Ocean is today. There was land then where today we take a boat from Europe to America. That was an early age, when land and water were distributed very differently from the way they are today.

In those days, five, six, seven millennia ago, the culture in Asia was the same as it was on this Atlantean continent which is today under the sea between Europe and America. Over there in Asia they had a culture that has survived in the clefts and underground caves of Tibet. When the sea came to the area between Europe and America and Europe began to rise, the Atlantean culture of that area was of course lost. But it survived over there in Tibet. However, this culture was really only appropriate to those ancient times when people lived under very different conditions than they do today. You have to realize that the air was not the way it is today, that humans were not as heavy as they are today but had much less weight, and the air was much denser. A dense mist really penetrated everything at that time, and because of this it was possible to live in a very different way.

People did not read or write in those days but they had

signs. These would not be put on paper. They did not have paper then. Nor did they write them on parchment but they would scratch them into rock surfaces. Those rocks had been hollowed out by the people, and on the inside they would scratch their secret signs, as they called them. We really need to understand the signs they produced if we are to understand how they thought.

Now you may ask how it has been possible for these people to keep it so well hidden. Well, you know, the earliest form of architecture had nothing to do with building above ground but people would originally dig into the rocks, making their homes in the rocks. That was the earliest form of architecture. So we need not be surprised that this was also the earliest form of architecture in Tibet. But such skills gradually grew decadent, falling into decline. And the things that developed later in Tibet are such that they cannot really be used any more today, Tibetan culture being older than Indian culture. Ancient Indian civilization developed only after the earth had reached its present form. Tibetan culture was therefore very early. And in this Tibetan culture something has been preserved in a bad form that originally had a relatively good form. Above all the ruler principle has taken a not very acceptable form. The individual who is to rule Tibet is actually venerated as divine; and this veneration is prepared in advance. I would say the choice is made in a supersensible way, really. The Dalai Lama was chosen to be ruler in the following way. Long before, when the old Dalai Lama was still there and people realized that he might soon die, a family was identified somewhere and it was said: The new Dalai Lama must come from this family. That is how it was in Tibet in earlier times. These were not hereditary rulers, but priests — who were the real rulers — identified a new family from which a Dalai Lama was to come.

If a child was born in such a family it would be held

available until the old Dalai Lama died. You can imagine that the worst kind of abuse was rife. If the old Dalai Lama was no longer wanted they would simply look for a child and say: The soul of the old Dalai Lama has to enter into the soul of this child. First he had to die, however. And the priests made sure that this happened at the right time. The people then believed that the soul of the old Dalai Lama had entered into the soul of the child. It was thus arranged that the whole of the populace really believed that the soul of any Dalai Lama had previously also been in the Dalai Lama who ruled thousands of years earlier. They thought it was always the same soul, and to them it was always the same Dalai Lama; he merely changed his outer body.

It was not like this in the original culture, but extra-ordinary mischief has developed out of it. You can see from this that the priests had gradually found ways of managing affairs in such a way that their supremacy was ensured.

This does not mean, however, that one does not discover great scientific secrets which people knew in the early days. These are engraved in the rocks, but Europeans have only been granted access on the rarest of occasions. It is true, however, that one can discover the great scientific secrets people knew in the early days, and all it needs is to develop this knowledge in a new form.

The situation is like this. The knowledge that once existed, coming to people in misty dreams, is to be made available again today through the science of the spirit. This cannot happen in the East, however. You see, new know-ledge, new insights will never be gained in the same way in the East as here in Europe, because oriental bodies are not made for this. The attempts one has to make to gain insights like those I have presented to you can only be done in the West and not in the East. Orientals are also much more conservative than Europeans; they do not want anything new, and the things we do here in Europe therefore do not impress them. But if you are able to say to them: Significant truths are to be found in those ancient crypts — which is the name for those rock caves — and they are ancient, this will make a tremendous impression on them.

Europeans also have some of this. Just look at the Free-mason's lodges of the higher order, if you are able to get into them. As to anthroposophy — it interests them a little, for they, too, are concerned with supersensible things; but they do not take a serious interest. But if you say to them: 'This is something that has been found; it is ancient Egyptian wisdom or ancient Hebrew wisdom,' then they'll be pleased. They'll immediately take it up, for that is the way people are. New discoveries do not impress them much; but something really ancient, even if they do not understand it, makes a considerable impression on them.

We may therefore assume that ancient knowledge if found in Tibet would provide fresh impetus. For much has been lost also to the people of Asia, with the most important Asian civilization, Indian civilization, only arising at a later stage. So it would be possible for many of the things other people do not know about in Asia to be found in Tibet.

The people who live there do not have much opportunity to make these things properly known, for the old Tibetan priest rulers did nothing to make them known; they wanted to keep the ancient rulership for themselves. Knowledge is power if it is kept secret. Europeans who went to Tibet did not understand the things they found. So there is not much prospect of the genuine Tibetan truths being made known; they live on in ancient traditions. For much has come down to posterity, and one can certainly get an idea of what lies behind it all. But it is difficult to imagine that it will really become widely known. It has grown decadent, as you said in your question; but if you go back to the signs in the crypts and not to what the priests say, you would certainly be able to discover extraordinary things. It will however be extraordinarily difficult to decipher them. It will be difficult to get at it without the science of the spirit. It can be deciphered using the science of the spirit, but there one discovers things for oneself, so the old things are not needed.

Question: Would it be possible for people in Europe to do something to help that downward-moving time stream in Asia to move upwards again?

Rudolf Steiner: That is a very nice question! For you see, if the people in Europe do nothing, the world will have to go into decline there. Over there in Asia — this will be obvious from what I have been saying — people hold on to the past. They do not know progress. You see that in China. China is at the same level as it was thousands of years ago. Long ago the Chinese had many things that were only discovered much later in Europe — paper, printing, and so on. But they do not accept progress but retain the old form.

The Europeans on the other hand, what do they do when they go to Asia? You know, the English gave the Chinese opium and such things in the first half of the nineteenth century. But until now the Europeans have not done anything to bring a real life of the mind and spirit to Asia. And it is difficult, of course, for these people simply do not accept it.

You see, the situation is interesting. As you know, European missionaries go there with European religion, European theology, and want to take European culture to Asia. This makes no impression whatsoever on the people of Asia. The missionaries speak to them of Christ Jesus as they see him. And the Asian person says: 'Well, if I look at my Buddha, he has much more excellent qualities.' So they are not impressed. They would only be impressed if one presented Jesus Christ to them the way he was presented here in these lectures some time ago, again in response to your questions. That would make an impression. But again one has to remember that Asians are conservative, reactionary, and initially suspicious.

It is a strange thing, gentlemen. You see, there are some who have studied the ancient wisdom. Over in Asia they have learnt something from Tibetan scholars, wise men, Tibetan initiates. The initiates themselves do not bother with the Europeans. But their students have done so. And this can really surprise one at times. I have told you a few things that will have surprised you, concerning the influence the universe has on human beings. It takes a great deal of time to investigate this fully. I can truthfully say that some of the things I am now able to tell you took 40 years until I was able to speak of them. These are things you do not find overnight, you have to look for them for years. And one then finds such things. One finds for instance that the moon has a population which is connected with the earth's population to such effect that reproduction is regulated by this, as I have told you. Truly, gentlemen, you do not find this along the avenues taken by present-day scientists, nor do you find it from one day to the next; you find it in the course of many years. That is the way it is. And then you have it. But then, when you have it, a strange light is suddenly cast on the things said by the students of oriental initiates. Before, you could not understand it at all. These people talk of moon spirits, for example, and the influence they have on the earth. European scholars will say it is all nonsense what they say. But when one finds these things for oneself one will no longer say it is nonsense. One is merely surprised how much those ancients knew thousands of years ago, things that have since been lost to humanity. It is a tremendous impression one may gain in this way. You investigate these things with tremendous effort and you then find that they were known in the past, though this was in a way people cannot understand today, not even those who speak of these things sometimes. So you gain respect, tremendous respect, for something that did exist in the past.

Now it would be necessary for Europeans who wanted to

do something over there in Asia to study anthroposophy before they do it. For otherwise they'll find they cannot do anything there. Today's European science and technology does not impress the people of Asia, for they consider modern European science to be childish, something that is entirely superficial, and as to European technology – they have no need of it. They say: 'Why should we stand at machines? That is inhuman!' It does not impress them in the least, and they consider it an encroachment on their rights when people build railways and machines over there. Europeans do this. But the people there really hate it. So again that is not the way to do it. We must also learn something about earlier days. And in those earlier days people did have some feeling as to how one should proceed.

You see, why should it not be possible for today's European culture to do something over there in Asia? Someone did manage to do something with Greek culture over there in Asia. That was in the fourth century before Christianity was founded. Alexander the Great was the man. He did take a great deal of Greek culture to Asia. And it is there now. It even came back again to Europe by a roundabout route through Spain with the Arabs and the Jews. But how did Alexander manage to take those things to Asia? Only by not proceeding the way modern Europeans do. Europeans consider themselves to be the clever ones, people who are altogether clever. When they go somewhere else they say: 'They're all stupid. We have to take our wisdom to them.' But the others do not know what to do with it. Alexander did not do that. He first of all went wholly into what the people had themselves. And very slowly, little by little, he let something flow into the things those people had. He respected and valued the things the others had.

And that is altogether the secret of how to bring something to some place. There is much to be said against the

British, and it is an infamous story in British history that they took opium to China, from sheer egotism. But one nevertheless has to say that not so much perhaps in the sphere of mind and spirit, though actually even there, the British always respect the customs and traditions of the nations they go to, especially in the economic sphere. They simply know how to respect it. The Germans are probably least able to do so. Because of this the Germans do not do well as colonizers, for they never consider what it feels like for the people where they want to have their colonies. They are expected to accept instantly what the Germans themselves have in central Europe. And that will not do, of course. As a result things have gone in such a way that the British are happily maintaining their colonies, even if the people rise at times, and all kinds of things, but economically the British still have the upper hand. The British do at least know how to consider the nature and character of foreign nations. The British also go to war in a very different way from the Germans. How does a German think of waging war against some nation? I don't want to speak against war at this point, but merely tell you how the Germans see it. They think one just has to set out and conquer. The English do not do this. They first of all observe, and perhaps even stir up another nation and let them fight among themselves. They'll look on for as long as possible, that is, they let people sort themselves out among themselves. That is how it has always been. And that is how the British Empire was established. The others, you see, never quite know what is going on. The British have a certain instinct to respect the particular nature of foreign nations. And this has made it possible for them to gain such a colossal economic advantage.

I am sure no one in England would have got the idea to do what people are now doing in Germany, which is to introduce the rentenmark currency. There is of course a

major money problem in Germany at the moment. No one
has any money. But when the rentenmark was introduced—as a stable currency—people thought it was
something terribly clever. It was, of course, the silliest thing
one could do. For as long as all the paper money in Britain
has gold coverage, the rentenmark must immediately lose
value. If the thing is done artificially, as is not the case with
a stable currency, it just means that the price of goods will
rise. You see, people have the rentenmark in Germany, and
it is always worth one mark. But, gentlemen, you can only
buy as much for it now as you used to get for 0.15 mark, and
so it is in reality worth no more than 0.15 mark. It is a
deception to say it will not go down and be stable. And that
is how it is. People think in Germany, but they have no
feeling for reality.

A nice little anecdote tells us how different nations study
the natural history of a kangaroo, let us say, or some other
animal, perhaps in Africa. The Englishman goes to Africa—
like Darwin did, who travelled around the world for his
nature studies[94]—and observes the animal in its natural
habitat. He can see how it lives there and what natural
conditions are. The Frenchman immediately removes the
animal from the desert and puts it in a zoo. He studies the
animal in the zoo, not in its natural environment but in a
zoo. And what does the German do? He does not bother to
look at the animal at all. He sits down in his study and
begins to think. The thing in itself does not interest him—
according to Kant's philosophy, as I told you—only the
ideas in his head. He spends some time thinking things out.
And having thought for a sufficiently long time he says
something. But it is not in accord with reality.

But the thing is also only relative where the British are
concerned. No one in modern Europe knows the ways used
in the past to influence human beings—for instance the way
Alexander the Great apparently left things exactly as they

were but little by little, slowly, introduced things that came from Greece in Asia. No one in Europe knows how to do this today. The first thing Europeans would have to learn, therefore, would be not simply to take things to Asia which are there already, but above all to go to some trouble to find out what the people of Asia know. They would then learn about Tibetan wisdom, for example. And they would then not speak of it to people in the old way but present it in a new way. But they would be using Tibetan wisdom. Thus respecting the local culture they would achieve something. This is something which Europeans in particular have to learn.

Europe is really a vast edifice of theories. Europeans produce theories, and basically have no practical approach. That is the way it is. Europeans also do business in a theoretical way, simply by thinking things up. This will work for a time. It never works in the long run. But Europeans above all fail in spreading their culture of mind and spirit because they do not know how to enter into the reality of other people.

Here, too, the science of the spirit must bring a change. But how does this go, even today? You see, gentlemen, it is important that in anthroposophy we make it a way of life, absolutely practical. One has to start somewhere, of course. What did I do myself, gentlemen? I once wrote about Nietzsche,[95] and people thought I had become a follower of Nietzsche. If I had written the way people would have wanted me to write, the way many people thought I would write, I would have written: Nietzsche is an absolute fool; Nietzsche has put forward foolish notions; Nietzsche must be fought to the death, and so on. I would thus have written in opposition to Nietzsche. It would have meant that I could be thoroughly abusive, almost as abusive as Nietzsche himself, but there would have been no point to it, it would have been useless. I gave careful consideration to

Nietzsche's teaching; I presented the things Nietzsche himself had said, and only let anthroposophical views flow into it. Today people come and say: 'He used to be a follower of Nietzsche; now he is an anthroposophist.' But it was exactly because I am an anthroposophist that I wrote about Nietzsche the way I did.

I wrote about Haeckel[96] using the same approach. I could of course have written that he was an out-and-out materialist, knowing nothing of the spirit, and so on. Well, gentlemen, again there would have been no point to it. Instead I took Haeckel as he was, and this is what I have always done. I have not denied the truth but taken things as they were. And this was at least a first step, through anthroposophy, in doing what should be done if our culture is to be taken to Asia. Going to India, one would need to know above all: 'That is what the ancient Brahmin said, and this is what the Buddhists say.' You have to tell people of Buddhism and Brahmanism, but also bring in the things you believe are needed. This is what the followers of Buddha themselves have done, for instance. Shortly before Christianity came into existence, the followers of Buddha spread Buddhism in the Euphrates and Tigris region, but they did it the way I have shown you, talking to people in a way they could understand. In antiquity people were not concerned with getting their own theories accepted in a completely selfish way. Asians have no understanding for European self-willedness. The relationship between Brahmins and Buddhists is not the same, for example, as that between Roman Catholics and Protestants. Roman Catholics and Protestants are highly theoretical in their teaching today, with one believing one thing, the other another. Probably the only difference between Brahmins and Buddhists is that Brahmins do not venerate the Buddha, whilst Buddhists do. And so they really deal with each other in a very different way from the way Protestants and Roman Catholics deal with one another in Europe.

You see, one must have a sense of reality if one wishes to disseminate culture. It really makes one want to cry to see how Europeans are going on in Asia today. Everything Asia has of its own also goes to perdition in the process, and nothing is gained at all. The big problem is, of course, that Europe is also in decline now, and cannot really get out of the damage caused by civilization unless people decide to accept a genuine culture of mind and spirit. Many do not yet believe this today. And so the situation is that all the people who have come to Europe from Asia, for example, have found the Europeans to be utterly barbaric.

You have probably also heard that all kinds of Asians, cultivated, clever Asians, are going about in Europe; but they all believe the Europeans to be barbarians. Because people in Asia still have much of the old knowledge of the spirit, ancient perception of the spirit, anything Europeans know seems childish to them. Everything which is so much admired in Europe seems incredibly childish to the people in Asia.

You see, the Europeans developed in such a way that their great technological advances are really all very recent. The following is interesting, for instance. If you go to some museums where they have things of early European times, you will sometimes be greatly surprised. You'll be amazed, let us say, in Etruscan museums, where they have things coming from Etruscan civilization, a civilization that once existed in Europe, and you'll find they had great skill in treating teeth, for example. They treated teeth very skilfully, putting in fillings made of stone. All this was lost in Europe, and barbarism truly came to Europe. At the time when the great migrations took place, in the third to seventh centuries AD, everything had really fallen into barbarism in Europe.

And it was only after this that things were regained. Today we are, of course, amazed at all the advances made. But those things did exist before. Where did they come from in those early times? They came more or less from Asia. The Asians then also lost the technology they used to have, though some of it still exists in China. But in the cultural sphere Asians truly are ahead of Europeans even today. And if we can find nothing in Europe which is better than the culture which exists in Asia, why should one have missions and that kind of stuff over there in Asia? That is totally unnecessary.

The sharing of culture will only be meaningful when Europeans themselves have a science of the spirit. If Europeans are able to give the Asians a science of the spirit, then the Asians will perhaps also accept European technology. But you see, for the moment they only see that apart from their technology Europeans know nothing at all. Educated, scholarly Asians are particularly impressed if they come to Germany, for instance, and you tell them about Goethe and Schiller. Then they prick up their ears. Such a scholar will say: 'Goethe and Schiller may not have been as clever and as wise as the ancient people of Asia, but they certainly had good minds.'

In the nineteenth century all this declined and disappeared rapidly. Today a Chinese scholar will see a German merely as a horrible barbarian. He'll say that German culture perished with Goethe and Schiller. The fact that the railways were invented in the nineteenth century will not impress him. Goethe's *Faust* will impress him to some extent, but he'd still say the great people of Asia were much wiser. This is something Europeans should begin to realize. They need to realize that Asians do not care for the kind of thinking we have in Europe. They want images, like the images you see in the monasteries of Tibet. Asians want images. The abstract notions Europeans have are of no interest to them, they make their heads hurt, and they do not want them.

A symbol such as the swastika [drawing], the ancient sun cross, was widely known in Asia, and the old Asians still remember it. Some Bolshevik government people had the clever idea of making the ancient swastika their symbol, just like the nationalists in Germany. This makes much more of an impression on the Asians than anything by way of Marxism. Marxism is a set of ideas that have to be thought, and this does not impress them. But such a sign, that does impress them. And if people do not know how to approach these people and come to them with things that are completely alien, nothing will be achieved at all.

Again we see that what matters above all in Europe is to have real insight again, a science of the spirit.

You may also have heard that a gentleman called Spengler—he even gave a lecture in Basle once, I have heard—has published a work called *The Decline of the West*, that is, the decline of Europe and America.[97] In it he speaks of everything that exists as European culture having to perish. Well, gentlemen, the superficial culture we have today must indeed perish. Something new has to come from inside, out of the spirit. But the outer, superficial culture must go. And because of this the book speaks of the decline of the West. One cannot really say anything against what Spengler says about the decline of the West, about what will be necessary with regard to external things. But he then speaks of the things he sees as positive, as something new. And what does he speak of, gentlemen? The Prussian spirit. He says Europe should take up the Prussian spirit. In his view, that should be the future civilization of Europe.

Now I do not know how he spoke in Basle, for I cannot imagine that he would have made a good impression on the Swiss by showing them that the Prussian spirit should rise from the decline. But you can see how an important man, a clever man like Spengler is able to see quite clearly that the existing civilization must perish. But, he says, brute force should rule in future. He is quite open about this: in future there can only be the conqueror, brutal and powerful.

If that is the most widely read book today, for Oswald Spengler is most widely read in Germany today, and an Oriental, an Asian compares what it says with his own culture, he will have to say to himself: 'That is one of the cleverest people in Europe,' and if he also has his own knowledge of the spirit — dreamlike, in the ancient way — he has to say: Well, what kind of people are these most clever Europeans? They have nothing to give us!

Gentlemen, that is the crux of the matter. And when the question is asked as to what Europeans can do to counter the downward-moving time stream in Asia, we simply have to say: The situation in Europe is such that Europeans must first of all find themselves, gain their own culture of mind and spirit, having lost it at the time of the great migrations. A true culture of mind and spirit was lost in those early Christian centuries. What came to Europe was not the deeper Christianity but words, really and truly words. You can see it particularly from the way Luther then translated the Bible. What did he make of the Bible? An incomprehensible book! For if you are honest you cannot understand Luther's Bible. You can have faith in it; but it cannot really be understood because that was already a time in Europe when people no longer knew of the spirit. There is spirit in the Bible. But it must be translated spiritually. But the things you find in the German Luther Bible, for example, are incomprehensible if one is honest about it. And it is really the same in all areas, except for wholly superficial insight into nature, but this does not really take us into the reality of the world. And if Europeans want to do something in Asia, my answer to the question must be:

They will be able to do something once they have really found themselves in the spirit.

I have to go to Paris now, gentlemen. I'll tell you when we'll be able to continue.

Nature of the sun. Origins of Freemasonry. Sign, handshake and word. Ku Klux Klan

Have you thought of something you'd like to ask, gentlemen?

Question: How do the sun's rays come about? Is that a substance? And how does it happen that they come to earth in a curve?

Rudolf Steiner: Am I right in thinking that you see the sun's rays as something real? And perhaps you can go a bit further and explain why you think they come to earth in a curve.

The questioner said he'd heard that they did not come to earth in a straight line but in a curve.

Rudolf Steiner: It's like this. The sun's rays, as we see them, are not actually a reality; but if we consider the sun the way it is, it is not really physical matter, it is in fact spiritual, a hollowed-out form created in space.

Now, you must get a real mental image of what such an empty space means. If you have a bottle of fizzy water — I have used this comparison before — the bottle is filled with water and one really hardly sees the water; we know there is water in there, but what we do see clearly are the beads in the water [drawing]. But you know that when you pour the water from the bottle those beads evaporate; they are in fact air. Being air, they are thinner than water. One is not seeing something denser than water, but one clearly sees the thinner element of air in there. That is how it is with the sun up there. Everything around the sun is really denser than the sun, and the sun is thinner than anything around it; and that is why you see the sun. It is an illusion to think that the sun is 'something' in space. In reality there is nothing there in space; you have a big hole there, just as with fizzy water you always have air, a hole, wherever there is a bead.

This immediately tells you that there can be no question of rays coming from that hole. The rays develop in a completely different way. You can understand this if you consider the following. Let us assume you have a street lamp, and there is a light in this street lamp. If you go out into the street and look at this lamp and the night is bright and clear, you'll see the lamp in steady, beautiful radiance. But imagine it is a foggy night, with mist and fog all around — then it will seem to you that rays come from the lamp, from the light! You then see those rays in there. But in fact you do not see rays of the light, for then you would also see them on a really good night. They do rather come from around the lamp; and the more mist and fog there is, the more do you see those rays. And so the sun's rays, too, are not something real, but something where you look through a mist at something that is less dense, an empty space. Can you understand this?

Now to go on. Looking into the distance through a mist, the object one looks at always appears in a different place from where it really is. If we are down here on the earth and look through the air at the sun, which is really empty, then, as we look, the sun actually appears lower down than it really is — it will be lower down in the emptiness of space. As a result, something which is not real anyway appears to be going in a curve [drawing]. So it is only that way because we look through the mist. That is the reality in this case. One can only be amazed, over and over again, that physicists today present the matter in such a way as if there was a sun there and rays were going along there, when in fact neither the sun nor the rays are outer, physical reality. And in that space, which is empty inside, there you do indeed then have something spiritual. And this is something one must always take into account. This is what I am able to say on this question.

Perhaps one of you may be able to think of something else?

Question: Might we hear something about Freemasonry and its purpose?

Rudolf Steiner: Well, you see, gentlemen, modern Freemasonry is really, one might say, only a shadow of its former self. I have talked to you about this on several occasions, saying that in very early times in human evolution they did not have schools like we have today, nor churches or centres for the arts of this kind, for it was all one then.[98] In the ancient mysteries, as they were called, you had school, art centre and religion all in one. They only became separate later. We could actually say that in our central European regions this happened only in the eleventh or twelfth centuries. Monasteries used to be memorials of times gone by, I would say. But in very early times the situation was that school, church and art centre were one. But everything that was done in those mysteries was taken much more seriously than things are taken in our schools today, for example, and also in our churches.

The situation was in those times that one had to go through a long period of preparation before one was allowed to learn. Today, the question as to whether one can learn something or not is really determined by a principle that has nothing to do with learning as such. I think you'll agree that today the decision is really entirely made on the basis of whether the money can be found for the person who is to learn, or if it cannot be found! That is of course something which has nothing to do with the abilities of the person concerned. And the situation was very different in earlier times, when people were chosen from among the whole of humanity — they had more of an eye for it in those days than people have today — who were perhaps the most

able. The whole thing went into a decline almost everywhere later on, because it simply is the case that people are
egotistical. But the principle used to be that people were
chosen who had abilities. And only they would be entitled
to learn in a spiritual way—not simply by drills and
dressage, and the kind of elements used in teaching today,
but they were able to learn in a spiritual way.

This learning in a spiritual way depended on people
learning to develop quite specific abilities in the course of
preparation. You merely have to consider that when we
touch something in ordinary life we have a rough and ready
sensation of it. The most people are able to achieve today is
that they can sometimes tell materials apart by the way they
feel, that they touch objects and are able to tell there is some
difference. But people's sentience—I am speaking of purely
physical sensation—is relatively crude today. They distinguish between hot and cold. At most it may be that people
who really depend on this develop more subtle sensation.
Blind people are an example. There are blind people who
learn to move across paper and feel the form of the letters.
Every letter is a little bit engraved in the paper. With subtle
sensation developed in the fingers it is possible to get
something of a feel of the letters. These are the only people
today who learn to have more subtle sensations. As a rule
sensation is not developed, though one learns a tremendous
amount if one develops sensation to be very subtle in one's
fingertips and fingers. Today people tell the difference
between hot and cold not just by feeling it. And they are able
to do this today because they are able to read a thermometer.
There the subtle differences in temperature are made visible.
But the thermometer has only been developed in the course
of time. Before that, people only had their sensations. And in
the preparation for the mysteries, sensation was specially
developed, above all in the fingers and fingertips. And
people were then able to sense things in a very subtle way.

So who was it who would initially be prepared to develop very fine sensation in the mysteries? Well, other people were not able to have such subtle senses. Let us assume now that there was a mystery site somewhere, in some place. People travelled a great deal in antiquity; they travelled almost as much as we do, and it is sometimes surprising how fast they travelled. They did not have railways. But they travelled because they were more nimble, able to walk faster, not getting tired so easily, also walking a bit better, and so on. And so they would meet on the way, these people. Well, when two such people, who were able to have subtle sensations, shook hands they would notice this in each other, and people would say: They recognize one another because of their fine sensation. This is what is known as the handshake, the handshake when you took hold of the other person in earlier times and realized that he had more subtle sensation.

Now to move on, gentlemen. Consider this second aspect. When it was realized that someone had subtle sensation, one would go further, for people learned even more than this. In the early days people did not write as much as they do today; they would really only write very rarely and then it would be something that was most sacred to them. There was a kind of correspondence in antiquity, but it was a correspondence in all kinds of signs. Many signs were developed for all kinds of things. And it was also the case that people who did not belong to the mysteries and therefore were not 'wise' people, as it was called, would only travel lesser distances; they would not go very far. But the scholars, the wise people, travelled a great deal. They would therefore have needed to know not only all languages but also all dialects. It is of course difficult for someone from the north of Germany to understand the Swiss German dialect. But those people in the mysteries had not only the language they spoke but all kinds of signs for things that interested them. They would make signs. For instance, the usual gesture, for which one already had a feeling, would be developed further: 'I understand'; or 'That is nothing, what you are telling me'; or 'We really understand one another'. They would sign a cross. A fully developed sign language thus existed especially among the wise people of old, and they would put everything they knew into those signs. You can see, therefore, that all the people who were in the universities of that time, which were the mysteries, had particular signs for everything. Let us say, for example, they wanted to record these signs at some point in time. It was only then that they would draw them. And this is how they came to put signs on things.

It is certainly interesting that there are still some scripts today where one can clearly see that they have developed from signs. An example is the script of the ancient Indians, Sanskrit. Here one can see everywhere that it has developed from a curved and a straight line [drawing]. Curved lines: dissatisfaction with something, antipathy; straight lines: sympathy. Just think of someone who knows that straight lines mean sympathy, curved lines antipathy. Now I want to tell him something. I have a sign for this, too. He wants to tell me something. This may be all right to start with, but then things may go wrong. You see, there it still works fine. Later he will draw a wriggly line — then it may be something bad. And so they had particular signs for everything. These signs provided a means of communication for those who were in the mysteries. So you had the handshake and the sign.

People also saw something very special in words in those times. You see, when people say words today, they really no longer have an idea of what there is to those words. But one can still have a feeling for what lies in the speech sounds. You will easily be able to tell when someone is in a particular life situation and starts to say: Ah. That has something to do with amazement, with awe. A — the letter

A [pronounced like the 'a' in father] is amazement. Now add the letter R — this is something rolling along, radiating. R = radiance. A = amazement, awe, R = rolling, radiance.

Now we know what we have just said about the sun's rays. But even if they are only seemingly there, and are not real, it looks as if they were streaming forth. Now imagine someone wants to say: 'Up there is something that tosses something to me here on earth, and when it appears in the morning it causes me to feel awe.' He would express his awe as A, but the fact that it comes from above with the sound R; so he would express it as RA. Yes, that is what the ancient Egyptians called the sun god — Ra. In each of these letters you have an inner feeling, and we have put the sounds together to make words. So there was feeling in there, feeling spread out. This has long since been forgotten. Take the sound I*, for instance. That is something like quiet pleasure, one comes to terms with something one comes across, something one perceives: I. And the laugh is also a heehee. That is quiet pleasure. And so every letter has a particular character. And there is a knowledge that enables one actually to create the words if one has an understanding of the sounds that make up the words.

Now you'll say one thing, gentlemen: 'Well, if that were the case, then there could be only one language.' Originally humanity did have just one language; when people still had a feeling for these speech sounds, these letters, there was just one language. Later different languages developed, when people went apart. But originally they had such feeling for it, and in the mysteries it was actually taught how speech sounds, letters, may be felt and made into words. They therefore had their own language in the mysteries. This was the language they would all speak among themselves. They would not use their dialects but this language, which all of

---

*Pronounced as the 'e' in 'me'.

them understood. When one of them said Ra, the other would know that this meant the sun. When one would say E [more or less like the 'a' in 'gate'] — just feel it: I shrink back a little. That does not suit me; E — I am a little afraid, something like fear! Take the L now. That is as if something is fading away, something is flowing, and EL, well, that is something that flows and from which we shrink back a little, which causes us to be afraid. That was El in Babylon, meaning 'god'. And everything was given its name on this principle. Take the Bible. If you say O — that is amazement, being taken aback by it. With the A you have a feeling you like, an amazement and awe you like. O and you want to step back; H, Ch [like the h in human] is the breath. So we may say: O = amazement, being taken aback; H = breath; I = one points to it, one takes quiet pleasure in it = I. And M, that is wanting to enter into it yourself. You feel, when you say M: M — the breath goes out, and you feel you are literally running after your breath; M thus is to go away. Now let us put this together. El, as we have seen is the spirit that comes in the wind, El; O is amazement that makes you step back, H is the breath; this is the more subtle spirit that acts as breath; I is quiet pleasure; M is to go towards it. There you have Elohim, and the Bible begins with this. You have these speech sounds in it. So that we are able to say: What are the Elohim? The Elohim are spirits in the wind of whom we are a little afraid, shrinking back a little, but with the breath they have pleasure in human beings, pleasure in going to the human beings — Elohim. And so one had to study the words originally for their speech sounds, their letters, to see what they really mean. Today people no longer have a feeling for how this really is.

What is the plural of *Wagen* here in Switzerland? Do you also say *Wagen* here, or is it *Wägen*? [Answer: *die Wagen.**] So

---

* The answer was wrong. It is *Wäge* in Swiss German, as Rudolf Steiner thought it might be.

it is still *die Wagen*. Then it has become blurred; originally it would have been *der Wagen, die Wägen*. With the plural we have this in all kinds of different ways. For instance we have *der Bruder, die Brüder*. Or, let us say, *das Holz, die Hölzer*. I expect here, too, one does not say *die Holzer*. *Das Holz, die Hölzer*. You see, gentlemen, when the plural is formed, the umlaut is used—a to ä, u to ü, o to ö.[99] Why is this done? You see, the umlaut indicates that the thing becomes blurred. When I see one brother, he is distinct, a single individual; when I see several brothers, it becomes blurred, and I have to differentiate between them, and if I cannot do this it becomes blurred. One has to look at them one by one. The umlaut always indicates things getting blurred. So when you have the umlaut in a word, something is blurred.

So there is something in language that allows us to see the whole human being; there you have the whole human being. And people would also bring to expression how there was a certain meaning even in the letters they wrote, in these signs. 'A' always was amazement, awe. When an ancient Hebrew had written the letter aleph like this: א [drawing], he would say to himself: Who is amazed in the earth world? Animals are not really amazed, only man is. And so he altogether referred to man as 'amazement'. When he wrote his aleph, the א, the Hebrew 'A', it therefore also referred to the human being.

And so it was that every letter also signified a particular thing or being. And the people who were in the mysteries knew all this. So when one of them was meeting another on his travels and they had that common knowledge, they would recognize one another by the word. So that we are able to say that in the early days the situation was that people who had learned things, who knew a great deal, recognized one another by handshake, sign and word. But you see, gentlemen, then there was something in it! You immediately had their whole scholarship in this sign, handshake and word. For people learned to distinguish between things by touching them. Having the signs, they had a way of imitating everything there is by way of nature's secrets. And in the word they got to know the inner human being. So we are able to say that in the handshake they had sensory perception; in the sign they had the world of nature, and in the word they had the human being, his inner amazement or shrinking back, his pleasure and so on. So they had nature and man and echoed them in sign, handshake and word.

In the course of human evolution a separation occurred into university and later schools on the one hand and the Church and the arts on the other. In all three of these, people no longer understood what had originally existed; and handshake, sign and word were lost completely. It was understood only by people who had then discovered: Wow! Those wise ancient people had some degree of power because they knew this. A person is justified in having this power because he knows something and it is for the benefit of others. If no one had known how to build a railway engine, humanity would never have had a railway engine. And it therefore benefits humanity if someone knows something; that is justifiable power. But later on people simply acquired the power by copying the external signs.

Just as this or that sign used to mean something in the past and people later no longer knew this meaning, so did all this lose its meaning. And mere aping, I would say, of the ancient mysteries then led to all kinds of things where you only have the superficial aspect. What did those people do? They no longer had the subtle sensation, but they agreed on a sign by which they would recognize one another. They shake hands in a particular way and one then knows: 'He belongs to the brotherhood.' They recognize one another by the handshake. Then they also make a sign in some other way. The sign and the handshake differ depending on whether someone has reached the first, second or third degree. People then recognize one another. But there is no more to this than a sign of recognition. And they also have special words for each degree, words they may say in certain Masonic associations. Thus if one wants to know the word for the first degree, for example, they may have the code word Jachin. One knows he has learned the word in the Freemason's lodge, otherwise he would not be a member of the first degree. It is merely a code word now. And he will then also make the sign, and so on.

Now this kind of Freemasonry has really only developed at a time when everything else about the mysteries had been forgotten. And some of the old things were imitated though they were no longer understood. So that the rites Freemasons have taken from the past are on the whole no longer understood by present-day Masons, for they do not know all the things that matter here. Thus they do not know that when they say the word for the second degree, Boas, that B is really a house, O means stepping back in amazement; A is pleasant amazement; S is the sign of the serpent. So it means: 'We recognize the world to be a great house built by the great world builder, and one has to be amazed at it both with slight fear and with pleasure, and evil, the serpent is also present in it.' Yes, people knew this in the past; they would look at nature in the light of this, look at the human being in the light of this. Today people who have reached the second degree in some Masonic associations utter the word 'Boas' without having a clue. And the same also in the third degree. You see, when people put their finger on the pulse in the past it really was recognition that the individual concerned had subtle sensation. This would be apparent from the way in which the finger lay on the pulse. Later this became the handshake for the third degree. Today, people only know that if someone comes along and takes one's hand in this particular way he is a Mason. So there really is something ancient, venerable, great in these things, something that contained the whole scholarship of earlier times. It has now become a mere formula, a nothing. Today the Freemasons have these things; they also have ceremonies, a ritual. This comes from the times when everything would also be presented in ritual form, in ceremonies, so that it would touch people more deeply. The Freemasons still do this today. And in this inner respect Freemasonry really no longer has significance today.

But it became terribly boring for people to join in with these things when the associations had been established. For it had really degenerated into a kind of tomfoolery. So something was needed, had to be poured into it, into Freemasonry. And the result was the Freemasons went more or less political, or they would spread more or less religious forms of enlightenment. The teaching that came from Rome was without enlightenment. The teaching that was in opposition to Rome was then spread by the Masons. Because of this, Rome, the people using the Roman rites, and Freemasons are completely at loggerheads. This no longer has anything to do with ritual, sign, handshake and word among Freemasons; it is something added on. In France the brotherhood was no longer called a brotherhood but Orient de France, for it had all come from the East. Grand Orient de France—that is the great French Free-masons' association. The rest—sign, handshake and word—exists only to keep people together; it is something by which they recognize each other. The communal rite is used when they gather on particularly solemn occasions. Just as others gather in church, so these Freemasons gather to hold ceremonies that originated in the ancient mysteries. This brings people together.

It was very much the custom when secret societies became established in the past, especially in Italy, to recognize one another by certain ceremonial elements—

sign and handshake—and to have gatherings. Political associations and societies have always picked up on this ancient mystery element. And it is really quite strange that when you go to some parts of Poland or Austria today you see posters; those posters show strange signs and strange letters which then combine to form words. Initially one does not know what the poster means. But such a poster, put up everywhere in areas of Poland and Austria, is the outward sign of a society established among young people by certain nationalist elements. They use the same things. This is really very widespread, and people know very well that the sign also has a particular power. Some associations, the German popular front, for instance, use an ancient Indian sign of two serpents intertwined, or, if you will, a wheel, which then became transformed into the present-day swastika [drawing]. They wear it on their lapels today. And you'll often hear that the swastika has been adopted by certain chauvinist nationalist groups. This is because tradition says that the ancients brought their power to expression in such signs. And it has always been like this on a large scale among Freemasons. Freemasonry really exists in order to keep certain people together, and this is done by ceremonial, sign, handshake and word. And hidden goals are pursued by keeping certain secrets among all the people who are connected by these ceremonies, by sign, handshake and word. Hidden goals can of course only be pursued if they are not known to everyone. And the situation with the Freemasons is that they often have political, cultural or similar goals.

Now there is something else you may say, gentlemen. You see, we cannot take exception to people coming together in Masonic bodies just because they do this, for they sometimes have the best and noblest intentions. It is only that they think people will not be interested in such aims in any other way but by having such organizations.

And many Masonic bodies also do extensive charitable work. It is good to practise charity and humanity to a major degree. And these organizations do so on a major scale. No wonder, then, that Masons are always able to say that Masonic organizations have founded and established an enormous amount of humanitarian and charitable work. Yet we have to say to ourselves that such things are really no longer right for the present age. For, you see, what is it that we cannot accept today in this respect? We cannot accept segregation. This soon leads to a cultural aristocracy which should not exist. And the democratic principle, which must increasingly come to the fore, really goes against both the Freemasons and the clerical bodies. We are thus able to say that it really is true that someone who is still able to understand what lies in many Masonic ceremonies of the first, second and third degree, which Freemasons themselves often do not understand, knows that they often go back to very ancient wisdom, but this is not really what counts. What really counts is that many Masonic associations have wide-ranging political or also social and charitable aims. The Roman Catholic Church and the Freemasons are fighting each other to the death, but this, too, is something that has only come in the course of time.

It is, of course, easy to get the wrong idea here. And that has also happened. Masons wear special garments for their ceremonies; they have a sheepskin apron, for instance. Some people came and said that Freemasonry is nothing but play-acting, pretending to be Masons, for stonemasons wear a sheepskin apron. But that is not true. The purpose of the apron — originally it was always a sheepskin one — is to show that someone who is a member of such an organization is not supposed to be rabid in his passions; the genitals are meant to be covered by the apron, and this is the sign. So it was something that reflected human character in signs. And that is how it is with very many signs which are also garments.

They also have higher degrees, when a priestlike robe is worn; everything has its meaning there. I have told you, for example, that apart from his physical body man also has an ether body. And just as the priest has a white linen garment, like a shift, to reflect the ether body, so certain high ranks among the Freemasons have such a garment. For the astral body – it is coloured – they have a toga, an over-garment. So it gives expression to all these things. And the cloak, which was then connected with the helmet, reflected the power of the I.

All these things take us back to ancient customs that had real meaning and significance but have now lost significance. Anyone who likes Freemasonry should not take the things I have said to be derogatory. I merely wanted to show how things are. There can, of course, be a Masonic order whose members are extraordinarily good people, and so on. And at the present time such a thing can become particularly important. The things people generally learn when they become physicians or lawyers – well, these do not touch their hearts. And many members of the legal and medical professions still become Masons because then they have at least the solemn ceremonials of old, and something which does no longer hold much meaning for them but is still something – sign, handshake and word, and what this does is to show that man does not live in outer, material things alone.

This is what I wanted to say to you. Is there anything else you'd like to ask?

Question: In America they have something called the Ku Klux Klan. What is this about? Could we hear from Dr Steiner what it signifies? One is always reading about it.

Rudolf Steiner: Well, you see, the Ku Klux Klan is one of the most recent inventions in this field, an invention that should certainly be taken more seriously than people generally do. As you know, gentlemen, some decades ago people were enthusiastic about a certain cosmopolitan way of thinking. It still exists today, of course, among the workers, among social democrats – these are an international element – but in middle class circles and in other circles nationalism is getting terribly out of hand, and nationalist tendencies are indeed getting very strong. And you will also remember that the people who supported Woodrow Wilson[100] – he himself was only a kind of figurehead – really counted on this nationalism, wanted to have nationalist states everywhere, incite nationalism everywhere, and so on. Well, one can have one's own ideas about this. But people are developing a tendency to take nationalism to extremes everywhere today. And in this drive to take nationalism to extremes the association known as the Ku Klux Klan has appeared in America. They are very much working with such things as special signs, in the sense in which I have spoken of this.

When one considers associations of this kind one needs to know that signs have a certain power to hypnotize. As you know, if you have a chicken [drawing], and let this chicken touch the ground with its beak, and you draw a line from there with chalk, the chicken will follow the chalked line. It is hypnotized, running after the chalked line. You just have to push its beak down on to it at the beginning and it'll follow the line, being hypnotized by it. And in this way every sign – not only the straight line for the chicken – has meaning, a particular hypnotic significance if you intend it to be that way. Some secret societies make use of this, choosing signs that will turn people's heads, putting them to sleep, so that they do not use their own powers of judgement.

Such means are above all used by secret societies. The Ku Klux Klan in America is one of them. And the Ku Klux Klan is dangerous because such societies do not concentrate on only one nation but want to see the nationalist principle everywhere. No one can say: 'The Ku Klux Klan can simply remain an American institution, for it aims to further American nationalism.' The members of the Ku Klux Klan do not say this. They say: 'One should promote nationalism everywhere – in Hungary, in Germany, in France.' All very well! What matters to them is not Americanism, they are not patriots, but they realize that the combined effect of people's insistence on nationalism in different nations will give them exactly what they want to achieve, and that is to throw everything into chaos. Sheer destructive frenzy lies in this. And you can't say it is an American element if it ever wants to spread here in Switzerland, for in that case it will be a Swiss national institution.

And basically that also held true for Masonic associations; they were international, but for individual countries always nationalistic. They would not rate this very highly, for they would do it more in response to the outside world, joining in whatever was going on outside. And we are able to say: 'People like that must surely be mad, wanting to encourage something like an absolutely nationalistic principle and wanting to destroy everything.' But people say: 'Everything has gone to rack and ruin today' – the leaders say this to themselves with reference to the others who follow them – and the others do not care in the least, so there is no point in looking after the things that exist today. 'One must first treat humanity as a confused mass. Then people will find themselves again and learn something decent.' So these people have an idea, and the Ku Klux Klan in particular has its ideas on the subject.

You think not?

Questioner: *Oh yes, I do, But it is funny!*

Rudolf Steiner: You see, many things in cultural life are funny, and we have talked about things that look funny. But funny things are sometimes rather dangerous. It seems funny to one, but it is extraordinarily dangerous.

Now, gentlemen, tomorrow sometime I have to be on my travels again, to Breslau.[101] I'll let you know when we can have our next session.

Man and the hierarchies. Ancient wisdom lost. *The Philosophy of Spiritual Activity*

Good morning, gentlemen. Perhaps you have been able to think of something during this slightly longer interval—a special question?

Question concerning the nature of the different hierarchies and their influence on humanity.

Rudolf Steiner: This, I think, will be a bit difficult for those of you who are here for the first time; not easy to understand because you need to know some of the things I have been discussing in earlier lectures. But I'll consider the subject, nevertheless, and try and make it as easy as possible.

You see, when you consider the human being, as he stands and walks on this earth, the human being really has all the realms of nature in him. In the first place man has the animal world in him; in a sense he also has an animal organization. You can see this immediately from the fact that human beings have upper arm and thigh bones, with similar bones also found in higher animals. But if one is able to gain good knowledge of them, one also finds related or similar elements in lower animals. Right down to the fishes you can more or less see elements corresponding to human bone. And what we can thus say about the skeletal system may also be said about the muscular system and also the internal organs. We find that humans have a stomach. Correspondingly we also find a stomach in animals. In short, the things that exist in the animal world can also be found in the human body.

Because of this, the materialistic view of the human being

came to be that he was simply an animal, too, though more highly developed. But he is not. Human beings develop three things which animals cannot develop out of their organism. The first is that humans learn to walk upright. Just look at animals that learn to walk more or less half-way upright, and you'll see the marked difference between them and human beings. In animals that are a bit upright, kangaroos, for instance, you'll see that the forelimbs, on which they do not walk, are stunted. The kangaroo's forelimbs are not made to be used freely. And with the apes we certainly cannot say that they are like humans in this respect; for when they go up trees, they do not walk, they climb. They really have four hands, not two feet and two hands. The feet are shaped similar to hands; they climb. An upright walk is thus the first thing to distinguish humans from animals.

The second thing that distinguishes humans from animals is the ability to talk. And the ability to talk is connected with the ability to walk upright. You will therefore find that where animals have something similar to the ability to talk — dogs, being highly intelligent, relatively speaking, do not have it, but parrots, for instance, do have it, being a little bit upright — you will find that the animal is upright in that case. Speech is entirely connected with this uprightness.

And the third thing is free will. Animals cannot achieve this, being dependent on their internal processes. These are the things that make up the whole internal organization of the human being, making it human.

But man nevertheless has animal nature in him. He does have this animal world in him.

The second thing man has in him is the plant world. What are people able to do because they have the animal world in them? You see, animals are sentient — humans, too; plants are not sentient. A strange science which has now come up does include the view — I have mentioned this here before[102] – that plants are also able to feel, because there is a plant, such as the venus fly-trap, for instance, and if an insect comes near and lands on it the venus fly-trap folds up its leaves and swallows the insect. That is a highly interesting phenomenon. But if someone says: 'This plant, the venus fly-trap, must feel the insect, that is, have sensory perception of it, when it comes near it,' this is just as nonsensical as if someone were to say: 'Such a tiny little thing which I set to snap shut when a mouse comes near – a mousetrap – is also able to sense that the mouse is entering into it.' Such scientific opinions are no great shakes, they are simply nonsense. Plants do not feel. Nor are plants able to move freely.

Sentience and mobility are therefore things man has in common with animals; there he has animal nature in him. It is only when he is able to think sensibly – which an animal cannot do – which makes him human. Man also has the plant world, the whole plant world in him. Plants do not move from place to place but they grow. Humans also grow and take nourishment. The plant world in them does this. This plant power is something humans also have in them. They have it in them even when they sleep. They let their animal nature go when they sleep, for they have no sentience of things, nor do they move around – unless of course they are sleepwalking, which is an abnormal development; in that case they do not let go of the ability to move around, and then they are sick. But in their normal condition people do not walk around when they are asleep, and they have no sentient awareness of things. When they need to have this, they wake up. In sleep, they cannot be sentient. Plant nature is something humans have in them also in their sleep.

And mineral nature, gentlemen, is also in us; it is present in our bones, for instance. They are a little bit alive, but they contain the lifeless element of calcium carbonate. We carry the mineral world in us. We even have brain sand in our brains. That is mineral. We have the mineral world in us. And so we have the animal world, the plant world and the mineral world in us.

But that is not all. If human beings only had mineral, plant and animal in them, they would be like an animal, they would walk about like an animal, for the animal, too, has mineral, plant and animal in it. Human beings, of course, are connected not only with those three realms of nature, which are visible, but also with other realms.

Let me draw a diagram for you. Imagine this to be the human being [Fig. 6]. He is now related to the mineral world, the plant world, the animal world. But he is a human being. You might say: 'Well, all right, animals can be

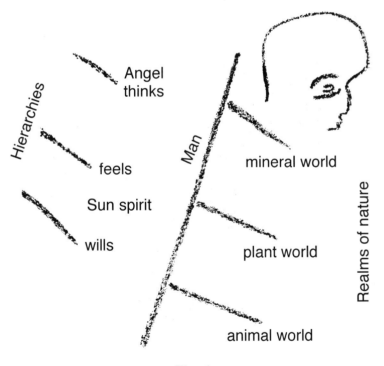

Fig. 6

tamed.' That is quite right. But have you ever seen an ox tamed by an ox? Or a horse by a horse? Animals, even if tamed, which gives them certain abilities that show distant similarity with human abilities, have to be tamed by humans! You'll agree there is no such thing as a school for dogs where dogs teach each other and make tame dogs out of wild dogs. Human beings have to intervene. And even if one were to think one might concede everything the materialists want, one would only have to take their own lines of thought further — you can concede everything, and if you like someone might say: 'The human being, as he is now, was originally an animal and has been tamed.' But the animal he would have been in that case cannot have tamed him! It simply is not possible. Otherwise a dog might also tame a dog. So there must have been someone originally who took humanity to its present level, and this someone, these entities — who may no longer be there now — cannot be from the three realms of nature. For if you imagine that you could ever have been tamed by a giraffe and made into a human being whilst still a little creature in your infancy — just as this would not have been possible, so it would not have been possible for you to have been tamed by an oak. You'd have to be a member of the German national front to believe that, people who may perhaps assume that the oak, a holy tree, has tamed humankind. And, you see, minerals even less so. A rock crystal is beautiful, but it certainly cannot tame the human being. Other entities must have existed, other realms.

You see, in human beings everything is truly called to higher things. Animals are able to form ideas, but they do not think. Ideas develop in animals. But they have no thinking activity. Human beings have thinking activity. And so they may have their blood circulation from the animal world, for example, but their thinking organ cannot come from the animal world. We are thus able to say: Man thinks, he feels, he wills. All this is freely done. And everything is different because man is a being who walks upright and who talks.

Just think how different your will intent would have to be, all your will impulses would be different if you always had to crawl around on all fours the way you do in the first year of your life. All human will impulses would be different in that case. And you would never get to the point of being able to think. And just as the things we have in our physical bodies connect us with the three realms of nature, so do thinking, feeling and will connect us with three other realms, with supersensible, invisible realms. We have to have a name for everything. Just as we call minerals, plants and animals the realms of nature, so we call the realms that bring about thinking, feeling and will in such a way that they may be free — the hierarchies. Thus we have here the realms of nature [Fig. 6], and with this, man extends into the natural world. And here we have the hierarchies. You see, man extends into three realms of nature on the one hand and into three hierarchies on the other. With his thinking he extends into the hierarchy — now you see, we do not yet have a name for it. We do not have a name for it because materialism takes no account of it; so we have to use the old names: angeloi, angels. People will immediately brand one as superstitious if one says this. It is true, of course, that we no longer have a real possibility of finding names for things, for humanity has lost the feeling for speech sounds. Languages were only able to evolve for as long as people still had a feeling for speech sounds. Today everyone uses words like 'ball' or 'fall'.[103] Each has the vowel 'a' in it. But what is that 'a' sound? It expresses a feeling! Imagine what would happen if you were to see someone opening that window from the outside and looking in. It would not be the right moment for such a thing, and so you would be surprised and amazed. Quite of few of you would probably react to this with an 'Oh!' – unless you felt this was not the place for expressing one's reactions. That sound always expresses surprise, being taken aback a little. And this is how every letter brings something to expression. When I say 'ball', I use that vowel sound because I am surprised at the strange way it behaves when I throw it, or if it is a ball where people dance, I am surprised to see all those lively gyrations. Only the way things have developed, people have got so used to it all that they are no longer surprised, you might just as well call it 'bull', or 'bill' but certainly no longer 'ball'. Let us take 'fall'. When someone takes a fall somewhere, we may also say 'Oh'. And the other important aspect lies in the 'f' – using an energy that lies in him. 'Oh' – whenever you are surprised, you also have that particular vowel sound.

And consider this. You believe that thinking takes place in the head. But if you were suddenly able to perceive that your thinking involves spiritual entities, just as there have to be animals on this earth so that you may be able to have sensation and feeling, this would come as another surprise to you. And to express this surprise you'd have to have a word that has that 'a' [as in father] sound in it. You would therefore also be able to give these thinking entities, known as angeloi, a name which has that 'a', and you would use the letter which indicates that you have the power of thinking, expressing power in a certain way: 'l'; and for the power that is taking effect you might perhaps use a 'b'. The word Alb,[104] used for something spiritual before, could indeed serve as a sign for these spirits who are connected with thinking, and not only for nightmares, which are the pathological side of it. The hierarchies are realms into which the human being extends, and which he has in him just as he has the realms of nature in him. And the spirits who were called Alb or angel are those connected with our thinking.

The feelings human beings have are connected with animal nature. What, animals? Well, you see, if one pays a little bit of heed and does not immediately go mad when something is mentioned that has to do with the spirit, but if people accept that one may be speaking of things of the spirit, quite a few things can be found out, even if one is not yet able to use a science of the spirit such as anthroposophy. Just consider—if you want to feel you need to have a certain warmth in you. A frog is much less alive in his feelings than a human being is, because it does not have warm blood. You really need to have warmth inside you when you feel. But the warmth we have in us comes from the sun. And so we are able to say that our feeling is also connected with the sun, but in a spiritual way. Physical warmth is connected with the physical sun; feeling, which is connected with physical warmth, is connected with the spiritual sun. This Second Hierarchy, which has to do with feeling, thus resides in the sun. You will definitely discover—providing you are not wholly brain-fixed, which many people are today, especially the scientists—you will discover that the Second Hierarchy are sun spirits. And because the sun only reveals itself on the outside in light and heat—no one knows the inside of the sun, for if physicists were to discover the sun as it really is they would be absolutely amazed to find that it does not at all look the way they think it does. They believe the sun to be a body of hot gases. That is far from the truth. It really consists of nothing but powers of suction; it is hollow, not even empty, but sucking. We can say that it reveals itself as light and heat on the outside; the spirits which are in there were known as 'spirits of revelation' in ancient Greek. When people still knew things—for the old instinctive knowledge was much wiser than the knowledge we have today—the spirits that revealed themselves from the sun were called Exusiai; we may just as well say 'sun spirits'. We just have to know that when we speak of feeling we enter into the realm of the sun spirits. Just as I say: Man has powers of growth and nutrition in him, and therefore the plant world, so I have to say: Man has in him powers of feeling, which are powers of the spiritual sun realm, the Second Hierarchy.

And the third thing is the First Hierarchy, which has to do with the human will. This is where human beings grow most energetic, not only moving but also bringing their actions to bear. This is in connection with spirits who are out there in the whole world and are altogether the highest spiritual entities we can get to know. Again we use a Greek or Hebrew name, for we do not yet have German ones, or altogether do not yet have the terms in our language — Thrones, Cherubs, Seraphs. That is the highest realm.

So there are three realms in the spirit just as there are three realms in nature. Man has to do with the three realms of nature and also with the three realms of the spirit.

Now you'll say: 'Well, I can believe that or not, for those three realms are not visible, they cannot be perceived by the senses.' Yes, but gentlemen, I have known people where one was asked to explain to them that there is such a thing as air. He would not believe that there was any air. When I tell him 'That's a blackboard', he'll believe it, for if he goes up to it he'll bump into it, or when he uses his eyes he can see the blackboard. But he does not bump into the air. He may look and will say: 'There's nothing there.' In spite of this everyone admits today that air exists. It is simply there. And one day people will also admit that the spirit is there. Today they still say: 'Well, it is not there, the spirit.' Which is what country people said about the air in the old days. In the place where I grew up, the country people would still say: 'The air simply is not there; that is just something the big-heads in the city say, wanting to be so clever. You can walk through there and there is nothing there where you are able to walk through.' But that was a long time ago.

Today even the cleverest people still do not know that spirits are present everywhere! But they will admit it in due course, for certain things cannot be explained in any other way, and they need to be explained.

If someone says today: 'There is no spirit in everything that exists by way of nature; everything scientists know about nature is in there, but nothing else.' Well, gentlemen, if anyone says such a thing that is just as if there is someone who has died, and the corpse lies there, and I come and say: 'You lazy fellow! Why don't you get up and move on!' I try hard to make him understand that he should not be so lazy and that he should get up. Well, I lack understanding in that case, believing that there is a living human being in there. And that is how it is. Everything a scientist is able to find in there he does not find in the living person, he finds it in the dead body. Out there in the world of nature he also finds only dead things; he does not find that which lives. He does not find the spiritual in this way, but this does not mean it does not exist.

This is what I wanted to say on this question concerning the hierarchies.

Mr Burle: In earlier lectures you spoke about the ancient peoples having knowledge of the science of the spirit. This has been lost to humanity today. Would you be able to explain to us how that happened? If it was all due to materialism?

Rudolf Steiner: Why the old knowledge was lost? Well, you see, gentlemen, that is a very strange thing. The people who lived in very early times did not have knowledge the way we have it today but they had it in an artistic, poetic form. They had great knowledge, and that knowledge has been lost to humanity, as Mr Burle said, quite rightly. Now we may ask what caused this knowledge to be lost. We certainly cannot say that it was all due to materialism; for if all people still had the old knowledge materialism could never have arisen. It was exactly because the old knowledge had been lost and people had been mentally crippled that they invented materialism. Materialism thus comes from the decline of the old knowledge, and we cannot say that the old knowledge went into decline because materialism was spreading. So the question is, what did actually cause the old knowledge to decline?

Well, gentlemen, it happened because humanity is in a process of evolution. Now you can of course dissect a person who exists today; if he dies you can dissect him. You can gain knowledge about the way in which the human being is made in our present time. The most we have from earlier times are, well, the mummies in Egypt, which we talked about recently, only they are so thoroughly embalmed that one really cannot dissect them properly any more. Scientists therefore cannot get an idea of what human beings looked like in earlier times, especially at the time when they were of a more subtle build. Ordinary science cannot help here, and one has to penetrate it with the science of the spirit. And then one will find that people were not at all the way they are today in those earlier times.

There was a time on earth when people did not have such hard bones as we have them today. People had bones like the bones children with rickets have today, so that they grow bow-legged or knock-kneed and are altogether weak. You can see that it is possible to have such soft bones, for one still finds them in cartilaginous fish today. Those bones are as soft as cartilage. Human beings once had such bones, for the human skeleton was soft at one time. Now you'll say: 'That must mean that everyone went around bow-legged or knock-kneed, and everything must have been crooked because the bones were soft.'

That would have been the case if the air had always been the same on earth as it is today. But it wasn't. The air was much thicker in earlier times. It has got much thinner. And the air contained much more water in those old times than it does today. The air also contained a lot more carbon dioxide. The whole air was denser. Now you begin to see that people were able to live with those soft bones in the past. We only have to have the bones we have today because the air is no longer supporting us. A denser air would support human beings. Walking was much more like swimming in those times than it is today. Today we walk in a terribly mechanized way; we put down one foot, and the leg has to be like a column; then we put down the other foot. People did not walk like that in the earliest times; they were aware of the watery air just as one can let the water carry one today. So it was possible for them to have softer bones. But when the air grew thinner—and even ordinary science can tell us that the air got thinner—hard bones began to make sense. Hard bones only developed then. Of course, in those times the carbon dioxide was outside; the air contained it. Today we have calcium carbonate inside us; and with this the bones have grown hard. That is how things go together.

But when the bones grow hard, others things, too, grow hard in the human being. The people who had softer bones also had a much softer brain mass. And the skull, the head of human beings was a very different shape in those times. You see, it was more like the heads of people with water on the brain. That was beautiful then; today it is no longer so beautiful. And they kept their heads the way very young children today still have it in the womb, for they had a soft brain mass, and the soft brain deposited itself in the front part of the skull [drawing]. Everything was softer then.

Now, gentlemen, when the human being was softer, his mental faculties would also have been different. Your thinking is much more spiritual with a soft brain than with a hard brain. The ancients still felt this; they would call someone who was only able to think the same thing over and over again and therefore insists on sticking to just this one idea a thick-head. This means that they had a feeling that one is really able to think better, to have better ideas, if one has a soft brain. The early people had such a soft brain.

And then there was something else they had. We are certainly able to say that when a child is born, its skull with its soft brain, and even the soft bones, are still very similar to the way they were in the early people. But you just sit or lay a small infant down—it cannot go anywhere, it cannot feed itself and the like; it cannot do anything! Higher spirits had to take care of this when people still had those soft brains. And the result was that people did not have freedom then, they did not have free will. But free will gradually developed in the course of human evolution. It means that the bones and the brain had to harden. But this hardening also meant that the old knowledge went into decline. We would not have become independent human beings if we had not become thick-headed, hard-headed, with hard brains. But we owe our freedom to this. And the decline of the old knowledge really went hand in hand with our freedom. That is it. Can you understand this? [*Answer: Yes.*] It comes with our freedom.

But now, having on the one hand gained freedom and independence, human beings have lost the old knowledge and fallen into materialism. But materialism is not the truth. We must therefore gain spiritual insight again, in spite of the fact that we have a denser brain today than people did originally. We can only do this through the anthroposophical science of the spirit. This gives insights that are independent of the body and are perceived with the soul only. Early humanity had their knowledge because their brains were softer and therefore more soul-like. We have our materialism because our brain has grown hard, no longer able to take in the soul. We therefore have to gain spiritual insights with the soul only, a soul not taken up by the brain. This is the way of the science of the spirit. We regain spiritual insights. But we live in an age now when humanity has bought freedom, the price being materialism. So we cannot say that materialism is something bad, even if it is untruth. Materialism, if not taken to extremes, is not something bad, for through materialism humanity has learned many things that were not known before. That is how it is.

Now there is another question that was put in writing before:

I have read the following statement in your Philosophy of Spiritual Activity:[105] *'We must make the content of the world the content of our thought; only then shall we find the wholeness again from which we have separated.'*

So the gentlemen has been reading something of the *Philosophy of Spiritual Activity.* His question is: *What belongs to this world content, since everything we see exists only in so far as we think it? And he goes on to say: Kant says the mind is unable to grasp the world of phenomena that comes before the world we perceive.*

Now you see, gentlemen, it is like this. When we are born, when we are little children, we have eyes, we have ears, we see and we hear; that is, we perceive the things that are around us. The chair which is there is not thought by a child, but it is perceived. It looks the same to a child as it does to a grown-up, only the child does not yet think the chair. Let us assume some artificial means could be found so that a child who does not yet have thoughts would be able to talk. In that case — and we are used to this today, for the very people who do not think are those who are most critical — the child would be inclined to criticize everything. I am actually convinced that if very young infants who are not yet able to think were able to chatter away they would be the greatest critics. You see, in ancient India, you had to be 60 before you were allowed to be critical; the others were not allowed to voice an opinion, for people would say: 'They have no experience of the world yet.' Now I won't defend this nor will I criticize it, I merely want to tell you how it was. Today anyone who has reached the age of 20 would laugh at you if you were to say he had to wait until he was 60 before he could give an opinion. Young people would not do that today. They do not wait at all, and as soon as they are able to hold a pen they start to write for the papers, to have opinions on everything. We've gone a long way in this direction today. But I am convinced that if very young infants were able to talk — oh, they would be severe critics! A 6-month-old infant, wow, he'd be criticizing everything we do if we could get him to talk.

Gentlemen, you see, we only start to think at a later stage. How did speech develop? Well, imagine a child of 6 months, not yet able to have the idea of the chair but able to see it just as we do. He would discuss the chair. Now you would say: 'I, too, have the idea of the chair; in the chair there is gravity, and so it stands on the floor. Some carving has been done on it, and so it has form. The chair has a certain inner consistency, and I am therefore able to sit on it without falling off, and so on. I have the idea of the chair. I think of something when I see the chair.' The child of 6 months who does not yet have the idea will say: 'Silly, you've grown stupid having grown so old. We know at 6 months what a chair is; later you have all kinds of fantasies about it.' Yes, that is how it would be if a 6-month-old child could talk. And something we are only able to do as we get older — being also able to think as we say things — with all this the situation is that the ideas do, after all, go with the chair; I merely do not know them beforehand. I only have the ideas when I have reached the level of maturity needed. But the solidity of the chair is not in me. I do not sit down on my own solidity when I sit down on the chair, otherwise I might as well sit myself down on myself again. The chair does not get heavy when I sit down on it; it is heavy in its own right. Everything I develop by way of ideas is already in the chair. I therefore perceive the reality of the chair when in the course of life I connect with it many times in my thoughts. Initially I only see the colours, and so on, hear when a chair rattles, and also feel if it is cold or warm; I can perceive this with my senses. But one only knows what is in that chair when one has grown older and is able to think. Then one connects with it again, creating a retroactive effect.

Kant—I spoke of him recently—made the biggest of mistakes in thinking that something a child does not yet perceive, something we only perceive later, i.e. the thought content, is something people put into objects themselves. So he was really saying: 'If that is a chair there—the chair has colour, it rattles. But when I say the chair is heavy, this is not a property of the chair, it is something I give to it by thinking it to be heavy. The chair is solid, but this is not inherent in it; I add it by thinking the chair to be solid.' Well, gentlemen, Kant's teachings are considered to be a great science, and I spoke about this a while ago. The truth is, however, that it is the greatest nonsense. Because of the particular way in which humanity has developed, great nonsense is sometimes considered to be great science, the most sublime philosophy, and Kant is of course also known as the man who ground everything to dust, who shattered everything. All I was able to see in him—I studied Kant from early boyhood, again and again—is a shatterer; but I have not generally found that someone who shatters soup plates creates the most sublime things, nor indeed that he was greater than the person who made the plates. It always seemed to me that the maker was the greater man. Kant has in truth always shattered everything.

Kant's objections should not concern us. But the thing is that when we are born we are disunited, having no connection with things. We only grow into them again as we develop concepts. The question that has been asked therefore has to be answered like this. What belongs to the world content? In my *Philosophy of Spiritual Activity* I wrote: 'We must make the content of the world the content of our thought; only then shall we find the whole again from which we separated in infancy.' In infancy we do not have the world content, we only have the sensual part of the world content. But the thought content is truly inside the world content. In infancy we thus have only half the world content, and it is only later, when we have developed and have thoughts, that we have the thought content not only in us, but we know that it is in the things, and we also treat our thoughts in such a way that we know they are in the things, and we then re-establish our connection with the things.

You see, in the 1880s—when everything had become Kantian and everyone kept saying that Kant's philosophy was the most sublime, and no one dared as yet to say anything against it—it was very hard when I stood up in those days and stated that Kantian philosophy was really a nonsense. But this is something I had to declare from the very beginning. For of course, if someone like Kant thinks that we actually add the thought content to things, he can no longer arrive at the plain and simple content, for he then has inner thoughts about things around him, and this is materialism indeed. Kant is in many respects responsible for the fact that humanity has not found its way out of materialism. Kant is altogether responsible for a great many things. I told you this on that earlier occasion when someone else had asked about Kant. The others, being unable to think anything else, created materialism. But Kant said: 'We cannot know anything about the world of the spirit, only believe.' What he was really saying was: 'You can only know something about the world perceived by the senses because you can drag thoughts only into this world perceived by the senses.'

And people who wanted to be materialistic felt even

more justified in this by referring to Kant. But this is another prejudice humanity must get out of the habit of using — meaning the part of humanity who at least know something of Kant — they have to get out of the habit of always referring to Kant when they want to say that one really cannot know anything about the world of the spirit. And so world content is sensory content and content of mind and spirit. But mind and spirit only gain that content in the course of life, as we develop ideas. We then re-establish the connection between nature and spirit. In the beginning, in infancy, we only had nature before us, and mind and spirit evolved gradually out of our own nature.

Would anyone have a very little question?

Mr Burle asked about human hair, saying: 'Many girls now have their hair cut short. Could Dr Steiner tell us if that is good for the health? My little daughter would also like to cut her hair, but I have not permitted it. I'd like to know if it is harmful or not.'

Rudolf Steiner: Well now, the matter is like this. The hair that grows is so little connected with the organism as a whole that it does not really matter very much if one lets one's hair grow or cuts it short. The harm is not enough to be apparent. But there is a difference between men and women in this respect. You know, for a time it was the case — it's no longer the case now — that one would see anthroposophists walking about, gentlemen and ladies — the gentleman would not cut his hair, wearing long tresses, and the ladies would have their hair cut short. People would of course say: 'Anthroposophy turns the world upside down; among the anthroposophists the ladies cut their hair short and the gentlemen let theirs grow.' Now it is no longer like this, at least not noticeably so. But we might of course also ask how it is with the difference between the sexes when it comes to cutting one's hair.

Generally speaking the situation is that a great head of hair is rather superfluous in men. For women it is a necessity. Hair always contains sulphur, iron, silica and some other substances. These are needed by the organism. Men need much silica, for as they assumed the male sex in the womb they lost the ability to produce their own silica. They absorb the silica that is in the air whenever they have just had their hair cut, absorbing it through the hair. It is of course too bad when the hair has gone, for then nothing can be absorbed. Going bald at an early age, which has a little bit to do with people's lifestyles, is not exactly the best thing for a person.

With women, cutting the hair short is not exactly good, and that is because women have the ability to produce silica more in the organism, and so they should not cut the hair really short too often; for then the hair absorbs silica — which the woman already has in her — from the air and forces it back into the organism. This makes the woman inwardly hairy, prickly; she then has 'hairs on her teeth' [German saying, meaning a tough woman]. This is then something that is not so apparent; one has to have a certain sensitivity to notice it, but a little bit of it is there. Their whole manner is rather prickly then; they become inwardly hairy and prickly; and cutting one's hair off does then have an influence, especially in young people.

Now you see, it can also be the other way round, gentlemen. It may be that modern youngsters come into an environment — children are all quite different today from the way we were in our young days — where their inner silica is no longer enough, for they want to be a bit prickly, scratchy. They then develop the instinct to cut their hair. This becomes fashionable, with one copying the other, and then we have the story the other way round, with children wanting to be prickly and having their hair cut. But if one managed to organize things so that they went a bit against such a fashion, this would not be such a bad thing if the fashion has gone a bit to extremes. In the final instance it all has to do with this, does it not—one person likes a gentle woman, another a prickly one. Tastes do change a little. But it cannot have a very great influence. Though of course if someone has a daughter who wants to or is supposed to choose a husband who likes a prickly woman, then she should get her hair cut. She then won't get a husband who likes a gentle woman. So that may indeed happen. So the business has more of an effect on things that are marginal in life.

Notes

Text source. The lectures were taken down in shorthand and transcribed by stenographer Helene Finckh (1883–1960). For the present edition, the original shorthand records were re-examined and re-transcribed. Changes in the text compared to the first German edition are due to this.

Blackboard drawings
The original drawings made by Rudolf Steiner have been preserved, for the boards would be covered with black paper for him to draw on at that time. The full set of drawings has been published in volume 28 of *Wandtafelzeichnungen zum Vortragswerk* (GA 353 and 354) (Rudolf Steiner Verlag, Dornach, Switzerland). The drawings in the text are based on the blackboard drawings.

The notes which follow are translated from the German edition, with additions made by the translator where appropriate for readers of the English edition.

GA = *Gesamtausgabe* (German edition of the collected works of Rudolf Steiner).

1 Neudörfl near Wiener Neustadt, at that time in Hungary.
2 Lecture given to the workmen on 23 February 1924, vol. 6 in the German edition of these lectures (GA 352).
3 The resort was called Sauerbrunn.
4 Lecture given on 3 March 1923. In vol. 3 of the series of workmen's lectures in German (GA 349).
5 Mahatma Gandhi (1869–1948), Indian reformer and statesman.

6 Syria historically included all of modern Syria and Lebanon, and parts of Israel, Jordan, Iraq, and Saudi Arabia. It was a province of the Ottoman Empire (1516–1918), becoming a French territory in 1920. The country gained its independence in 1944.

7 Lecture given to the workmen on 21 February 1924, vol. 6 in the German edition of these lectures.

8 Homer, *Odyssey*, 11th canto.

9 Plato (*c.* 427–347 BC), Greek philosopher. After living for a time at the Syracuse court, Plato founded the most influential school of the ancient world, the Academy, in Athens.

10 Tacitus, Publius Cornelius (*c.* AD 55–120), Roman public official and historian. His greatest works, *Histories* and *Annals*, covered the period from the death of Augustus to the death of Domitian (AD 14–96).

11 'The originator of this name (Christianian), Christ, was executed during the reign of Tiberius, under the Procurator Pontius Pilate.' *Annals*, Book 15, 44.

12 Rudolf Steiner was able to use wordplay in German here that cannot be reproduced in English. The two German verbs *hören* and *zuhören* are 'to hear' and 'to listen'. The *zu* prefix signifies attention. Steiner said this had been omitted in referring to university students, who may hear but not necessarily listen. Translator.

13 Du Bois-Reymond, Emil (1818–86), physiologist in Berlin. The quote comes from his *Über die Grenzen der Naturerkenntnis*, 7. Aufl. S. 46; Leipzig 1916.

14 Stresemann, Gustav (1878–1929), German foreign minister (1923–29). He shared the 1929 Nobel Peace Prize.

15 Louvier, Ferdinand August, *Sphinx locuta est. Goethes Faust und die Resultate einer rationellen Methode der Forschung* (2 Bände), Berlin 1997.

16 Gaius Caesar Germanicus, called Caligula (AD 12–41), Roman emperor AD 37–41.

17 William or Wilhelm II (1859–1941), German emperor 1888–1918.

18 Quidde, Ludwig, *Caligula*, Leipzig 1894.

19 What is said here about Caligula refers to Commodus (AD

161–192; Emperor of Rome 180–192). See lecture of 5 May in this volume, also the lecture of 20 May 1917 in *Mitteleuropa zwischen Ost und West* (GA 174a). The probable source was H.P. Blavatsky's *The Secret Doctrine* (vol. 3): 'Ragon [J.-M. Ragon, *Orthodoxie maçonnique*, Paris 1853, p. 101] speaks of rumour accusing the emperor Commodus — on an occasion when he played the role of initiator — to have taken his role in the initiation drama so seriously that he actually killed the seeker when he struck him with the axe.'

20   Augustus, originally called Octavian (63 BC–AD 14), first Emperor of Rome (27 BC–AD 14).

21   Strictly speaking 29, but Rudolf Steiner used the ages a bit loosely here, and in the light of what follows it seems better to make it 30.

22   Julian the Apostate (331?–363), Roman emperor (361–63).

23   Heinrich II (973–1025), king from 1002, emperor from 1014, canonized by the Pope in 1146.

24   The first Crusade was from 1096 to 1099, with Godfrey of Bouillon (d. 1100) establishing the kingdom of Jerusalem in 1099.

25   Peter the Hermit (*c.* 1050–*c.* 1115), French soldier and then monk, born at Amiens.

26   Walther von Habenichts (the name means 'have-not', the 'pauper'), French knight who joined the Crusade in 1095 and was killed in the battle with the Turks at Nicaea.

27   John 8:32.

28   Otto von Guericke (1602–86).

29   Nicolas Copernicus (1743–1543), canon of Frauenburg Cathedral, founder of modern astronomy.

30   See note 7.

31   Ulfila, or Wulfila (*c.* 311–83).

32   *Codex argenteus* (silver book), Gothic sixth-century Gospel manuscript written in silver and gold letters on deep crimson parchment originating in northern Italy; contains Ulfila's Gospel translations.

33   Attila, king of the Huns from 434 to 453.

34   See note 10.

35   *De origine et situ Germanorum* (about the origin and home-

lands of the Germanic tribes), written in Latin, probably in about the year 100, and generally known as the *Germania*.

36 German: *Wotan weht im Winde* — German W is English V sound. See pronunciation table.

37 German: *Donar dröhnt im Donner*. See pronunciation table.

38 German: *Ziu zwingt Zwist* (Ziu forces strife, see pronunciation table) — all three phrases were written on the blackboard. Translator.

39 Mohammed (Arabic for 'the one who is praised') (570–632).

40 Charlemagne (742–814).

41 Harun al-Rashid (763?–809), Caliph of Baghdad 786–809.

42 Martin Luther (1483–1546).

43 Huss, John, Czech Jan Hus (1369–1415).

44 Mark 1: 32. 'When evening came and the sun had set, they brought to him all those who were sick or possessed by demons and the whole town was gathered round the door. He healed many people...' (*The Gospel of Mark*, translated by Kalmia Bittleston, Edinburgh: Floris 1986).

45 The next talk was, in fact, not given on the Saturday but on the following Wednesday.

46 This was a long process which culminated in decisions taken at the 8th Ecumenical Council held in Constantinople in 869.

47 Lecture given on 12 March 1924.

48 *Evangelienharmonie* (Harmony of the Four Gospels) written by the Alsatian monk Otfried von Weissenburg *c.* 800–70 in Old High German verse.

49 *Heliand*, Gospel Harmony written in stave-rhyme between 822 and 840.

50 Marcus Aurelius Augustinus (354–430). The 'strange words' may be found in his *Retractiones* I, 13, 3.

51 So far it has not been possible to trace this.

52 Good Friday. Good is not Indo-European but an entirely Germanic word derived from *gath-* (as in 'gather' and 'together'), to 'bring together', meaning 'brought together in the right way'. The *kara* in the German *Karfreitag* relates to English 'care', meaning 'sorrow'. Also, Middle English *chari*, 'careful', 'sorrowful' derives from Old English *cearig*, sorrowful. Translator.

53 Constantine I, the Great (285?–337), Emperor of Rome (306–37).

54 See note 22.

55 Justinian I (483–565), Byzantine emperor 527–65.

56 The editors are aware that what Rudolf Steiner is saying in the given context seems to contradict the statements he made on 1 and 5 March in this course of lectures.

57 Dr Elisabeth Vreede (1879–1943), member of the first Council of the General Anthroposophical Society and leader of the Section for Mathematics and Astronomy.

58 This refers to a passage in H.P. Blavatsky's *Isis Unveiled*:
'Deleuze has collected, in his Bibliothèque du magnétisme animal, a number of remarkable facts taken from Van Helmont, among which we will content ourselves with quoting the following as pendants to the case of the bird-hunter, Jacques Pélissier. He says that "men by looking steadfastly at animals oculis intentis for a quarter of an hour may cause their death; which Rousseau confirms from his own experience in Egypt and the East, as having killed several toads in this manner. But when he at last tried this at Lyons, the toad, finding it could not escape from his eye, turned round, blew itself up, and stared at him so fiercely, without moving its eyes, that a weakness came over him even to fainting, and he was for some time thought to be dead."' (Paris 1817–18, Vol. I, pp. 67–68.)
Pélissier, Jean Jaques (1794–1864), Duc de Malakoff, French military leader who served in Spain, in the Morea and in Algeria. French ambassador in London 1858–9, later governor of Algeria.
The Rousseau referred to was not Jean-Jacques Rousseau.

59 Helmont, Jan Baptiste van (1577–1644), Flemish physician, chemist and physicist.

60 Monkshood, *Aconitum napellus*. See van Helmont's *Demens Idea* § 12.

61 Lucius Domitius Nero, Roman emperor 54–68.
Lucius Aelius Aurelius Commodus (161–192), Roman emperor 180–192.

62 See note 20.
63 Paracelsus, Philippus Aureolus (1493?–1541), Swiss physician and naturalist, originally named Theophrastus Bombastus von Hohenheim and known as 'the father of medicine'.
64 See note 29.
65 Svedberg, Theodor (1884–1971), Swedish chemist, wrote a book on matter in 1912; 1926 Nobel Prize winner.
66 The origins and arrangement of the Sephiroth Tree are presented somewhat differently in Cabbalistic literature than here by Rudolf Steiner.
67 Maimonides, Moses (1135–1204), originally Moses Ben Maimon, Jewish philosopher born in Spain.
68 Lully (or Lull), Raymond (1235?–1316), Catalan philosopher.
69 Alexander the Great (356–323 BC).
70 Aristotle (384–322 BC).
71 Kant, Immanuel (1724–1804), German idealist philosopher.
72 Joseph Mayer, who taught German literature at the secondary school specializing in the sciences in Vienna-Neustadt.
73 Steiner, R., *Rudolf Steiner, an Autobiography* (GA 28), tr. R. Stebbing, New York: Rudolf Steiner Publications 1977.
74 Reclam's Universalbibliothek, publishing venture of Philipp Reclam Jun., Stuttgart, producing the classics in reasonably priced paperback editions. Still exists today. Translator.
75 Schopenhauer, Arthur (1788–1860), German philosopher.
76 Steiner, R., *The Philosophy of Spiritual Activity. A Philosophy of Freedom* (GA 4), tr. R. Stebbing, London: Rudolf Steiner Press 1989.
77 Leibniz, Gottfried Wilhelm (1646–1716), German philosopher and mathematician.
78 Wolff, Christian (1679–1754), German mathematician and philosopher who made the work of Leibniz popular.
79 Kant, I., *Prolegomena*, tr. by P.G. Lucas in 1953.
80 von Hartmann, Karl Robert Eduard (1842–1906). His *Philosophie des Unbewussten* (1869) was translated into English by Coupland, with a new edition in 1931.

81   'Eduard von Hartmann, his teaching and significance' first published (in German) in the monthly *Deutsche Worte* (Vienna), vol. XI, No. 1 (Jan. 1891) and reprinted in GA 30.

82   In the work referred to in note 93, vol. 2: Metaphysics of the unconscious, chapter 14: The goal of the world process and the significance of the conscious mind (numerous editions!).

83   Haeckel, Ernst (1834–1919), German philosopher and naturalist.

84   Schmidt, Oscar (1823–86), German zoologist, student of Haeckel.

85   *Das Unbewusste vom Standpunkte der Physiologie und Deszendenztheorie. Eine kritische Beleuchtung des naturphilosophischen Teils der Philosophie des Unbewussten aus naturwissenschaftlichen Gesichtspunkten*, Berlin 1872.

86   *Das Unbewusste vom Standpunkte der Physiologie und Deszendenztheorie*, 2. verm. Aufl. der 1872 anonym erschienenen Schrift nebst einem Anhang: 'Oscar Schmidts Kritik der naturwissenschaftlichen Grundlagen der Philosophie des Unbewussten', Berlin 1877.

87   Except for circumpolar stars.

88   Tycho Brahe (1546–1601), Danish astronomer.

89   Ptolemy or Claudius Ptolemaeus (*c.* AD 87–165), Egyptian geographer, mathematician and astronomer.

90   Halley, Edmund (1656–1742), English astronomer.

91   This is the phrase Rudolf Steiner used. Translator.

92   Steiner, R., *Kosmogonie* (GA 94). Lectures given in Paris, 25 May–14 June 1906. The summaries by E. Schuré in this volume do not include Steiner's statements concerning the comet atmosphere.

93   Moses (thirteenth century BC).

94   Darwin, Charles (1809–82).

95   Steiner, R., *Friedrich Nietzsche, Fighter for Freedom*, tr. M. Ingram deRis, Englewood, NJ, 1960.

96   Steiner, R., 'Haeckel and his Opponents' (in GA 30).

97   Spengler, Oswald (1880–1936), German philosopher, considered that civilizations and cultures to be subject to growth and decay just as human beings are. *The Decline of the West* (1918–1922).

98　See the lectures in Steiner, R., *The Temple Legend* (GA 93), 20 lectures, Berlin 23 May 1904–2 January 1906, tr. J. Wood, London: Rudolf Steiner Press 1985, and Steiner, R., *Zur Geschichte und aus den Inhalten der erkenniskultischen Abteilung der Esoterischen Schule von 1904 bis 1914* (GA 265), Dornach: Rudolf Steiner Verlag 1987.

99　The umlaut (meaning sound-changer) is not an accent but actually the letter 'e'. It used to be written on top of the a, o or u originally, and gradually became reduced to two short vertical lines or two dots. If you look at the pronunciation table given in this book and try and pronounce the words Rudolf Steiner gave here as indicated, you'll feel that the original sound is made to go more in the direction of the German 'e', which is like 'ay', but without going up into an 'i' sound at the end.

100　Woodrow Wilson (1856–1924), US Democratic politician, president 1913–21. Presented his Fourteen Points as a peace programme in January 1918.

101　Breslau, formerly capital of Lower Silesia. Now in Poland, called Wroclaw. Rudolf Steiner was going there to give the Agriculture Course. Translator.

102　Lecture of 21 April 1923, in GA 349. Tr. by M. Cotterell entitled 'The Nature of Christianity' in MS R59, Rudolf Steiner House Library, London.

103　As vowel sounds differ greatly between German and English, which reflects the spirit of each nation and its language, I have only taken the first two of the three words given by Rudolf Steiner (*Ball, Fall, Kraft*), as it is possible to make his point more or less well in English with these two. I have used 'oh' instead of 'ah', as it matches the English sounds and (fortunately) we know from previous lectures in this volume that both vowels express amazement. Concerning the third, *Kraft*, he went on to say, after discussing *Fall*, that the 'f' also has special significance, using an energy to propel oneself. Translator.

104　The German *Alb* means sprite, goblin, and also nightmare, incubus. The change from plural to singular occurs in the original. Translator.

105   Steiner, R., *The Philosophy of Spiritual Activity. A Philosophy of Freedom* (GA 4), tr. R. Stebbing, London: Rudolf Steiner Press 1989.